AIRLINERS
WORLDWIDE

Over 100 Current Airliners Described and Illustrated in Colour

TOM SINGFIELD

Dedicated to the memory
of my long-time friend
Colin Ballantine, 1944-2004.

Airliners Worldwide – 2nd Edition
© 2005 Tom Singfield

ISBN 1 85780 189 X

First published in 2005 by Midland Publishing
4 Watling Drive, Hinckley, LE10 3EY, England.
Telephone: 01455 254 490   Fax: 01455 254 495
E-mail: midlandbooks@compuserve.com

Midland Publishing is an imprint of
Ian Allan Publishing Ltd

Worldwide distribution (except North America):
Midland Counties Publications
4 Watling Drive, Hinckley, LE10 3EY, England.
Telephone: 01455 254 450   Fax: 01455 233 737
E-mail: midlandbooks@compuserve.com
www.midlandcountiessuperstore.com

North American trade distribution:
Specialty Press Publishers and Wholesalers Inc.
39966 Grand Avenue, North Branch, MN 55056, USA
Telephone: 651 277 1400   Fax: 651 277 1203
Toll free telephone: 800 895 4585
www.specialtypress.com

Design concept and layout
© 2005 Midland Publishing and NARA-Verlag

Printed in England by Ian Allan Printing Ltd,
Hersham, Surrey KT12 4RG

Title page: One of Air France's regional
franchise operators is Morlaix-based Brit Air.
CRJ100ER F-GRJM seen from Gatwick control
tower. (Author)

Opposite page: The author poses alongside an
equally scruffy but serviceable DC-3 in Georgia,
USA. (Maggi Singfield)

Contents

Colourful Moldovan-registered Antonov An-24 ER-AZB operates out of Brazzaville for Aero-Service in the Congo (afavia-photos.co.za)

Second-hand L-410 Turbolets are very popular in Africa. L-410UVP 5X-UAG is operated by Precision Air Services in Tanzania. (Afavia-photos.co.za)

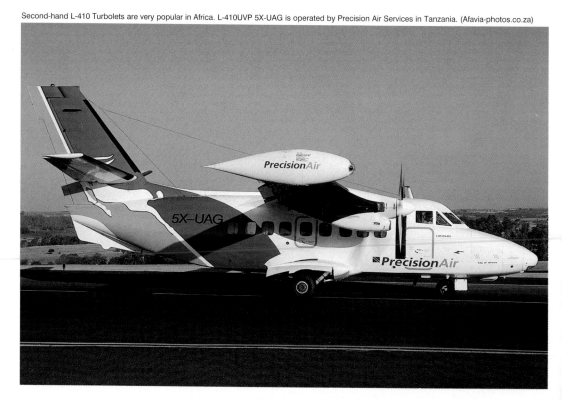

This book is a fully revised, corrected and updated edition of the original *Airliners Worldwide* that was published in 1997. New photographs depicting current colour schemes are provided throughout and the lists of operators for each type include deliveries and cancellations up to the fourth quarter of 2004. This book is a sister publication to *Airlines Worldwide* by B I Hengi, also published by Midland Publishing. Between them, the two titles provide a comprehensive library on modern-day airliners and airline operations.

The decision to omit, or include, a particular type of airliner was dictated by its passenger capacity, or by the number of that airliner type remaining in worldwide service at the time of writing. Most airliners in current commercial use that have more than 15 passenger seats are included in this book. This therefore excludes the smaller 'commuter' types, such as the BN-2 Islander, Beechcraft 99 and the Swearingen/Fairchild Merlin. Other types excluded from this book because of their limited numbers in current commercial operations include the Antonov An-8 and An-22, Aviation Traders ATL-98 Carvair, Beriev Be-32, Douglas DC-7, GAF Nomad, IAI Arava, IPTN CN-235 and Vickers Viscount. Another one not included is the Caravelle; sadly the last airworthy one crashed in 2004. Some of these, plus many more interesting airliners, can be found in my book, 'Classic Airliners' which was published in 2000. Despite the genuine 'airline' activities of many helicopters worldwide, it was decided to exclude them, and refer only to fixed-wing aircraft.

Major Changes

Sadly, since the first edition was published, airliners have become the tools of terrorists. The aftermath of the World Trade Center attack on 11th September 2001 caused many potential passengers to avoid flying if at all possible. Airlines went bust, security costs rose and the manufacturers suffered when the surviving airlines reduced or cancelled their orders and reservations. These problems continued for a couple of years but recent growth in low-cost airlines and the incredible rise of the regional jet has once again filled the order books. Sadly this is not the case in the former Soviet Union. Despite some excellent products, the major airliner constructors there struggle to compete with the western designs.

In the last seven years, there have been many major changes in the airliner manufacturers' business. Most significant was when McDonnell Douglas, ever hopeful for significant airliner sales, was 'merged' into arch rival Boeing in July 1997. SAAB shut down their regional airliner production lines in December 1997 and, like BAE Systems and Raytheon Aircraft, they kept in the business by concentrating on asset management and aftermarket support. Let, from the Czech Republic, builders of fine aircraft since 1950, failed to sell their promising L-610 commuter aircraft and consequently the company collapsed. The Bombardier turboprops continue steady sales while their regional jets sold in large numbers. Embraer's venture into the regional jet market has proved to be a great success and their new ERJ170/175/190/195 series is gaining significant orders. They are now the fourth largest civil airliner manufacturers in the world. ATR, once the king of the turboprop commuterliner manufacturers, delivered only nine new civil aircraft in 2003. However, they endure by selling and servicing pre-owned ATRs while their cargo door conversion programme has already found a buyer in Alaska.

The Big Players

Airbus continues its march towards supremacy in the airliner manufacturing business and now achieves more sales per year than Boeing. In 2003, Airbus delivered 284 airliners compared to 240 from Boeing and in 2004 they revealed details of their proposed A330-based A350, a rival to Boeing's 787, and the A30X, a short-haul widebody replacement for the A300. After 30 years of production, the 5,000th Airbus was ordered in August 2004. Their airliner portfolio now stretches from the 107-seater A318 up to the giant A380, able to squeeze up to 840 passengers into its double decks. This book should appear soon after the first Airbus A380 has climbed away from the runway at Toulouse Blagnac and into the history books. Its first flight will probably create as much interest in the world press as any previous event in aviation.

Boeing caught the imagination of the public with their 2000 proposal for a Sonic Cruiser, but in reality it was a non-starter. However, the official launch of their sleek 7E7 (now 787) in April 2004 has once again brought them into the forefront of airliner technology. Boeing's other airliner designs continue to be refined and updated although their 757 line has been closed down.

The End of Airliner Production in Britain

Most significant for British readers was the appearance of the last airliner ever to be built in the UK. Since the Second World War, the British aircraft industry has built more than 3,500 airliners ranging in size from small twin-props to the mighty Super VC-10. In November 2001 that all came to an end when British Aerospace Regional Aircraft cancelled their Avro RJX programme after the world airline downturn post 9/11. British airliner designers and engineers now have to be content building engines, wings and other components whilst employed by multi-national companies such as Airbus.

With the last commercial flight of the much-admired Concorde in October 2003, the chance of supersonic airline travel appears to have disappeared for a long time. A full-size supersonic passenger airliner would now be considered to be environmentally unfriendly, costly to design and a waste of resources. With the price of aviation fuel continuing to rise, the new generation large airliners have to be ultra fuel-efficient as well as have a low environmental impact. Rightly so, but because they all conform to the same aerodynamic restrictions and have to operate from established airport layouts, sadly, just like motor cars, they are all starting to look the same.

Tom Singfield
Horsham, West Sussex
February 2005

Acknowledgements

This book would not be half as interesting without the splendid pictures taken by my aviation photographer friends from around the world. Many of them travel thousands of miles in search of rare and unusual types in the hope of capturing them on film. These trips often involve negotiation with airport, airline and even military authorities in order to gain the necessary passes to get the vitally important 'Airside Pass'. With airport security at an all time high, this can now be a real problem, so I would like to thank all the photographers who made such great efforts and who kindly allowed their work to be published.

Mark Abbott, Jonny Andersson, Mike Barth, Colin Ballantine, Tony Best, Malcolm Bezzina, Peter J.Bish, Art Brett, Chris Buckley, Phil Camp, Aldo Ciarini, Chris Doggett, Tony Dixon (Airliner World), Romano Germann, Julian Gill, Eddy Gual (Aviation Photo of Miami), Jacques Guillem, Chris Herbert, Oliver Herting, Richard Hunt, Kevin Irwin, Dmitry Karpezo, Tommy Lakmaker, Peter Linden, Philippe Loeuillet (AVIMAGE), Chris Mak, Ian Malcolm (Afavia-fotos.co.za), Andy Marsh, Dave Mathieson, Frank McMeiken, John Mounce, Berni Muller, Hiro Murai, Hans Oehninger, Alan Pardoe, Derek Pedley (airteamimages.com), Pierre-Alain Petit, Joe Pries, Michael S Prophet, Eda Radnic, Robbie Shaw, Tim Spearman, Christian Volpati, Christofer Witt, Richard Vandervord, Jarrod Wilkening and Paul Zethof,

I would also like to thank the following who have assisted me with research, photography and writing: Gordon Bain, M Balaraman (HAL-Dornier), Roy Blewett, Keith Brooks, Dave W Carter (Raytheon), Wende Cover (AvCraft), David Dorman (BAE REGIONAL Aircraft), Mary E Cane (Boeing), The Gatwick Aviation Society, Peter Hillman, Juliet Kennedy (EGKK ATC), Philippa King (Bombardier), Valery Kuzenkov (AVIANT), Frederic Lahache (ATR), Francesca Pecci (Blue Panorama), Dave MacMillan (SAL), Andy Ramsay, Rovos Air, Bob Ruffle, Sophie Terrier (ATR) and Tim Travis (Raytheon). Special thanks goes to my wife Maggi for tolerating my hobby and slow writing and to Julian Gill who did a fantastic job compiling the lists of current operators, supplying photos and helping with the 'in service' numbers.

Notes

Manufacturer's addresses are hopefully current for types which remain in production. For some of the older types the manufacturers may have gone out of business, merged or relocated. In such cases the (sometimes abbreviated) addresses quoted are not valid for correspondence but serve only as an indication of their location at that time.

The fleet data is current to late 2004 and includes expected deliveries up to early 2005. Several of the types listed within are also operated by military forces and these have been excluded from the operators lists, except where they are known to provide 'commercial' services in addition to any military flying. Unless specified, military airliners are included in the 'number built' and 'number in service' figures.

Current operator information is divided into regions to provide a rough guide as to where they can be found.

To keep the list manageable and straightforward, not because of poor geography (!), various liberties have been taken with the 'region' titles.

Africa: All on the African continent.
Asia: Includes Afghanistan, China and India.
Australasia: Includes all the Pacific Islands except Hawaii.
Europe: Includes Bulgaria, Cyprus, Czech Republic, Greenland, Hungary, Iceland, Poland, Romania and the Slovak Republic.
Former Soviet Union (FSU): Covers all countries that, prior to the break up of the Soviet Union, had aircraft registered with a CCCP prefix.
Middle East: Includes Israel, Jordan, Turkey and all of the Arab States (except those in continental Africa).
North America: Includes Canada and Hawaii.
South America: Includes Mexico and all of the Caribbean Islands.

The two most popular jetliners in the world are the Airbus A320 and the Boeing 737. Passengers may not notice much difference from their perspective, but the pilots certainly do. The Thomas Cook A320 (above) has a FBW cockpit with sidestick controllers while the retro-coloured American Airlines 737-400 (below) has the more conventional floor-mounted columns. (Author)

Standard (and some non-standard) abbreviations are used to save space within the text.

AC — Air Charter/Air Cargo
AL — Airline/s
AS — Air Service/System
AT — Air Transport/Aero Transport
AW — Airway/s
AEW — Airborne Early Warning – aircraft-mounted surveillance system
APU — Auxiliary Power Unit – on-board power unit for ancillaries
AWACS — Airborne Warning and Control System – surveillance and co-ordination platform
BAe — British Aerospace – UK manufacturer
CAA — Civil Aviation Authority – UK legislative and administrative body
CIS — Commonwealth of Independent States – essentially what is now termed 'Russia'
CofA — Certificate of Airworthiness – national (or international) approval of an aircraft
CRT — Cathode Ray Tube – 'television' type cockpit instrumentation
EICAS — Engine Indication and Crew Alerting System – computer monitored display system
EFIS — Electronic Flight Instrument System – CRT-based cockpit instrumentation
ehp — Estimated shaft horsepower
ER — Extended Range – increased tankage
EROPS — Extended Range Operations – procedure for twin-engined types
ETOPS — Extended Twin-Engined Operations – over-water procedure for twin-engined types
FAA — Federal Aviation Administration – US legislative and administrative body
FADEC — Full Authority Digital Engine Control – 'fly-by-wire' control of engines and sub-systems
FCS — Flight Control System – digital inputs controlling flight surfaces ('fly-by-wire')
FMC — Flight Management Computer – monitoring of control/systems/propulsion
FMS — Flight Management System – monitoring of control/systems/propulsion
FSU — Former Soviet Union – used to denote the regions/nations previously within the USSR
ft — foot/feet – Imperial unit of length, 1ft = 0.3m
ft^2 — square foot/feet – Imperial unit of area, 1ft^2 = 0.93m^2
ft^3 — cubic foot/feet – Imperial unit of volume 1ft^3 = 0.02m^3
GAZ — Government Aircraft Production Plant – FSU
GE — General Electric – US engine producer
GPS — Global Positioning System – satellite-based navigation system
GPWS — Ground Proximity Warning System – altitude monitoring/alerting system
HGW — High Gross Weight – airframe capable of taking extra capacity/fuel tankage

IAE — International Aero Engines – multi-national engine producer
ICAO — International Civil Aviation Organisation – legislative/administrative authority
IGW — Increased Gross Weight – strengthened airframe for 'growth' version
ILFC — International Lease Finance Corporation – leasing company
in — Inches – Imperial unit of length 1in = 25.4mm
INS — Inertial Navigation System – computer controlled navigation system
Intl — International
kg — Kilogram – SI unit of weight, 1kg = 2.2lb
km/h — Kilometres per hour – SI unit of velocity, 10km = 6.2mph
kN — Kilonewton – SI unit of force (static thrust), 1kN = 224.8lb = 101.96kg
kt — Knots – one nautical mile per hour, 1kt = 1.15mph = 1.85km/h
kW — Kilowatt – SI unit of power (force), 1kW = 1,341shp
LA — Lineas Aereas – Spanish for airline(s)
lb — Pounds
m — metre – Imperial unit of weight, or force (static thrust, st), 1lb = 0.45kg
m^2 — square metre – SI unit of area, 1m^2 = 10.76ft^2
m^3 — cubic metre – SI unit of volume, 1m^3 = 35.3ft^3
MDC — McDonnell Douglas Corporation – US manufacturer
MTOW — Maximum Take-off Weight
NATO — North Atlantic Treaty Organisation – multi-national military alliance.
nm — Nautical mile – unit of length, 1nm = 1.15 mile = 1.85km
PIP — Performance Improvement Programme – enhancement through re-engineering
P&W — Pratt & Whitney – US engine producer
P&WC — Pratt & Whitney Canada – subsidiary of P&W
QC — Quick Change – from passenger to freight and vice versa
QT — Quiet Trader – see BAe 146 and AI(R) RJ
RAF — Royal Air Force – UK
RJ — Regional Jet – see AI(R) RJ and Canadair RJ
RR — Rolls-Royce – UK engine producer
shp — Shaft horsepower – Imperial unit of force (power), 1shp = 0.746kW
SP — Special Performance – enhanced parameters
SR — Short Range – generally, high capacity
SUD — Stretched Upper Deck – Boeing 747 with increased accommodation behind cockpit
TCAS — Traffic Alert and Collision-Avoidance System – radar monitoring and alerting system
UAD — United Air Detachment – FSU aircraft operating group
UHB — Ultra High Bypass – large turbofan
USAF — United States Air Force
USN — United States Navy
USSR — Union of Soviet Socialist Republics (see CIS)

Farnair Switzerland's ATR42-320 HB-AFF seen landing at its EuroAirport Basel/Mulhouse base in July 2004. (Author)

ATR 42

ATR Integrated
1 Allée Pierre Nadot, PO Box 16
Blagnac Cedex, F-31712, France

Avions de Transport Régional (ATR) was formed in October 1981 to develop and manufacture a range of twin-engined turboprop regional airliners. Aérospatiale of France, and Aeritalia of Italy, who were both studying their own turboprop projects, took equal shares in the company. The ATR 42 designation was given in recognition of the type's baseline passenger capacity. Until 2001, ATR production and design work was shared equally between Alenia Aeronautica and EADS with manufacture is split between various sites including Naples, St Nazaire, Meulte and Nantes. The final assembly, test flights, certification and deliveries are made at Toulouse.

First flown in August 1984, the early -100 and -200 versions were quickly revised into the standard -300 model which had a maximum take-off weight of 34,725lb (15,750kg). Initial deliveries of this model commenced in 1986 to customers including Brit Air from France who remarkably are still operating some of those early production aircraft.

In 1989, the type suffered a setback when engineers discovered wing structure faults. ATR had to pay for modifications to every ATR 42. Despite this, the type has been a huge success and, with the ATR 72, has achieved over 12 million flight hours and has been sold to more than 100 operators worldwide.

In 1993, the 'new generation' 50-seater ATR 42-500 was launched. This model

had more powerful PW127E engines, six-bladed props and a quieter and more comfortable cabin. First delivery of a -500 was to Air Dolomiti in 1995. CSA Airlines of the Czech Republic launched the PW121-powered -400, with first deliveries in March 1996. The same engine was also offered for the ATR 42-320A.

In 1996, the regional airliner activities of BAe (Avro) and ATR combined to form a new marketing and production operation – Aero International (Régional) or AI(R), but this alliance only lasted two years because BAe withdrew its financial support for a new AI(R) 70-seater jet.

The ATR family includes a number of specialised cargo versions. Both the 42 and 72 have convertible passenger/freight versions with a forward cargo door. Also ATR, in association with the outfitter Aeronavali, has a 'Large Cargo Door' conversion programme in order to accommodate ULD containers; launch customer, Northern Air Cargo of Alaska, received their first in 2003. ATR is still improving their range. In 2004 ATR was planning a 50% increase in the design life and even more powerful engines.

Details

Span: 24.57m (80ft 7in)
Length: 22.67m (74ft 5in)
Engines: Two P&WC turboprops,
 42-300 1,340kW (1,800shp) PW120;
 42-500 1,790kW (2,400shp) PW127

Cruise speed:
 ATR 42-300 490km/h (265kt) max
 ATR 42-500 563km/h (304kt) max
Accommodation: 50 maximum

First service: Air Littoral, Dec 1985
Number built (ordered): 376 (5)
Number in service: 319

Current Operators

Africa: Air Botswana, Air Madagascar, Air Malawi, Air Mauritius, ALS, Antrak Air, ASECNA, Avirex, DHL Avn, Ethiopian AL, Precisionair, Regional AL, Rossair, Royal Air Maroc, Solenta Avn, TACV, Tuninter, Zambian AW.

Asia: Air Deccan, Air Mandalay, Alliance Air, Dirgantara AS, Transasia AW, Trigana AS.

Australasia: Air Caledonie, Air Tahiti, Air Vanuatu.

Europe: Aer Arann, Air Atlantique, Air Contractors, Air Dolomiti, Air Exel, Airlinair, Air Wales, Alitalia Express, Avanti Air, Brit Air, Cimber Air, City Air, Coast Air, Contact Air, Croatia AL, CSA, Danish AT, Eurolot, Euromanx, European Air Express, Eurowings, Falcon Air, Farnair Switzerland, Globus AL, Islandsflug, Islas AW, Italy First, Olympic AL, Swiftair, Tarom, Titan AW, Viaggio Air, White Eagle Avn.

Middle East: Israir, Oman Air.

Former Soviet Union: Air Lithuania, Armavia.

North America: American Connection, Bradley AS, Cape Air, FedEx, First Air, Northern AC, Trans States AL, West Wind Avn.

South America: Aero Caribbean, Aerogaviota, Aeromar AL, Air Antilles, Air Caraïbes, Air Guyana Express, Air Saint Pierre, Bonaire Exel, Cubana, DHL de Guatemala, Islena AL, LAI, Pantanal, Pluna, Santa Barbara AL, Total LA, Trans Am, TRIP LA, Vensecar Intl, West Caribbean AW.

Tunisair's subsidiary airline Tuninter operates an ATR42 and two ATR72s including TS-LBC seen departing Malta in 2003. (Author)

ATR 72

ATR Integrated
1 Allée Pierre Nadot, PO Box 16
Blagnac Cedex, F-31712, France

The stretched version of the original ATR 42 was announced at the 1985 Paris Air Show and was officially launched in January 1986. With the Fokker 50 and the BAe ATP both offering more seats than the ATR 42, the Franco-Italian consortium decided to counter this threat to sales by modifying the ATR 42 with more powerful engines and lengthening the fuselage by 4.5m (14ft 9in). The stretch was made up of two plugs, one forward and one aft of the wing, thus increasing the standard capacity to 64, with a maximum of 74 if a reduced seat pitch was used. In addition to the fuselage stretch, other changes included an increase in the use of chemical bonding and carbon fibre composites to save weight, a revised door fitment, a simplified wing flap arrangement and an increase in wing span. The ATR 72 became the first commercial aircraft to have carbon fibre outer wings.

First flight was from Toulouse in October 1988 followed later in 1989 by type certification in France and the USA. The first delivery was to launch customer KarAir, a subsidiary of the Finnish national airline, a year later.

The basic model ATR 72-200 is also available as a freighter, able to carry 13 small containers. There is also a 'hot-and-high' ATR 72-210 version with more powerful engines and different propellers. The first ATR72-210 was delivered to American Eagle in

December 1992. The ATR72-500 (originally referred to as the ATR 72-210A) has even better 'hot and high' performance because of its PW127F engines and can be identified by its six-bladed propeller units, similar to those on the ATR 42-500.

The ATR 52C was a proposed, but unbuilt, freighter version with a revised tail and a rear-loading ramp. A 'Petrel 72' Maritime Patrol version and a long fuselage ATR 82 were also planned but neither were built. Like the ATR 42, the '72 can be converted to the latest 'Large Cargo Door' configuration. The first customer for this conversion was Farnair of Switzerland.

Worldwide sales of both the ATR 42 and 72 have been excellent, with many of their 115 operators in 74 countries operating both types. The operator with the largest ATR 72 fleet has been American Eagle who operate 46. In January 2005 the Indian low cost operator Air Deccan placed the largest ATR order in many years, for 30 aircraft to be delivered at 6 to 8 a year.

ATR is currently discussing plans to update the avionics and cabin interior, and improve performance by using more powerful engines, in addition, they are planning a 50% increase in design life.

Details

Span: 27.05m (88ft 9in)
Length: 27.17m (89ft 2in)
Engines: Two P&WC turboprops,
  72-200 1,611kW (2,160shp) PW124B;
  72-500 2,050kW (2,750shp) PW127F
Cruise speed: 518km/h (280kt)
Accommodation: 74 maximum

First service: KarAir, October 1989
Number built (ordered): 295 (42)
Number in service: 286

Current Operators

Africa: Air Algérie, Air Austral, Air Mauritius, Safair, Tuninter.

Asia: Air Mandalay, Bangkok AW, China Xinjiang AL, Jet AW, Lao AL, Siem Reap Air, Thai AW, Trigana AS, Vietnam AL, Yangon AW.

Australasia: Air Tahiti, Mount Cook AL.

Europe: Aer Arann, Air Atlantique, Air Contractors, Air Dolomiti, Airlinair, Air Nostrum, Alitalia Express, Alsace Exel, Aurigny AS, Binter Canarias, CCM AL, Cimber Air, CSA, Danish AT, Eurolot, Europe Airpost, Eurowings, Farnair Switzerland, Finnair, Islas AW, JAT, Olympic AL, Swiftair.

Middle East: Arkia, Iran Aseman.

Former Soviet Union: Aero AL.

North America: American Connection, Atlantic Southeast AL, FedEx, Trans States AL.

South America: Aero Caribbean, Air Caraïbes, LA IAACA Venezuela

In 2004, Air Scandic flew holiday charters from Manchester with two Airbus A300B4s leased from Finnair. They now use MD-83s and B757s. (Author)

AIRBUS A300

Airbus Integrated Company
1 Rond Point Maurice Bellonte
Blagnac Cedex, F-31707, France

In the mid-1960s, Britain and France studied designs for a twin-engined 300-seater wide-bodied medium-range airliner for their national airlines, BEA and Air France. These studies widened and later, with the German aircraft industry involved, eventually became the multinational Airbus A300. In 1969, after much dithering due to the lack of orders, the British government withdrew their support for the A300, leaving the French and Germans to continue work on the project. Thankfully for the British economy and its collapsing aircraft industry, Hawker Siddeley (later to become part of BAe) remained in the consortium with responsibility for the design and construction of the wings. The first A300 to be built was the 252-seater A300B, powered by General Electric CF6 engines. This first flew from Toulouse in October 1972.

All the early A300s were poor performers in comparison to current models, and this was reflected in slow sales of this, the world's first wide-bodied twin-jet. The major boost to the A300 sales drive came in 1978 when US carrier Eastern Airlines ordered 19 A300B4s after it had operated four leased examples.

Airbus produced several variants over the A300s lifetime. In 1974, the popular A300B2 with a 2.65m (8ft 8in) stretch appeared with Air France, followed in 1975 by the longer range 'B4 that first flew with Germanair. The 'C4 was convertible to freight while the 'F4 was all-freight. Production of the 'B4 was stopped in May 1984 when the programme switched to the much improved A300-600.

The A300-600 has a two-crew EFIS cockpit, drag-reducing wingtip fences and airframe modifications, more powerful engines, a new APU and a high level of composite materials. It also has two more rows of seats than the earlier models because it uses the same rear fuselage as the A310. The extended-range/higher MTOW A300-600R that entered service in 1988 was the last passenger version built.

FedEx encouraged the design of the all-freight -600F and this type first flew in December 1993. It has a reinforced floor and a large upper-deck cargo door. The current model, first delivered in September 2004, is the A300-600F 'General Freighter'. This has a cargo loading system and revised side freight door. Production of the A300-600 continues at one per month but in January 2005 FedEx cancelled 37 of their remaining 50 A300-600F orders. Two companies developed freight conversion programmes, BAESAS at Filton and EADS-EFW at Dresden. BAE have since sold their conversion line to Flight Structures in the USA.

Mention should be made here of the A300-600ST Super Transporter. This outsize purpose-built freighter is designed solely to carry wings and large airframe components between Airbus factories.

Details

Span: 44.84m (147ft 1in)
Length: 54.08m (177ft 5in)
Engines: Two 262kN-273kN (59,000-61,500lb) GE CF6-80C2A or two 258kN (58,000lb) PW 4158s or two 249kN (56,000lb) PW JT9D turbofans
Cruise speed: 890km/h (480kt)
Accommodation: Typical 267, Max 375
(Details above are for the A300-600)

First service:
  (A300-B4) Air France, May 1974
  (A300-600) Saudia, March 1984
Number built (ordered): 535 (17)
Number in service: 400

Current Operators

Africa: Afriqiyah AW, Fly Intl AW, Libyan Arab AL, Sudan AW, Tunisair.

Asia: Air Hong Kong, Air Paradise Intl, Ariana Afghan AL, Astro Air, China AL, China Eastern AL, China Northern AL, Indian AL, JAL Domestic, Korean Air, Pakistan Intl AL, Thai AW.

Europe: Air Contractors, Air Scandic, Channel Express, Europe Airpost, European AT, Islandsflug, Kuzu AL Cargo, Lufthansa, Monarch AL, Olympic AL, Pan Air, TNT AW.

Middle East: AMC AL, Egyptair, Fly Air, Iran Air, Kuwait AW, Kuzu Cargo AL, Mahan Air, MNG AL, Onur Air, Orbit Express AL, Qatar AW, Saga AL, Tristar Air.

North America: American AL, Express.Net AL, FedEx, Tradewinds AL, UPS AL.

South America: Aerounion, VASP.

Tehran-based Mahan Air operate a mixed fleet of Soviet and Western types including A310 F-OJHH. (Julian Gill)

AIRBUS A310

Airbus Integrated Company
1 Rond Point Maurice Bellonte
Blagnac Cedex, F-31707, France

The designation A300B10 was given to one of the many proposed versions of the original A300 Airbus. This version later developed into the Airbus programme that was officially launched in July 1978 after Eastern Airlines, Lufthansa and Swissair showed interest in the type.

The A310 has the same fuselage cross-section as the A300 but the fuselage is shortened by 13 frames. Its British-built high aspect ratio two-spar wing has a slightly shorter span than the A300 and the horizontal tail surfaces are smaller, but the tail fin is the same. The two-crew cockpit has a six-screen EFIS layout and conventional control columns. The initial engine choice offered by Airbus was between the JT9D and the CF6, and although Rolls-Royce's RB211 was also offered, it failed to attract the necessary airline interest to warrant development.

The type's first orders were announced from Lufthansa, Swissair and KLM in spring 1979 followed by the first flight in April 1982. By September of that year, the order book stood at 102. Excellent performance and fuel economy were evident in the test flights; indeed, a 4% improvement in fuel consumption was discovered over pre-production forecasts.

Initially Airbus offered two versions, the standard -100 and the longer range -200. All orders received were for the -200, and

therefore no Series 100s were built. The further improved -300 with a range of 9,580km (5,170nm) was launched in 1982 with an order from Swissair. This had a computerised fuel distribution system and the extra fuel carried in the tailplane was used as a trimming device similar to the one used by the Concorde. The small winglets that first appeared on the -300 were also fitted to late model -200s.

Production of the A310 ceased in mid 1998 and the type is now disappearing from front line passenger service; however, it has found a significant new life as a freighter. Originally, a single A310-200C Combi passenger/cargo was built for Martinair Holland in 1984. This aircraft now flies for FedEx having been converted to all-cargo configuration. FedEx also operate nearly 50 of the A310-200F freighter, all of them being ex-passenger A310-200s converted in Germany by EADS EFW. The air forces of Germany and Canada operate A310-300s converted to freighters while the first civilian A310-300F conversion was first flown in February 2001 prior to delivery to FedEx. A multi-role Transport Tanker conversion of the A310 entered service in Germany in late 2004.

Details

Span: 43.89m (144ft 0in)
Length: 46.66m (153ft 1in)
Engines: Early versions, two 213.5kN (48,000lb) PW JT9D-7R4D1 or 222.4kN (50,000lb) GE CF-6-80A3A1. Later versions, two 238.0kN (53,500lb) GE CF6-80C2A2, 262.4kN (59,000lb) GE CF-6-80C2A8, 231.2kN (52,000lb) PW4152 or 249.1kN (56,000lb) PW4156A turbofans.
Cruise speed: 897km/h (484kt) max
Accommodation: Typical 212, Max 280

First service: Lufthansa, April 1983
Number built: 255
Number in service: 189

Current Operators

Africa: African Safari AW, Air Algérie, Fly Intl AW, Libyan Arab AL, Yemenia.

Asia: Air India, Air Paradise Intl, Biman Bangladesh AL, China Eastern AL, MIAT Mongolian AL, Pakistan Intl AL, Singapore AL.

Europe: Air Plus Comet, CSA, Eagle Avn, Hapag Lloyd, Islandsflug, Lufthansa, SATA Intl.

Middle East: AMC AL, Emirates, Iran Air, Jordanian Avn, KTHY, Kuwait AW, Mahan Air, Midwest AL, Royal Jordanian, Turkish AL, World Focus AL

Former Soviet Union: Sibir AL, Uzbekistan AW.

North America: Air Transat, FedEx.

South America: Aerolineas Argentinas.

The evening light at Paris Charles de Gaulle Airport highlights the taller tail of A318-111 F-GUGE used by Air France on European services. (Julian Gill)

AIRBUS A318

Airbus Integrated Company
1 Rond Point Maurice Bellonte
Blagnac Cedex, F-31707, France

In the mid-1990s, Airbus, Alenia, Singapore Technologies and AVIC of China announced a joint programme for a 100-seater airliner which would be assembled in China. The AE31X specification covered two types, a 95-seater AE316 and a 115/125-seat AE317. However, this project was cancelled by Airbus in 1998 after they revealed that they had been studying a smaller version of the A319 that would involve minimum changes to the airframe. Initially given the name A319M5 (The M5 suffix indicating 'Minus 5 fuselage frames') the model was revealed by Airbus at the 1998 Farnborough Air Show. However it was not until April 1999 that Airbus could announce the official launch after it had secured 109 orders from Air France, ILFC, Frontier and Egyptair.

Airbus engineers had a difficult task in reducing the length of the A319, as this was already a reduced length airliner with common parts relating to the much larger A320 and A321. The goal of 95% of common parts between the single-aisle range was made difficult partly because of the higher weight of the structures required for the larger aircraft. In the end Airbus settled for four major differences. First and most obvious was the reduction in length from the A319 by the deletion of 4.5 frames (2.4m). This caused a knock on problem because the position of the baggage compartment door was now too close to the engine

nacelle for ground vehicles to manoeuvre up to it. A new, smaller door was therefore designed at great cost. To preserve the in-flight longitudinal stability, the fin height was increased slightly (0.8m/ 2ft 8in), and, perhaps the most radical change, and the one that was to cause much grief, was the development of a specially tailored engine, the PW6000, designed for the 100-seater market.

The PW6000-powered prototype first flew on 15th January 2002. The engine, offered exclusively for the A318, had been built with fewer parts and fewer compressor stages for simplicity and lightness. Sadly, it proved to have less power and burnt 6% more fuel than promised. Airbus therefore switched powerplants to the heavier CFM56 for the rest of the certification flights. The A318 was eventually certified by Europe's JAA and the FAA in the USA in spring 2003. The certification of the PW-powered version has been delayed until mid 2005.

Built at Finkenwerder, Hamburg, the A318 has failed to sell in quantity. British Airways, Air China and GATX/Flightlease have either cancelled or changed their orders, while an order for 50 from TWA collapsed along with that airline in 2001. Mexicana commenced A318 services in November 2004.

Details

Span: 34.10m (111ft 10in)
Length: 31.45m (103ft 2in)
Engines: Two 97.9kN-106.8kN (22,000lb-24,000lb) PW6122 or PW6124 or two 97.9kN (22,000lb) CFM56-5B turbofans
Cruise speed: Mach 0.78
Accommodation: Typical 129, Max 107

First service: Frontier, July 2003
Number built (ordered): 14 (68)
Number in service: 14

Current Operators

Europe: Air France.
North America: Frontier AL.
South America: Mexicana.

Seen on delivery at London Gatwick in October 2004, A319-111 G-EZEV shows its extra overwing emergency exit that is unique to EasyJet's aircraft. (Author)

AIRBUS A319

Airbus Integrated Company
1 Rond Point Maurice Bellonte
Blagnac Cedex, F-31707, France

Market research and proposals for this shortened version of the best-selling Airbus A320 commenced in May 1992 and in December that year, Los Angeles-based leasing company ILFC ordered six aircraft (ILFC was also the first customer for the IAE V2500-powered version in June 1995). Airbus officially launched the type at the Paris Air Show in June 1993. Basically, the A319 is an A320 shortened by seven fuselage frames thereby reducing the maximum seating to 142. Because of its lower weight, the A319 has a greater range (maximum 6,845km/3,697nm) than the A320/A321. It can even fly further than the smaller A318.

Because of the type's commonality with the other Airbus narrowbodies and the fact that A320/321 flight crew can fly the A319 using a 'common type rating', it has attracted many orders from airlines that already operate the A320/321. The A319's entry to the US market came with an 'opening' order from United Airlines for 24 units (later increased to 51) – a significant inroad into firm Boeing 737 territory. Air Canada has over 110 Airbus single-aisle airliners including 48 A319s.

The first 124-seater, CFM-56-5A-powered prototype Airbus A319 was rolled out at the Deutsche Airbus factory in Hamburg in August 1995. First flown on the 25th August 1995, European JAA certification for the CFM-powered version was granted in April 1996 after 650 hours of test flying. Swissair commenced A319

services at the end of that month. The prototype was then re-engined with V2524s and commenced further certification trials on 22nd May 1996, leading to certification of this version in December.

In 1997, Airbus revealed their 10-60-seater A319 'Airbus Corporate Jetliner'. With an 11,690km (6,300nm) range, it was advertised as 'The world's most spacious corporate jet'. First flown in November 1998, on 16th June 1999 it set a distance world record of 12,812km (6,919nm) when it flew from Santiago to Le Bourget. The A319CJ's customers include the Italian and French Air Forces, Privatair, Volkswagen, DaimlerChrysler and Qatar Airways. The 44-seat A319 'Executive' is also available.

Other versions are the extended range A319ER and long range A319LR. The ER has two extra 3,000-litre (700-gal) fuel tanks in the rear hold. In 2004 Air France announced that it would use four 82-seat A319ER aircraft for new 'thin' routes to Africa and the Middle East. In February 2003, the Airbus A319LR made its debut at an exhibition in Hamburg with an all-business class layout with 48 seats and a range of 8,250km (4,500nm). In 2003, EasyJet became the launch customer for a 156-seater version that can be identified by the extra overwing exits.

Details

Span: 34.10m (111ft 9in)
Length: 33.84m (110ft 11in)
Engines: Two 99.7-106.6kN (22,500-24,000lb) turbofans, either CFM International CFM56-5, or IAE V2522/V2524.
Cruise speed: 833km/h (459kts)
Accommodation: Normal 124, Max 145

First service: Swissair, April 1996.
Number built (ordered): 637 (362)
Number in service: 637

Current Operators

Africa: Air Burkina, Air Mauritius, South African AW, Tunisair.

Asia: Air China, Air Macau, China Eastern AL, China Northern AL, China Southern AL, Druk Air, Royal Brunei AL, Sichuan AL, Silkair.

Europe: Aeroservices, Air France, Air Malta, Alitalia, Austrian AL, BMI, British AW, CCM AL, Croatia AL, Cyprus AW, EasyJet AL, EasyJet Switzerland, Finnair, Germanwings, Iberia, Lufthansa, Meridiana, Privatair, SN Brussels AL, Swiss Intl AL, TAP Air Portugal.

Middle East: Lotus Air.

Former Soviet Union: Aeroflot.

North America: Air Canada, America West AL, Blue Moon Avn, Frontier AL, Independence Air, Northwest AL, Sky Service AL, United AL, US AW, Virgin America.

South America: LAN Chile, LAN Express, Mexicana, TACA Intl AL, TACA Peru, TAM LA.

JFK-based jetBlue anticipate having 202 A320s by 2012. Each aircraft is given a name containing the word 'blue'. This is N506JB 'Wild Blue Yonder'. (Author)

AIRBUS A320

Airbus Integrated Company
1 Rond Point Maurice Bellonte
Blagnac Cedex, F-31707, France

Having had some success with their A300/A310 airliners in a market dominated by the Americans, Airbus launched their A320 design in 1984 as a competitor to the Boeing 737 and the McDonnell Douglas MD-80 series. By equipping their 'mini-Airbus' with the very latest in cockpit technology and ultra fuel-efficient engines, the European consortium managed to create a state-of-the-art airliner that sold, and still sells, in huge numbers worldwide. Indeed, the A320 made aviation history by receiving more airline orders before its first flight than any previous airliner.

First flown in February 1987, the A320 completed its certification tests in 1988. The first airline A320 entered service the following year with Air France, which had ordered examples of both the -100 and -200. Only 21 -100s were built before Airbus decided to concentrate on the new -200 with wingtip fences, greater fuel capacity and higher MTOW. The first delivery of an A320-200 was to Ansett of Australia in June 1988.

The A320 uses significant amounts of composite materials, for weight saving and it was the world's first subsonic airliner to be built with a computerised fly-by-wire control system incorporating a fully integrated EFIS cockpit together with 'sidestick' control columns.

The A320 design subsequently evolved into the stretched A321 and the smaller A319/318 versions. All of them retain the same cockpit and flight controls allowing flightcrews to fly any of the series using a common type rating. The A320 is built at Toulouse using components from Airbus subsidiaries in Europe. The wings are built in the UK and flown to France in A300-600ST Super Transporters while the centre and rear fuselage and fin are built in Germany.

The type is in service with scheduled and charter operators worldwide. One of the largest fleets of A320s is with New York-based jetBlue Airways. Their future plans foresee a fleet of 202 A320s by 2012. All jetBlue A320s offer passengers single-class accommodations of 156 all-leather seats, each equipped with 24 channels of DIRECTV(r) programming.

Airbus is currently analysing whether the A320 family would benefit from the addition of larger winglets. Designs for these winglets up to 2m (6ft 6in) long have been tested on the company's A340-300.

Details

Span: 34.09m (111ft 9in)
Length: 37.57m (123ft 3in)
Engines: Two 104.5-117.9kN (23,500-26,500lb) turbofans, either CFM International CFM56-5, or IAE V2525-A5
Cruise speed: 903km/h (487kt) max
Accommodation: Normal 150, Max 180

First service: Air France, April 1988
Number built (ordered): 1,331 (437)
Number in service: 1,290

Current Operators

Africa: Afriqiyah AW, Nouvelair, Orion Air, Tunisair.

Asia: Air Blue, Air China, Air Deccan, Air Macau, ANA, Asiana AL, Bangkok AW, China Eastern AL, China Southern AL, Dragonair, First Cambodia AL, Indian AL, Jetstar Asia, Lao AL, Pacific AL, Philippines AL, Royal Brunei AL, Sichuan AL, Silkair, Srilankan AL, Tiger AW, Transasia AW, Valuair, Vietnam AL.

Australasia: Air New Zealand, Jetstar AW.

Europe: Adria AW, Aer Lingus, Aeroflight, Air France, Air Luxor, Air Malta, Air Prishtina, Alitalia, Austrian AL, BH Air, Bluewings, BMI, British AW, British Mediterranean AW, CCM AL, Condor Berlin, Croatia AL, Cyprus AW, Dutchbird, Edelweiss Air, Eurofly, Finnair, First Choice AW, GB AW, Germanwings, Hellas Jet, Iberia, Iberworld, LTU, LTU Austria, Lufthansa, Martinair, Monarch AL, My Travel AW (UK), My Travel AW (DK), My Travel Lite, Niki, Ocean AW, SATA Intl, Spanair, Star AL, Swiss Intl AL, TAP Air Portugal, Thomas Cook AL, Thomas Cook AL Belgium, Volar AL, Vueling AL, Windjet, Wizzair.

Middle East: Air Arabia, Air Memphis, Atlas Jet, Egyptair, Freebird AL, Gulf Air, Jordanian Avn, Kuwait AW, Lotus Air, MEA, Mena Jet, Onur Air, Qatar AW, Royal Jordanian, Syrianair, Turkish AL.

Former Soviet Union: Aeroflot, Air Moldova, Armavia, Armenian Intl AW, Azerbaijan AL, LAT Charter, Um Air.

North America: Air Canada, Air Tran AW, America West AL, Jetblue AW, Northwest AL, Ryan Intl AL, Sky Service AL, Ted, United AL, US AW, USA 3000 AL, Virgin America.

South America: Air Jamaica, LAN Chile, LAN Express, LAN Peru, Mexicana, TACA Intl AL, TACA Costa Rica, TAM LA, TAME.

Aeroflot have replaced Boeing 737s with A320s. Other Western types in their inventory include the A319, A321, A310, B767, B777 and DC-10. (Julian Gill)

Airbus A321-231 B-2371 is flown by Sichuan Airlines who in 2003 bought the 'luckiest' telephone number in China, 88888888! (Colin Ballantine)

Undoubtedly one of the most colourful schemes seen in Miami belongs to Air Jamaica's six A321s. This is A321-211 6Y-JMD 'City of Westmoreland'. (Author)

AIRBUS A321

Airbus Integrated Company
1 Rond Point Maurice Bellonte
Blagnac Cedex, F-31707, France

With their groundbreaking A320 selling well, Airbus were able to plan for a 'minimum change' A320 'stretch' version using as much of the A320 airframe as possible. In June 1989 this became the A321 and the programme was officially launched in November that year.

The A320 design was stretched by extending the fuselage with a 4.27m (14ft) plug inserted forward of the wing and a 2.67m (8ft 9in) plug behind. This allows the seating capacity to be raised to 185 in a two-class layout (or a maximum of 220 in a high-density configuration at 29-inch seat pitch) and increases the hold volume by 40%. Despite the emphasis on a straightforward fuselage stretch, several modifications were needed to the original design. These included a stronger undercarriage with larger tyres, local strengthening to the centre fuselage section, a simplified fuel system and the addition of two extra overwing exits. The revised wing was very similar to the A320's but was provided with double slotted flaps rather than the 320's single slotted devices. The flap alterations allowed the flight characteristics of the A321 to match the A320. The A321 cockpit is identical to the smaller A320/319/318 allowing aircrew to fly any of them under the common type rating system.

Late in 1992, an IAE V2500-powered example and a CFM56-powered aircraft were both approaching completion at DASA's Hamburg factory. The first to fly was the V2500-powered example on 11th March 1993 followed by the CFM version on 23rd May. JAA certification for the IAE-powered version was completed in December allowing launch customer Lufthansa to accept its first A321 in January 1994. Alitalia was the launch customer for the CFM-powered A321 and after JAA certification in February, they received their first in March.

In March 1995, the basic A321-100 was complemented by the extended-range A321-200. This version has a 2,900-litre (766-US gal) ACT 'Additional Centre Tank' in the rear cargo hold. This tank is shaped to the same dimensions as an LD-6 cargo container. The extra fuel allows the A321-200 to fly similar distances to the smaller A320 aircraft. Other changes to the -200 were the more powerful engines and additional structural strengthening. Aero Lloyd ordered the first A321-200 in April 1995 and accepted delivery of it a year later. Currently the largest A321 fleets are operated by US Air and Alitalia.

Details

Span: 34.09m (111ft 9in)
Length: 44.51m (146ft 0in)
Engines: Two 133-146.8kN (30,000-33,000lb) turbofans, either CFM International CFM56-5, or IAE V2530/V2533
Cruise speed: 903km/h (487kt)
Accommodation: Normal 185, Max 220

First service: Lufthansa, March 1994
Number built (ordered): 317 (85)
Number in service: 317

Current Operators

Africa: Air Ivoire, Orion Air, Royal Air Maroc.
Asia: Air Macau, ANA, Asiana AL, China Eastern, China Northern AL, China Southern AL, Dragonair, Pacific AL, Sichuan AL, Transasia AW, Vietnam AL.
Europe: Aer Lingus, Aeroflight, Aigle Azur, Air France, Air Mediterranée, Alitalia, Austrian, Bluewings, BMI, British AW, British Mediterranean, Finnair, First Choice AW, GB AW, Iberia, Livingstone, LTU, Lufthansa, Monarch AL, My Travel AW (UK), My Travel AW (DK), Niki, Novair, SAS, Spanair, Swiss Intl AL, TAP Air Portugal, Volar AL.
Former Soviet Union: Aeroflot.
Middle East: Air Cairo, Egyptair, KTHY, Mahan Air, MEA, Onur Air, Qatar AW, Turkish AL.
North America: Air Canada, Spirit AL, US AW.
South America: Air Jamaica.

This is one of the two Stockholm-based Novair A330s seen on final approach to runway 08R at London Gatwick in September 2004. (Author)

AIRBUS A330

Airbus Integrated Company
1 Rond Point Maurice Bellonte
Blagnac Cedex, F-31707, France

The A330 (and A340) medium/long-range high-capacity airliner can trace its lineage back to the early 1970s when Airbus considered future designs based on the A300. The smaller A300B10 project developed into the A310, and in 1980, the larger twin-engined A300B9 and four-engined A300B11 evolved into the Airbus A300TA9 and TA11 (TA=Twin Aisle)

By 1982 the two designs were proposed with a common wing, one with two engines, the other with four, and an extended 194ft 10in fuselage common to both types. The cockpit would be fly-by-wire with sidesticks and EFIS instruments. In January 1986, the type designators changed with the A300TA9 becoming the A330 and the A300TA11 becoming the A340. The advanced concept of a twin-engined and a four-engined aircraft with a shared airframe, wing and cockpit design was unique in the world of airliners. By 1986 the design was stretched by 5 frames (10ft 7in) to add an extra 24 passengers at the expense of some range. The A330 would also have an additional centre section auxiliary undercarriage (standard fitting on the A340) offered as an option.

Airline interest in the baseline A330 (by now given the suffix -300) was confirmed early in 1987 when French carrier Air Inter ordered 5 (+ 15 options) and Thai International ordered 4 (+ 4 options). Airbus then officially launched the A330 in time for the Paris Air Show that summer with orders for 38 from three customers.

The twin-engined A330-300 first flew in November 1992, over a year after its sister, the A340. Aer Lingus became the first airline to operate trans-Atlantic flights with the A330 after the type had been granted ETOPS approval in May 1994.

First flown with CF6 engines, the A330 later became available with the PW4000 or the Rolls-Royce Trent, both of which share the same pylon and mount. Versions include the basic A330-300 and the longer-range -200 that was launched in November 1995 as a competitor to the Boeing 767-300ER. The series 200's fuselage is 10 frames (5.33m/17ft 6in) shorter than the -300, it has a bigger fin and tailplane and has an additional centre fuel tank allowing it to fly over 12,350km (6,650nm). First operator of the -200 was Canada 3000 in May 1998. In June 2003 Northwest Airlines received their first A330-300 'Enhanced'; this has a fly-by-wire rudder control, LCD instrumentation and an updated cabin.

The A330-200 MRTT 'Multi-Role Tanker/Transport' has been ordered by the RAF to replace their VC-10 and TriStar tanker fleet. Other MRTT orders are from Germany, Canada and Australia.

In 2004, Airbus revealed plans for an A350 model that would replace its two earliest models, the A300 and A310. Based on the A330, the A350 would use similar engines to those on the Boeing 787 and have significant amounts of carbonfibre reinforced plastic components.

Details

Span: -300 and -200 60.30m (197ft 10in)
Length: A330-300 63.60m (208ft 11in); A330-200 58.32m (191ft 5in)
Engines: Two 300-322kN (67,500-74,000lb) turbofans, either General Electric CF6-80E1, Pratt & Whitney PW4164/4168 or Rolls-Royce Trent 772.
Cruise speed: 880km/h (475kt)
Accommodation:
A330-300 440 max, normal 295
A330-200 380 max, normal 253

First service: Air Inter, January 1994
Number built (ordered): 319 (179)
Number in service: 319

Current Operators

Africa: Air Algérie, Yemenia.
Asia: Asiana, Cathay Pacific, China AL, China Southern, Dragonair, Eva Air, Garuda, Korean Air, Malaysia AL, Philippines AL, Srilankan AL, Thai AW.
Australasia: Air Calin, Qantas AW.
Europe: Aer Lingus, Air France, Air Greenland, Air Luxor, Air Madrid, Austrian, BMI, Corsair, Cyprus AW, Edelweiss Air, Eurofly, Iberworld, Livingstone, LTU, Lufthansa, Monarch AL, My Travel AW (UK), My Travel AW (DK), Novair, SAS, SN Brussels AL, Star AL, Swiss Intl AL, Thomas Cook AL.
Middle East: Egyptair, Emirates, Etihad AW, Gulf Air, MEA, Qatar AW.
North America: Air Canada, Air Transat, Northwest AL, Sky Service AL, US AW.
South America: Air Caraïbes, TAM LA.

Fast growing Middle East airline Etihad operates this A330-200 A6-EYX on flights EY303/4 between Heathrow and its Abu Dhabi base. (Richard Vandervord)

Although this A340-212 V8-BKH flies in the colours of the national airline, it is actually a VIP aircraft belonging to the Sultan of Brunei. (Jacques Guillem)

The only airline on the beautiful island of Mauritius is Air Mauritius. Founded in 1967, it has 5 Airbus A340s including 3B-NBD seen here at Manchester. (Author)

AIRBUS A340

Airbus Integrated Company
1 Rond Point Maurice Bellonte
Blagnac Cedex, F-31707, France

The A340 is a direct descendant of the A300/A310 series and retains the same fuselage diameter. The design was originally planned as a four-engined version of the A310 with the designation A300B11. This was later changed to TA11, (TA = Twin Aisle) and finally it became the A340 in 1986. In June 1987, the A330/340 joint programme was launched; the two types became the world's first airliners to be designed completely using computers and to use the same airframe, wing and cockpit but with both two and four engines.

The A340 is currently available in four fuselage lengths. First flown in October 1991, over a year before the first A330, the A340 gained its Joint European certification in December 1992. Air France and Lufthansa both commenced scheduled A340 services in March 1993.

The basic version of the A340 is the -300 that typically seats 295 in a three-class arrangement and has a range of 13,150km (7,100nm). Singapore Airlines ordered the A340-300E, a high gross weight version with an extra centre fuel tank, stronger landing gear and wing structure.

The shorter fuselage/longer range -200 first flew in April 1992; it normally seats 263 in three classes and has a range of 13,805km (7,450nm). When the first A340 entered service in 1993, it was the first entirely new long-haul airliner to enter service for more than 20 years. The stretched Trent-powered A340-500 and -600 versions were launched in 1997. The -500 was designed as an ultra long-range airliner while the further stretched -600 sacrificed some range for extra capacity. Both have longer spans than the A340-200/300, a larger fin and tailplane and a four-wheel centre bogie to cope with the extra weight. The A340-500 has the longest range of any commercial airliner in service, able to fly 15,742km (8,500nm). First delivered to Emirates Airlines, it commenced non-stop Dubai to New York and Dubai to Melbourne flights in June 2004. The Emirates A340-500s can be fitted with an $8 million ICE (Information Communication & Entertainment) system that can show live news broadcasts, 50 TV channels and 100 movies. Singapore Airlines' A340-500s fly the world's longest scheduled service, Singapore to New York.

The Airbus A340-600 version holds the title as the longest commercial airliner in the world, indeed, the -600 is even longer than the giant A380. Lufthansa's -600s, complete with a lower deck washroom and kitchen, first entered service in December 2003.

Details

Span: -200 & -300 60.30m (197ft 10in), -500 & -600 63.45m (208ft 2in)
Length: A340-200 59.39m (194ft 10in); A340-300 63.65m (208ft 10in) A340-500 67.90m (222ft 9in); A340-600 75.30m (247ft 0in)
Engines: -200 & -300 Four 151.2kN (34,000lb) CFM International CFM-56-5C4 turbofans -500 236kN (53,000lb) Rolls-Royce Trent 553, -600 249kN (56,000lb) Trent 556.
Cruise speed: 494kt/914kmh max
Accommodation: 440 maximum, normally 239 to 380.

First service: -200 Lufthansa, Mar 1993, -600 Virgin Atlantic, August 2002.
Number built (ordered): 285 (67)
Number in service: 285

Current Operators

Africa: Air Mauritius, South African AW.
Asia: Air China, Cathay Pacific, China Eastern AL, China Southwest AL, Philippines AL, Srilankan AL, Singapore AL, Thai AW.
Australasia: Air Tahiti Nui.
Europe: Air Bourbon, Air France, Austrian, Iberia, Lufthansa, Ocean AW, Olympic AL, SAS, Swiss Intl AL, TAP Air Portugal, Virgin Atlantic.
Middle East: Egyptair, Emirates, Etihad AW, Gulf Air, Kuwait AW, Royal Jordanian, Turkish AL.
North America: Air Canada.
South America: Aerolineas Argentinas, Air Jamaica, BWIA, LAN Chile.

With 45 double-deck Airbus A380s on order, Emirates Airlines will eventually become the world's largest operator of the world's largest airliner. (Airbus)

AIRBUS A380

Airbus Integrated Company
1 Rond Point Maurice Bellonte
Blagnac Cedex, F-31707, France

The A380 (initially designated A3XX), the world's first twin-deck, twin-aisle airliner, was formally announced in December 2000 after seven years of design studies. The launch of the $10.7billion project came on the back of firm orders for 50 aircraft from five airlines (Virgin Atlantic, Qantas, Emirates, Singapore and Air France) and the aircraft lessor ILFC.

Airbus has contracts with at least 25 companies worldwide to provide A380 structures. The airliner will be assembled in Toulouse from parts that will arrive by land, sea and air from all over Europe and Asia. Because of the huge size of some of the components, even the A300-600ST 'Beluga' transport will not be large enough to carry them. The UK-designed wings, 36.6m (120ft) long, 17.7m (58ft) wide at the root, are built at Broughton in Wales and will be transported to France using a huge, Chinese-built roll-on roll-off vessel. The same ship will carry sections from Hamburg in Germany, St Nazaire in France and Puerto Real in Spain. Special river barges and road trailers will then haul the items to the new 50 hectare Airbus A380 site at Blagnac airport.

Design features include a four-leg main landing gear with high-density carbon brakes designed to bring the 560 tonne airliner to a stop from 174kts (322km/h) in 32 seconds. Structural weight reduction is helped by the use of composite materials that make up 22% of the A380 by weight. The two separate

cabins are in twin-aisle format with up to eight abreast on the top deck and ten abreast on the lower. The standard 3-class layout will seat 555, but 840 could be carried if it was fitted for a high-density single class.

Power for the A380-800 is provided by either the Rolls-Royce Trent 900 or by the GP7020 built by Engine Alliance, a 50/50 partnership of P&W and General Electric. The A380 Freighter has even higher power Trent 977s or GP7277s.

The roll-out ceremony for the first aircraft took place on 18th January 2005. Initial A380 production will start with five aircraft that will be flown by Airbus on flight tests. Four of these will later be reworked and sold to Etihad Airlines. Certification is planned for first quarter of 2006, followed by first deliveries to launch customer Singapore Airlines in March that year. A380s for European and Middle Eastern customers will be flown from Toulouse to the Hamburg-Finkenwerder factory where they will be customised, fitted out and then delivered. Current versions offered are the baseline A380-800 and the all-freight A380-800F with a payload of 152,400kg (150 tons). Future versions could be a 480-seat A380-700 and a 650-seat A380-900. In 2004, both Virgin Atlantic and Air France delayed their delivery dates, mostly because some airport's ground infrastructures required to allow A380 operations would not be ready in time.

Details

Span: 79.60m (261ft 2in)
Length: 72.70m (238ft 6in)
Engines: Four 311kN (70,000lb)
Rolls-Royce Trent 970 or GE/P&W
Engine Alliance GP7270 turbofans.
-800 Freighter has 340kN (76,500lb)
Trent 977 or GP7277s.
Cruise speed: Mach 0.85
Accommodation: 555 normal, 840 max

First service: planned for March 2006.
Number built (ordered): None (129)
Number in service: None

Orders received

Asia: Korean Air (8), Malaysia AL (6), Singapore AL (10), Thai AW (6).
Australasia: Qantas AW (12).
Europe: Air France (10), Lufthansa (15), Virgin Atlantic (6).
Middle East: Emirates (45), Etihad AW (4), Qatar AW (2).
North America: FedEx (10).

Y5B-100 B-8447 is operated by Jihua Airlines of Shijiazhuang. The winglets are designed to reduce drag and increase rate of climb. (Colin Ballantine)

ANTONOV An-2 & SAMC Y-5

PZL Mielec, ul.Wojska Polskiego 3, PL-39-300 Mielec, Poland; SAIC, 19 Beierhuan West Rd, Shijiazhuang, Hebei, China.

With up to 20,000 of this large, single-engined biplane produced, the An-2 (NATO reporting name 'Colt') is the world's best selling commercial aircraft. Oleg Antonov's post war design bureau set out to create a rugged aircraft that could fulfil a design specification set by the Soviet Ministry of Agriculture and Forestry. The result was the SKh-1 (Selskokhozyaistvennyi-1 or Agricultural-economic-1). First flown on 31st August 1947, the design was re-designated An-2.

The An-2 is built almost entirely of metal; however, the wings aft of the front spar, the rudder and the tailplane are fabric covered. The An-2's exceptional operating characteristics are mostly due to the biplane layout and the clever use of high-lift wing devices, which permit true STOL operations and allow the aircraft to fly very slowly with a stalling speed of only 95km/h (52kt).

In addition to the standard passenger-carrying An-2T, An-2P and An-2TP, Antonov created other versions including the An-2S ambulance, the An-2L water bomber and the An-2Skh and An-2M agricultural models. The An-2M can be identified by the larger, square-shaped tail fin. The An-2 can also be operated on skis or on floats (An-2V) and there was even a twin-finned military An-2F version with a clear perspex rear fuselage for artillery observation.

In the 1960s, production was gradually switched from the USSR to WSK-Mielec

in Poland, where the majority of An-2s were completed as the utility An-2R. Around 1982, the Poles developed a turboprop conversion, designated An-3. Conversions continue at AVIANT, Kyiv, with 9 being converted in 2003/4. Versions available are the Transport An-3T and agricultural sprayer An-3Agr.

728 An-2s were built in China under license as the Fonshu 2 'Harvester' at Nanchang from 1957 before production was switched to SAMC at Shijiazhuang where it was known as the Yunshuji Y-5. At least 16 versions are known including the Y-5A 11-passenger version for CAAC, the Y-5B agriculture/forestry model (first flown in 1989), the Y-5B-100 with Chinese avionics and high-lift wing-tip devices, the Y-5B(K) for export and the Y-5B 'PARA' for parachute training. Small numbers of Y-5s are still being built in 2005.

Details

Span: 18.18m (59ft 8in)
Length: 12.74m (41ft 9in)
Engine: One 746kW (1,000hp) PZL Kalisz ASz-62IR radial piston.
Cruise speed: 185km/h (100kt)
Accommodation: Max 19, normally 12
(Details above are for PZL-built An-2P)

First service: Aeroflot, 1948.
Number built: 20,000 approximately.
Number in service: 1,071, most in the Former Soviet Union and China.

Current Operators

Asia: Eastern General Avn, Guangdong General Avn, Jiangnan Universal Avn, Jihua AL, Jingmen United General Avn, VASCO, Xinjiang General Avn, Zhejiang Donghua General Avn, Zhongfei AL.

Europe: Abas, Acvila Air, Aero Gryf, Aero Slovakia, Aero Smed, Agrolet, Air Adria, Air Albatross, Air Mizia, Air Patrol, Air Service CS, Air Special, Air Tempelhof, Anhaltisher Verein für Luftfahrt, AVS, Bohemia AS, Boniair, Budapest Aircraft Services, Classic Wings, Donau AS, Falcon Air, Fitoplant, FMU, Freunde der Antonow, Hanseflug, Jas Air, JAT Privredna Avijacija, Macedonian Commercial Avn, Motorflugverein, North Adria Avn, OFC, Polkart, Primex, SFS, Tessel Air, Trener Air.

Middle East: THK.

Former Soviet Union: Aerobratsk, Aeroflot-Nord, Air Klaipeda, Air Livonia, Air Zena, Alrosa, Altai AL, Amur Avia, Antex Polous, AS Avia, Avialesookhrana, AZAL Agro Air Company, Barkol Avia, Bel Flight, Bellesavia, Berkut West, Bravia, Bugulma Air Enterprise, BURAL, Chukotavia, Concordavia, Dauria, Delta-K Enterprise, Gintarines Avialinijos, Grodno Avia, ILIN, Kazan Air, Kirensk Air, Kiro Vohradavia, Komaviatrans, Krylya Samotlora, Lugansk AL, Lukiaviatrans, Meridian, Mold Aero Service, Murmansk Avn, Naryan-Mar Air, Nikolaeusk-Na-Amure Air Enterprise, Nikolaev-Air, Nizhneudinsk Air, Novosibirsk Air, Odessa AL, Orel Air, Orenburg AL, Polar AL, Polet AL, Privolzhskaya-Regionalaya, Ryazanaviatrans, Saramsk Air, Sibaviatrans, Sibia Avia, Sverdlovsk 2nd Air Enterprise, Tambov Avia, Tian-Shan, Tiramavia, Tura Air Enterprise, Turukhan Avia, Tuva AL, UAL, UTair Avn, Volgodonsky Ask, Vologda Air Enterprise, Vostock AL, Yaroslavl Avn, Zapolyarye Avia, Zhezair, Zonalnoe Air Enterprise.

South America: Aerobol, Aerogaviota, Aerotaxi, Aguilas Mayas Intl, At la Montana, Rutaca AL, Tranaca, Transmandu.

EX-163 'Julia' is one of four Kyrgyzstan-registered An-12B freighters operated by British Gulf International Airlines from its base at Sharjah in the UAE. (Author)

ANTONOV An-12/YUNSHUJI Y-8

Antonov ASTC, 1 Tupolev Str, Kyiv, 252062, Ukraine;
Shaanxi Aircraft Industry (Group) Co Ltd
Hanzhong, Shaanxi, China

Developed alongside the 90-seater An-10 Ukraina, the An-12 (NATO reporting name 'Cub') was designed to meet a Soviet Air Force requirement for a turboprop-driven freighter. The An-12 was built from 1957 to 1973 at Tashkent, Voronezh, Kazan and Irkutsk in the Soviet Union.

First flown in December 1957, the Soviet equivalent of the C-130 Hercules also has a large rear cargo ramp. This allows direct loading from the rear of a truck and the delivery of cargo in flight by using extraction parachutes. An internal overhead gantry crane assists in the loading of bulky cargo. The typically Soviet robust undercarriage allows the An-12 to operate from grass, sand, pebbles or snow, while in Polar Regions a version equipped with heated skis was used to supply ice stations. The rear tail gun turret used on the military versions can still be found on current civil An-12 freighters, but this is often removed and the area faired over. In 1962, the design team of the An-12 was presented with the Lenin Prize for their excellent work.

A few months after the An-12 made its Western debut at the 1965 Paris Air Show, Aeroflot began scheduled passenger/freight services between Moscow and Paris. The 14 passengers were accommodated in a small, pressurised, cabin immediately behind the crew stations.

In 1969, the Shaanxi Aircraft Company in China commenced license production of the An-12 as the Yunshuji Y-8. This upgraded An-12B has four 3,170kW (4,250shp) Chinese-built Zhuzhou WJ6 engines and earlier versions are identifiable by the longer nose. The prototype Y-8 aircraft flew in December 1974 followed by the first SAC-built aircraft at Chengdu a year later. Several versions were available, including the Y-8A helicopter carrier, the Y-8B, the fully pressurised Y-8C, the Y-8D with some western avionics and the Y-8E drone carrier. Also offered was the Y-8F for carrying up to 500 sheep or goats in special cages, the Y8-H for aerial reconnaissance and the Y8-X for maritime patrol work.

In the late 1990s, Shaanxi produced several advanced models. The Y-8F-100 had more powerful engines, EFIS, colour weather radar, TCAS and GPS. The pressurised Y-8F-200 had a 2.2m (7ft 10in) stretched fuselage. The Y-8F-400, with Honeywell avionics, a 3-crew cockpit, shortened solid nose, re-shaped fuselage and reduced empty weight, made its first flight in August 2001 and a further version, the PW150B-powered Y-8F-600 is under development and should enter service in 2006. It is thought that up to 100 Y-8s have been completed in China.

Details

Span: 30.00m (124ft 8in)
Length: 33.10m (108ft 7in).
    An-12BP 34.05m (114ft 8in)

Engines: Four 2,493kW (3,495shp) Ivchenko AI-20K or 'M turboprops
Cruise speed: 670km/h (361kt)
Accommodation: 14 passengers plus freight
Payload: 20,000kg (44,090lb)

First service: Aeroflot, February 1965
Number built: 1,243 An-12, 100 Y-8
Number in service: 170 civil, most in the Former Soviet Union

Current Operators

Africa: Aero Fret Business, Aerolift, Afrika Avn, Air West, Astral Avn, Azza Transport, Daallo AL, Data Intl Avn, El Magal Avn Services, Fresh Air, Goliaf Air, Juba AC, King Transavia Cargo, Lotus AW, Natalco AL, Sarit AL, Shoa AL, Sudanese States Avn, Trans Air Congo, Trans Attico, Universal Arabian AL, Wimbi Dira AW.

Asia: Air People Intl, China Postal AL, Expo Avn, Imtrec Avn, Jiangnan Universal Avn, Royal AL.

Australasia: Pacific Air Express.

Europe: Air Sofia, Bright Avn Services, Heli Air, Inter Trans Air, Scorpion Air, Vega AL.

Former Soviet Union: Aerocom, Aeroflot-Don, Aerovis AL, Aerovista AL, Air Armenia, Airline Transport, Airstars, Alamaty Avn, Antex-Polus, Antonov AL, Armenian AL, ATRAN, Avia Leasing Avn, Avial NV, Aviast, AZAL Cargo Air Company, Berkut Air, British Gulf Intl AL, Gorlista AL, Gromov Air, GST Aero, Irbis, Khors Air Company, KNAAPO, Kosmos AL, Lasare AL, Lviv Al, Miras Air, Motor Sich, NAPO-Aviatrans, Pecotox-Air, Phoenix Avia, Polar AL, Shovkoviy Shlyah, Silk Way AL, Tesis, Tiramavia, Ukrainian Cargo AW, Uzbekistan AW, Valan Intl, Vaso AL, Veteran AL, Volare AL, Yakutia AL, Zapolyarye Avia.

North America: Skylink Avn.

One of several African-registered Soviet-built propliners that could be found at Sharjah in March 2004 was Inter Congo's An-24B TN-AHB. (Author)

ANTONOV An-24

Antonov ASTC
1 Tupolev Str, Kyiv
252062, Ukraine

The An-24 is another remarkable aircraft from the design group led by Oleg Antonov. When it first entered service with Aeroflot, the west took very little interest in the neat 44-seater with engines specially designed for it, but it became a huge success and was sold all around the world. The design later spawned the An-26, the An-30, the An-32 and the Chinese-built Y-7, all of which have the same basic structure.

The prototype was first flown from Kiev-Svyetoshino on 20th December 1959. This was followed by three further prototypes before series production commenced at Kiev. From 1965, about 180 An-24s were built at Ulan Ude and between 1967 and 1971; the An-24T/TV and RT were built at Irkutsk.

The An-24 (NATO reporting name 'Coke') was designed as a replacement for the twin-piston powered Ilyushin IL-14 and Lisunov Li-2, able to operate from small airfields with unprepared runways. This called for a strong undercarriage and a high wing to keep the propellers clear of debris. Extensive flight-testing using the two prototypes built at Kiev-Svyetoshino was completed in September 1962.

Exported to 23 countries, foreign customers included Air Guinée, Air Mali, Balkan Bulgarian, Cubana, CAAC, Egyptair, Iraqi Airways, Interflug, Mongolian Airlines, LOT and Tarom. The type also found use as a freighter/troop transport with several air forces.

Versions include the 50-seat An-24B (An-24V in Cyrillic letters), the An-24B Series II with water injection engines and the An-24TV and RT freighters. The An-24RV and the RT have a Tumansky Ru-19A-300 auxiliary turbojet in the starboard engine nacelle to assist in take-offs at 'hot-and-high' airfields. They are also fitted with a dropdown cargo ramp under the tail, smaller than that on the An-26. A special fire-fighting version, the An-24P (Protivopozharny) was first tested in 1971. It was used to carry fire-fighting parachutists and their equipment.

After production stopped in 1979, the An-24 continued to serve in both passenger and freight roles for many years, especially with Aeroflot. The type can still be found all over the FSU but its poor fuel economy compared with modern turboprops means that many are now grounded, replaced by later models. The new generation of economical turboprops including the IL-114 and the An-140 will cause further examples of this remarkable aircraft to be grounded.

Details

Span: 29.20m (95ft 9in)
Length: 23.53m (77ft 2in)
Engines: Two 1,901ekW (2,550ehp) or 2,103ekW (2,820ehp) Progress AI-24 (Series 2) or AI-24T turboprops
Cruise speed: 450km/h (243kt)
Accommodation: 50 maximum

First service: Aeroflot, October 1962.
Number built: 1,342
Number in service: 329, most in FSU

Current Operators

Africa: Aerolift, Aero Service, Air Atlantic Congo, Air Boyoma, Air Libya, Canadian AW Congo, COAGE, Daallo AL, Djibouti AL, GETRA, Guinee Paramount AL, Inter Congo, Malift Air, Marsland Avn, Satgur AT, Sudan AW, Tobruk Air, Trans Air Congo, UTA de Guinee, UTAGE, Weasua AT, West Coast AW.

Asia: Air Koryo, Ariana Afghan AL, Hangard AL, Kam Air, MIAT Mongolian AL, PMT Air, President AL.

Europe: Aviostart, Flying Dandy, Vivant Air.

Middle East: Syrianair.

Former Soviet Union: Adygheya Avia, Aerocom, Aeromost, Aeromost-Kharkov, Aerovista AL, Air Moldova, Airline Transport, Air Urga, Alrosa, Altyn Air, Angara AL, Armenian AL, ARP 410 AL, Asia Continental AL, Astair, Astrakhan AL, Avia Jaynar, Avia-Urartu, Aviant, AVL, Belavia, Bravia, Bural, Chukotavia, Chuvashia AL, Dalavia, Dauria, Donbassaero, Euro-Asia Air, Gomelavia, Gorlista AL, Izhavia, Karat, Kate Kavia, Kirov Air Enterprise, Komiinteravia, KRYM, KVZ, Lugansk AL, Lviv AL, Motor Sich, Novosibirsk Air, Omskavia, Orenburg AL, Pecotox-Air, Perm AL, Phoenix Avia, Podillia Avia, Polar AL, Progress TSSKB, Regional AL, Riga Aero Club, Rubystar, Ryazanaviatrans, Saransk Air Enterprise, Saravia, SAT AL, SCAT, Sevastopol Avia, Sibaviatrans, Sir Aero, Specavia, State Flight Academy of Ukraine, Tajikistan AL, Tambov Avia, Tandem-Aero, Tatarstan Air, Tomskavia, Tulpar Avia Service, Turkmenistan AL, Ukraine Intl AL, Ukraine National AL, Ural AL, UTair, Uzbekistan AW, Valan Intl, Vaso AL, Vladivostock Air, Yakutia AL, Yamal AL, Zapolyarye Avia.

South America: Aero Caribbean, Aero Condor, Aerosegovia, Cubana, Star Up.

Another colourful propliner undergoing maintenance at Sharjah in early 2004 was An-26B ST-SAL of Khartoum-based freight airline Sarit. (Author's collection)

ANTONOV An-26

Antonov ASTC
1 Tupolev Str, Kyiv
252062, Ukraine

The Antonov An-26 (NATO reporting name 'Curl') was derived from the An-24RT passenger turboprop transport, with particular attention being made to the potential use by the Soviet military forces. In the late 1960s, the Antonov factory at Kiev-Svyetoshino built the first An-26 and this aircraft first flew on 23rd May 1969. A second prototype was also flown and this one was the first to be revealed to the Western world when it was shown at the Paris Air Show in June 1969.

The aircraft is basically a freight version of the An-24 but with a highly modified rear fuselage incorporating a large loading ramp. In order to load freight from a truck, this unique and patented ramp is lowered and then rolled forward under the rear fuselage, enabling the truck to reverse up to the freight floor.

Other differences to the basic An-24 include more powerful engines, larger fuel tanks and a stronger basic structure to cope with the higher weights. The starboard engine nacelle also has an auxiliary turbojet engine for boosting take-off performance and for use as an APU. The An-24, An-26 and An-30 all have interchangeable wings, empennage, engine nacelles and landing gear providing valuable economic savings for operators of these aircraft.

Versions include the basic An-26, the improved An-26B, the An-26M ambulance version, the An-26L airfield calibrator and the An-26P (Protivopozharny) firefighter. Many An-26s have been exported, particularly to those countries influenced by the then USSR. Most are military operated but several civil airlines have bought the An-26 for freight/passenger use including Tarom, Syrianair, Cubana, MIAT Mongolia and Lao Aviation.

In 1988, the Chinese Xian Aircraft Company first flew a home produced military version of the An-26 called the Y-7H. The civil version of this aircraft, the Y7H-500, first flew in March 1992. Differences to the An-26 include the winglets that were first used on the Y7-100, larger cockpit windows and Chinese built 2,082Kw (2,790shp) Dongan WJ5E engines. Like the Antonov version, the Y7H-500 has an auxiliary turbojet in the starboard nacelle for additional thrust when required. In this case it is a Chinese built copy of the Tumansky PY19A-300 of 800kg (1,764lb) thrust.

Details

Span: 29.20m (95ft 9in)
Length: 23.80m (78ft 1in)
Engines: Two 2,074kW (2,780ehp) ZMKB Progress AI-24VT turboprops
Cruise speed: 440km/h (235kt)
Accommodation: 40 maximum
Payload: 5.5 tons

First service: Aeroflot, 1969
Number built: 1,400
Number in service: 218 civil, mostly in the Former Soviet Union

Current Operators

Africa: Ababeel AV, Air Boyoma, Air Libya, Bentiu AT, COAGE, Compagnie Africaine d'Aviation, El Magal Avn Services, Libyan AC, Sarit AL, Uhusu AL.

Asia: Ariana Afghan AL, MIAT Mongolian AL, President AL, Royal AL, Vietnam Air Services.

Europe: Air Sofia, Avio Piva, Cityline Hungary, Exin, Ion Tiriac Air, Scorpion Air.

Middle East: Syrianair.

Former Soviet Union: Adygheya-Avia, Aero-Charter AL, Aerocom, Aeriantur-M AL, Air Kharkov, Airline Transport, Air Moldova, Air Urga, Alrosa, Amur Avia, Angara AL, Antonov AL, ARP 410 AL, Artem-Avia, Asia Continental AL, Atran, Avialesookhrana, Aviant, Aviastar-Tu, Avia-Urartu, Avialeasing Avn, Aviavilsa, AVL, AZAL Cargo Air Company, Belavia, Chukotavia, Dalavia, Dauria, Gorlista AL, GST Aero, Irbis, Izhavia, Jet Line Intl, KAPO, Kirov Air, KMPO, KNAAPO, Kroonk AL, Perm AL, Petropavlovsk-Kamchatsky Air, Pecotox-Air, Phoenix Avia, Podillia Avia, Polar AL, Progress TSSKB, Pskovavia, RAF-Avia, SAT AL, Saturn Avia, Sir Aero, Specavia, Tajikistan AL, Tatarstan Air, Tbilaviamsheni, Tepavia Trans, Tomskavia, Transavia-Garantia, Tura Air Enterprise, UAA, Ukrainian Cargo AW, Ulyanovsk Higher Civil Avn School, UTair, Vichi Air, Yakutia AL, Yamal AL, Zapolyarye Aviakompania.

South America: Aero Caribbean, Aerogaviota, Aerosegovia, Aero Transporte, SELVA, Star Up.

RA-41901 is a 1998-built Antonov An38-100 leased to Layang-Layang Aerospace in Malaysia by Vostok Airlines. (John Mounce)

ANTONOV An-28/-38/PZL M28 SKYTRUCK

Antonov ASTC, 1 Tupolev Str, Kyiv, 252062, Ukraine
PZL Mielec, ul.Wojska Polskiego 3, 39-300 Mielec, Poland

After a 1968 Aeroflot request for a light passenger and utility transport, Antonov proposed their An-14M turboprop update of the unsuccessful twin-piston An-14 and Beriev offered the all-new turboprop Be-30. A competition declared the An-14M as the winner, and the first of three prototypes first flew at Kiev in September 1969. Flight-testing commenced on the Isotov TVD-850 powered aircraft but the trials were not completed until 1972. This delay prompted Aeroflot to order large numbers of the Czech-built L-410 Turbolet.

In 1973, the type was given the new designation An-28 (NATO reporting name 'Cash'). The prototype initially had a retractable undercarriage, but the small performance improvement gained could not justify the complication and extra weight, so it was redesigned with fixed gear. It was first displayed at Sheremetyevo in 1974 and by 1975 the An-28's engines were switched to the 716kW (960shp) Glushenkov TVD-10B.

In 1978, the complete production line was moved to PZL at Mielec in Poland. The first Polish-built example flew in July 1984 and deliveries to Aeroflot started around 1986. The design is very rugged, and great attention has been paid to single engine performance. It has a large under-tail clamshell-door cargo hatch (1.4m x 2.4m – 4ft 7in x 7ft 9in) and a 500kg (1,102lb) hand-winch attached to

the cabin roof. A few sub types, TD, B1, B1R and RM2 have been noted. Around 1993, after 185 had been built, the Polish An-28 production line switched to the updated M28 version.

The PT6A-powered PZL M28 Skytruck (originally An-28PT) was built for export. It has Hartzell five-bladed propellers, colour weather radar and some Western-built avionics. First flown in July 1993, the Skytruck has an optional 200kg (440lb) under fuselage cargo pod and a port side passenger door. From 2004 the Skytruck Company in Florida marketed the M28 after it received FAA certification. Further development includes the wingletted M28 Skytruck Plus; one version has a rear under-tail door or ramp, and the other has a starboard side freight door and a roller floor able to accept three LD-3 containers. In 2003 the M28 Bryza B1R-bis (maritime patrol/search and rescue) version with retractable undercarriage was first flown. In 2004, the first civil M28 orders were announced from Air Guyane, Air Antilles Express and Vieques Air Link while development of a civil stretched version, the AM -128 Plus, was started.

Work on the stretched 15.67m (51ft 5in) long and upgraded An-38 started in 1989. Designed by Antonov and built in Novosibirsk, this 26-seater utility transport was first flown at Chkalovskaya in June 1994. Available either as the Series 100 with two 1,227kW (1,645shp)

AlliedSignal TPE-331 turboprops driving Hartzell five-bladed props, or as the Series 200 with Omsk MKB Mars TVD-20 engines, by mid 2004 ten An-38-120 had been ordered. The An-38K freighter, able to carry four LD-3 containers, is also available.

Details

Span: 22.06m (72ft 5in)
Length: 13.10m (43ft 0in)
Engines: Two 820kW (1,100shp) P&W
   PT6A-65B turboprops
Cruise speed: 355km/h (191kt) max
Accommodation: 18 maximum
(Details above are for M28 Skytruck)

First service: An-28 – Aeroflot 1986?
Number built: 185 An-28, 50 M28
Number in service: 51

Current Operators

Africa: Goliaf Air, Malift Air, Malu Avn.
Asia: Air Mark Indonesia Avn, Layang-Layang Aerospace, Vietnam AS.
Europe: Baltic Helicopters.
Former Soviet Union: Air Livonia, Alrosa, Avial NV, Chukotavia, Enimex, Koryakavia, Riga Aero Club, Tajikistan AL, Tepavia Trans, Ukrainian Pilot School, Vologda Air Enterprise, Vostock AL.
South America: Blue Wing AL, Comervia.

Antonov An-30 VN-B376 is used for freight and survey work by VASCO (Vietnam Air Service Co) from its base at Ho Chi Minh City. (Author's collection)

ANTONOV An-30

Antonov ASTC
1 Tupolev Str, Kyiv
252062, Ukraine

The aerial survey version of the An-26, the Antonov An-30 (NATO reporting name 'Clank'), was first flown in 1973 and was shown to the West at the Hanover ILA airshow in 1974. The An-30 was initially developed as a conversion of the An-24 known as the An-24FK and was conceived partly as a replacement for the survey versions of the Ilyushin IL-14 'Crate', but also able to be operated as a freighter with the camera hatches covered by special plates.

In 1966, the design work associated with the development of the An-24FK was assigned to the Beriev bureau at Taganrog who converted an An-24B into the FK version. This hybrid made its first flight in August 1967. After the flight trials were completed, the An-30, as it was now known, commenced limited production alongside An-24s and An-26s at Kiev.

The requirement for accurate maps in a country as vast as the former USSR was essential and a sizable fleet of 65 An-30s were purchased by Aeroflot for aerial photography in order to make topographic and special maps. Several examples were also exported to countries including China, Bulgaria, Mongolia, Vietnam and Romania. With an obvious military use, the Soviet Air Force and the air forces of Czechoslovakia, China, Ukraine, Bulgaria, Romania, Afghanistan and Cuba also operated the An-30.

In order to accommodate the equipment in the much-modified glazed nose section and to allow normal visibility for the crew, the design of the An-30 incorporated a raised cockpit in a hump above the forward fuselage. It has an onboard darkroom and five camera windows with sliding shutters in the cabin and navigator's floor. It can also take oblique and strip photos from the side windows. Photographic scales covered are from 1:10,000 to 1:150,000. Sub versions include the An-30B, An-30D and the An-30-100. In 1996, the United Nations operated an An-30R that was specially fitted out to detect airborne radiation. Production stopped in 1980 after 123 had been completed, all of them at Factory No 473 at Kiev-Svyatoshino. Current civil operations are in Russia, Ukraine, Vietnam and Mongolia while some of the military versions are now seen in the West carrying out 'Open Skies' observation missions.

Details

Span: 29.20m (95ft 9in)
Length: 24.26m (79ft 7in)
Engines: Two 2,074kW (2,780ehp) ZMKB Progress AI-24T turboprops
Cruise speed: 530km/h (286kt)
Accommodation: 22 maximum

First service: An-30 – c1975
Number built: 123
Number in service: 31 civil, mostly in the Former Soviet Union

Current Operators

Asia: Vietnam AS.

Former Soviet Union: ARP 410 AL, AS Aviakompania, Geodynamica Centre, Gromov Air, Kazaviaspas, Lukiaviatrans, Novosibirsk Avia, Polyot, Ukraine National AL.

The An-32 has found many operators in South America. Here is Selva Colombia's An-32B freighter HK-4052X at Villavicencio. (Christian Volpati)

ANTONOV An-32

Kyiv State Aviation Plant
100/1 Peremohy Prospect
Kyiv, 03062, Ukraine

First seen by the western world at the 1977 Paris Air Show, the prototype An-32 (NATO reporting name 'Cline') was built from an Antonov An-26 airframe at the Kiev-Svyetoshino factory and first flew on 19th July 1976.

Developed primarily for export by the Antonov Aviation Science and Technology Complex as a short-field/hot and high tactical transport, the An-32 is basically an An-26 with very powerful engines, beefed-up undercarriage and various modifications including a new power supply and engine starting system. With an APU and onboard cargo handling, the An-32 is self-sufficient at remote sites. The three-crew cockpit is pressurised and air-conditioned while the freight hold temperature can also be controlled

Unlike its cousin the An-26, the An-32 can operate at very high airfields (up to 4,500m) and where the surface temperature reaches 50°C. This remarkable performance has not gone unnoticed by the United Nations who regularly charter An-32s from civilian operators for use in humanitarian relief flights in Africa. The An-32 can be used as an Air Ambulance, and with its large (2.4m/7ft 10in)-wide rear-loading door opened in flight, the type can also deliver palletised freight by airdrop. On the ground, the lower door section can either be rolled out of the way under the rear fuselage or it can be lowered to the

ground for use as a ramp. Freight loading and unloading is assisted by use of a 3-ton overhead crane in the fuselage roof. The roller floor can be locked semi-automatically to speed up the handling of pallets and the rollers can either be removed or stored at the sides of the fuselage if necessary.

The basic An-32 was followed by the slightly more powerful An-32B in 1995. The An-32P 'Firekiller' is a water bomber variant that can carry 8 tons of fire retardant. It has seen real action in both Spain and Portugal while on demonstration flights. The higher weight An-32B-100 has Series 5M engines that have longer times between overhauls and an assigned service life up to 20,000 hours. The An-32B-110 has two crew and new metric instruments while the An-32B-120 has imperial instruments. The further developed An-32B-200 has an advanced engine control system able to input 'extreme power mode' in the event of an engine failure. If required it can also be supplied with a two-crew cockpit with western avionics and extra 'strap-on' fuel-tanks fitted on the outside of the fuselage.

Around 22 countries have operated the An-32; however, most of the exported examples are military operated. The Indian Air Force received the first of 123 An-32 'Sutlej' in 1984.

Details

Span: 29.20m (95ft 9in)
Length: 23.78m (78ft 0in)
Engines: Two 3,760kW (5,042ehp) ZMKB Progress AI-20D Series 5 turboprops
Cruise speed: 530km/h (286kt) max
Accommodation: 50 maximum

First service: Indian Air Force, July 1984
Number built: 375 approx
Number in service: 38 civilian worldwide, mostly in the FSU

Current Operators

Africa: Aerolift, ALADA, Business Avn, Gira Global, Malift Air, Uhuru AL, Valon.
Asia: Airmark Avn.
Former Soviet Union: Airline Transport, Antonov AL, Armenian AL, Aviant, Azal Cargo Air Company, KMPO, KNAAPO, Pecotox-Air, Sibaviatrans, Tura Air Enterprise, UAA, Valan Intl.
South America: Aerosegovia, SADELCA, SAEP, SELVA.

This typical Sharjah ramp shot in March 2004 shows various An-12s and Il-18s in addition to this Georgian-registered Antonov An-72 operated by IAP. (Author)

ANTONOV An-72 & An-74

Antonov ASTC
1 Tupolev Str, Kyiv
252062, Ukraine

The distinctive Antonov An-72 (NATO reporting name 'Coaler') made its first flight at Kiev in August 1977 and was designed as a turbofan-powered light STOL replacement for the An-26, able to operate from the numerous unprepared strips that still seem prevalent in the CIS.

The two huge engines, designed under the leadership of V Lotarev, are placed high and forward of the wing to protect them from the ingestion of debris and also to employ the Coanda effect to achieve extra lift from the exhaust gases ejecting over the upper wing surface. They are also placed very close to the fuselage to alleviate the asymmetric problems caused by a single engine failure. Six An-72 pre-series aircraft were completed at Kiev-Svyatoshino prior to production being transferred to the KhGAPP factory at Kharkov in 1985.

In 1984, design work commenced on the An-74. This is externally similar to the An-72, but when it first appeared in the West at the 1987 Paris Air Show, it was advertised as an An-72A (A = Arkticheski/ Arctic) specifically designed for use in Polar regions. The main differences are its ability to operate on a wheel/ski landing gear, its increased fuel capacity and a de-icing system for the engine intakes, tail and wing. On most examples there is a large bulged observation window on the port side. Distinguishing between the 72 and 74 is normally achieved thanks to the practice of

painting the type designation on the nose of each aircraft.

Versions include the first two short-nose prototype An-72s and the standard An-72 with longer wings and fuselage. Others include the armed An-72P maritime patroller that was seen at Farnborough in 1992 (also reported as an An-76), the An-72R communications relay aircraft, the An-72S VIP transport, the An-74T-200 freighter, the An-74TK-200 convertible for passengers or freight, and the four-crew An-74T-100 and TK-100. Two AEW examples of the An-72 with fin-mounted radomes were built for the Soviet military. Known as the An-71 (NATO reporting name 'Madcap'), these had more powerful engines and an RD-38A booster engine in the rear fuselage. The An-74TK-300 is a Progress D-426D1-powered version with the engines mounted below the wings. The proposed airline version of this has been dropped in favour of a 5,200km (2,800nm) bizjet.

Foreign operators of the 72/74 include the Peruvian Air Force and the Iranian Revolutionary Guard, while the vast majority are employed as freighters inside the FSU. The largest fleet is currently operated by Moscow-based Gazpromavia whose fleet of 12 are used as freighters or 52-seater passenger liners. They also have an An-74D that is used as a 12-seater VIP transport.

Details

Span: 31.89m (104ft 7in)
Length: 28.07m (92ft 1in)
Engines: Two 63.74kN (14,330lb) ZMKB Progress D-36 turbofans.
Cruise speed: 580km/h (310kt)
Accommodation: 68
Payload: 10,000kg (22,045lb) max

First service: Unknown
Number built: 200
Number in service: 56, most in the Former Soviet Union.

Current Operators

Europe: Atlantic AL, Instone Air.

Former Soviet Union: Aero-Charter AL, Air Van, Alliance Avia, Antonov AL, Aviapaslauga, BAL, Bashkirian AL, Cabi AL, Enimex, Gazpromavia, Kharkov State Aircraft, Khoriv-Avia, Koryakavia, KS Avia, MCHS Rossii, Motor Sich, RAF-Avia, Shar Ink, Sibaviatrans, Sverdlovsk 2nd Air Enterprise, Vichi Air, Yamal AL.

An-124-100 UR-82073 is flown by Antonov Airlines, a division of the Antonov Design Bureau. Note the 20 wheels on the main undercarriage. (Tony Best)

ANTONOV An-124

Antonov ASTC
1 Tupolev Str, Kyiv
252062, Ukraine

Named 'Ruslan' after a Russian knight and folklore hero by Antonov and given the reporting name 'Condor' by NATO, the An-124 first flew at Kiev in December 1982. Since then it has broken many world records including the carriage of the heaviest single item of cargo (124 tonnes) from Düsseldorf to New Delhi in 1995. This record has since been broken by the An-225 (see below) with a 142.5 ton (285,000lb) transformer from Austria to the USA.

Designed specifically for use by the Soviet Air Force, the An-124 is now mostly involved in worldwide civilian charters. Normally crewed by two pilots, two flight engineers, a navigator, a loadmaster and a radio operator, it has an upper deck comprising the cockpit, relief crew area and loadmaster's cabin and in the upper rear fuselage there is a pressurised cabin for up to 88 passengers. The pressurised lower deck is completely clear of obstructions and has two winches and two 10 tonne moving cranes. Self-contained loading ramps at the front and rear extend hydraulically when either the front upward-hinging nose door or the rear clamshell doors are opened. To assist operations, the front fuselage can be made to 'kneel' by retracting the nose undercarriage and extending two short struts to support the weight and keep the fuselage clear of the ground. This creates a continuous slope into the cabin

from ground level, thereby allowing easier loading/unloading, particularly of very long items of cargo.

In 1992, the civilian version of the An-124 was given the designation An-124-100. The current work involves the upgraded An-124-100M. It has a longer service life, Western avionics, onboard equipment to move items weighing up to 40 tons, a new navigation system and radar, and only four crew instead of six. It has 55,000lb D-18T-4S engines and a maximum payload of 150 tons compared to the earlier versions' 120 tons.

In 2003/4, the Aviant factory at Kyiv completed an unfinished Series 100, which had initially been laid down in the Soviet era. Originally intended for Moscow-based Atlant-Soyuz, it was sold to the UAE in 2004 for $38m.

In September 2004 it was announced that the ZAO Aviastar factory would re-start An-124 production with 80 new An-124-100M aircraft being built between 2006 and 2020. Possible future models include the An-124-130 with General Electric CF6 engines and the An-124-200 with Rolls-Royce RB211-524Gs. Long term plans include the stretched An-124-300 powered by 80,000lb thrust engines.

Mention must be made here of the world's largest aircraft – the An-225 Mriya (Dream) is a highly modified, six-engined An-124. First flown in 1988, it has twin tail fins and a maximum payload of

250,000kg (551,100lb). It was designed originally to carry the Soviet Space Shuttle 'Buran' on its back. It set a new payload record in June 2004 when it flew oil pipeline machinery weighing 247 tons to Tashkent. Only one An-225 was completed; however, work on an uncompleted second was continuing until 2002 when finance problems forced a stop.

Details

Span: 73.30m (240ft 6in)
Length: 69.10m (226ft 9in)
Engines: Four 229.5kN (51,630lb)
   Ivchenko Progress D-18T turbofans
Cruise speed: 850km/h (459kt)
Max payload: 120,000kg (264,550lb)
(Details above are for the An-124-100)

First service: January 1986
Number built: 60
Number in service: 34

Current Operators

Africa: Aldawlyh Air.
Former Soviet Union: Antonov AL, Polet Aviakompania, Volga-Dnepr AL.

First visit to the UK of the new An-140 commuterliner was made by Ilyich Avia's UR-14007 at the Farnborough Air Show in September 2004. (Author)

ANTONOV An-140

AVIACOR, 32 Pskovskaya St, 443052 Samara, Russia; Kharkov State Aircraft Manufacturing Co Sumskaya Str 61023, Kharkov, Ukraine; HESA Iran Aircraft Manufacturing Industries Co, 107 Sepahbod Gharany Ave, Tehran, Iran

Designed for use in the CIS and as a potential export winner, this regional commuter turboprop was first revealed at the 1993 Paris Air Show. Intended as a replacement for the hundreds of An-24s, 26s and Yak-40s in CIS service, it was officially launched the following year but design and development was a very extended affair, taking more than three years from the launch until its first flight at Kyiv-Svyatoshino in September 1997.

Like the An-24/26 series, the An-140 is strong and easily maintained. It is also self-reliant at remote airfields thanks to its built-in airstairs and an APU, but unlike its predecessors, the An-140 is quiet, fast (575kmh/310kts max), comfortable, fuel-efficient and has a greater range. Powered by the Motor-Sich-built AI-30 turboprop (a licence-built version of the Klimov TV3-117VMA-SBM1) it is relatively inexpensive to build and has low operating costs. The AI-30 is based on a helicopter engine and requires a rear gearbox and long shaft above the engine to transfer the power to the propeller. Cost-saving measures employed in construction include analog instruments rather than EFIS and the use of the front fuselage of the An-74. After the flight-testing was completed in 1999, the tailplane was modified with 6° of dihedral. Certification was achieved in April 2000 after more than 1,000 flights were performed at both hot-and-high and freezing locations.

In October 1995 the type was chosen by Iran to be their next-generation commuter airliner and an agreement was signed to allow them to license-build 80 aircraft in Iran. A production line was built at Shahin-Shahr near Isfahan and uncompleted kits were shipped there where the first Iranian assembled aircraft, appropriately dubbed the IR.AN140 'Farazs', was first flown in February 2001. The Iranian military may well order this aircraft.

The Aviacor factory at Samara in Russia is the third location for the assembly of the An-140. They rolled out their first An-140 on 25th December 2003 and will be responsible for all production for the Russian market. Local airline Samara Airlines was the launch customer for the Samara-built aircraft.

Initial versions offered included the base line 52-seater, a 20-seat/3,650kg (8,030lb)-combi model and another combi with a 36 passenger/1,650kg (3,630lb) freight split. An all-freight An-140T version with a large cargo door, an AWACS version, a VIP model, a military rear-loading version and a 68-seater stretched airliner are all being considered. The current model, first delivered to Ilyich Avia in April 2004, is the An-140-100. This has 2,000 design changes including extended wings, larger fuel tanks and various aerodynamic modifications that improve range, operating height and fuel

efficiency. In 2004, AZAL Azerbaijan Airlines ordered 4 An-140-100s to replace their elderly Yak-40s. In 2003, Tibesti Air Libya announced that they would buy 5 An-140s with the first delivery expected in 2004.

Details

Span: 24.50m (80ft 5in) -100 25.50m (83ft 5in)
Length: 22.60m (74ft 2in)
Engines: Two 1,838kW (2,466shp) Motor-Sich AI-30 turboprops
Cruise speed: 520kmh (280kts)
Accommodation: 52
Max payload: 7,000kg (15,500lb)

First service: Odessa Airlines March 2002
Number built (ordered): 12 (10)
Number in service: 11

Current Operators

Africa: Air Libya (5 on order).
Asia: Iran Asseman AL.
Former Soviet Union: Aeromost, Azerbaijan AL (4 options), Ilyich Avia, Motor Sich, Odessa AL, Samara AL (1 on order), Tulpar Avia Service.

A BAC 1-11 in airline service is now almost impossible to find except maybe in Africa. This is Air Katanga's BAC 1-11 201AC 'Fatima'. (Afavia-fotos.co.za)

BAe (BAC) 1-11

British Aerospace, Bournemouth, Dorset, UK
Romaero SA, Bucharest, Romania

This successful short-haul airliner can trace its lineage back to a 1956 Hunting Aircraft design for a twin jet Vickers Viscount replacement. Launched as the British Aircraft Corporation BAC 1-11 in April 1961, the first order for ten aircraft came from Gatwick-based British United Airways in May that year.

The first 1-11 to fly in August 1963 was a Series 200 with Rolls-Royce Spey 506 engines. On 22nd October, on its 53rd flight; it was carrying out tests to measure the stability and handling when approaching the stall. Sadly, the aircraft suffered what was later known as a deep stall and crashed. All seven on board were killed and the loss of the prototype and the subsequent investigations caused severe delays to the trials. After rectifying the problem, orders for the One-Eleven poured in from Europe and the USA.

Production of the various 1-11 components was carried out a BAC sites at Hurn, Weybridge, Luton and Filton, with the final assembly at Hurn. First services were flown in 1965 by BUA, Braniff, Mohawk and Aer Lingus. The type was subjected to continuous modifications and uprating, which produced the -300 and -400 with Spey Mk.511s and higher operating weights. In January 1967, BEA ordered the unbuilt stretched -500 for use on their extensive European routes. A 12.30m (13ft 6in) fuselage stretch and uprated Spey

512DW engines gave the -500 a 97-seat capacity, which, with higher weights granted, increased to 119.

The last British-built example of the One-Eleven was the -475. This had Spey 512s and the short fuselage of the -200. Only nine of this 'hot and high' version were built, including one all freight 1-11-487GK(F) for Tarom.

In 1981, the entire One-Eleven production was transferred to Romaero SA in Bucharest and the first Romanian-assembled ROMBAC 1-11 Series 560 flew in September 1982. All nine examples built were delivered to the Romanian national airline, Tarom.

In the 1980s, efforts to reduce the engine noise of the 1-11s involved the fitting of hushkits to the engines. Although this allowed continued use of the type, the impending requirement of Stage 3/Chapter 3 compliance throughout the Western world prompted the appearance of the Rolls-Royce Tay 650-powered 1-11 which was offered by Dee Howard in 1990. A Stage 3/Chapter 3 hushkit that was developed by the Quiet Nacelle company and European Aviation was evaluated during mid-1997. At least 6 executive 1-11s currently have Stage 3 hushkits fitted.

The last stronghold for the 1-11 in passenger service was Africa. In the 1980s and 1990s dozens of airworthy examples were sold in Nigeria with 11 going to South Africa. These sturdy

airliners coped well for several years but after a series of accidents, the Nigerian aviation authority grounded all the 1-11s on 9th May 2002. More than 50 1-11s are currently in 'store' worldwide.

Details

Span: 28.50m (93ft 6in)
Length: 32.60m (107ft 0in)
Engines: Two 55.8kN (12,500lb) Rolls-Royce Spey 512-14DW turbofans
Cruise speed: 851km/h (470kt)
Accommodation: 119 maximum

First service: British United Airways, April 1965.
Number built: 243 (UK and Romania)
Number in service: 6 (plus around 20 in executive and military use)

Current Operators

Africa: Air Katanga, Chrome Air, Jetline Intl, Libyan Arab AL.
Europe: Aravco, Romavia.
North America: Business Jet Services, Flight Source Intl, Kori Air, Select Leasing.
Also operated by Northrop Grumman, Qinetiq and the Sultan of Oman AF

Steadily growing Eastern Airways has a large fleet of J32 and J41 Jetstream aircraft. J32 G-CBCS was seen in May 2002 at Linkoping in Sweden. (Author)

BAe JETSTREAM 31/32/32EP

BAE Systems
Prestwick International Airport
Ayrshire, Scotland KA9 2RW

Originally designed in the mid-1960s by the famous Handley Page company at Radlett in Hertfordshire as the HP.137, this attractive pressurised 19-seater was first powered by two 635kW (840ehp) Turboméca Astazou XIV turboprop engines, and given the name Jetstream 1. This first flew in August 1967 and 36 were built.

HP had forecast a market for up to 1,000 aircraft and with an early order (later cancelled) for up to 87 Garrett TPE331-powered Jetstream 3Ms for the USAF (designated C-10A), the future looked good. Early Jetstreams suffered with poor performance so Handley Page commenced work on a more powerful version, the Jetstream Mk.2 with 800kW (1,073shp) Astazou XIVCs. Before the Mk.2 and a civil version of the 3M could be developed, huge financial problems forced Handley Page into liquidation in August 1969 and several unfinished Jetstreams were broken up

In 1970, Scottish Aviation and Jetstream Aircraft redeveloped the Mk.2 theme into the Jetstream 200, which was built in small numbers for the RAF and Royal Navy as an aircrew trainer. By 1978, British Aerospace had absorbed Scottish Aviation and they commenced development of the Garrett-powered version known as the Jetstream 31. Built at Prestwick in Scotland, the J31 was first revealed at the Paris Air Show in 1978 and was vigorously marketed alongside

the BAe 146. First flight of the J31 was in March 1980 followed by UK type certification in June 1982. The J31 achieved impressive sales, particularly in North America where it met a newly emerging requirement for large numbers of aircraft in the 18/19-seater bracket to serve as feederliners.

In October 1988, the improved Jetstream Super 31 (also known as the J32) was certificated. This had more powerful engines allowing higher weights, more fuel capacity, better brakes and undercarriage and had an upgraded cabin interior with more headroom. The Super 31/J32 was also available with either a corporate or a company shuttle interior. The J32EP 'enhanced-performance' version was designed for hot-and-high and short field operations. This was certificated in 1988 and had uprated engines, higher operating weights and was able to carry an additional 360kg. Production of the Jetstream stopped in 1993 after the US commuter market began to demand higher seating capacities.

The J31/32 series were highly utilised throughout the late 1990s, but since the dramatic downturn in air traffic in the USA since 9/11, and additionally because of the staggering rise of the Regional Jets, dozens of Jetstreams have been withdrawn from use and parked up on desert airfields.

Details

Span: 15.85m (52ft 0in)
Length: 14.37m (47ft 1in)
Engines: Two 760kw (1,020shp) AlliedSignal TPE331-12UAR turboprops.
Cruise speed: 482km/h (260kt) max
Accommodation: 19
(Data above for Super 31)

First service: Bavaria Flug, Oct 1969
Number built: 67 Mark 1/200/T.1; 220 J31; 161 Jetstream Super 31
Number in service: 183, mostly in North America

Current Operators

Asia: Air Andaman.

Australasia: Air National, Maroomba AL, O'Connor AL, Origin Pacific AW.

Europe: Aceline Air, Bromma Air Maintenance, Coast Air, Direktflyg, Eastern AW, Eurojet Romania, European Executive Express, Hellas Wings, Highland AW, Homac Avn Services, Quest AL, Sun Air, Tulip Air.

Former Soviet Union: Avies Air Company.

North America: Air East, Air Mikisew, Akins Avn, Alberta Citylink, Alta Flights, Boston-Maine AW, Corporate AL, Corporate Express, Empire AW, Mid America Jet, Murray Avn, Northwestern Air, Paladin Canada, Peace Air, Sky Service Avn, Skyxpress AL, Starlink Avn, Swanberg Air, Transwest Air, Vee Neal Avn, Vision Air, West Wind Avn.

South America: ACSA, Aerocaraibe, Aerolinea de Antioquia, Aerolineas SOSA, Aeromet, Cancun Express, Caribair, Mapiex Aero, SAVE, TAG, Venezolana.

Swaziland Airlink flies this single J41 ZS-NRK using the familiar 'Springbok' callsign as part of the South African Airlink network. (Afavia-fotos.co.za)

BAe JETSTREAM 41

BAE Systems
Prestwick International Airport
Ayrshire, Scotland KA9 2RW

In the late 1980s, the 30-seater twin-turboprop market was hotly fought between many of the world's commuterliner manufacturers. Types such as the SAAB 340, EMB120 Brasilia, and the Fairchild Dornier Do 328 were all selling well. However, despite the competition, the British Aerospace designers at Prestwick decided to enter this market by producing a scaled-up version of the 19-seat Jetstream 31.

Given the name Jetstream 41, the programme was publicly announced in May 1989 followed by the demonstration of a full-scale cabin mock-up at that year's Paris Air Show. The J41 was generally externally similar to its predecessor Jetstream 31 with the same fuselage cross section, but had many modifications and improvements. These included a 4.88m (16ft) longer cabin, longer wings, a revised cockpit with a new windscreen and Honeywell four-tube EFIS instrumentation, larger tail surfaces, more fuel capacity and a forward airstair. The larger engine nacelles housing the TPE-331 turboprops and the new, forward-retracting main gear, were also fitted further from the fuselage to reduce internal cabin noise. The huge fairing where the low-mounted wing meets the fuselage provided a ventral baggage hold as well as allowing the wing spar to be routed underneath the cabin, leaving the cabin aisle clear of obstruction. Like many current designs, a risk-sharing

agreement was established by British Aerospace that saw Field Aircraft Ltd, Pilatus Flugzeugwerke AG, ML Slingsby and Gulfstream Aerospace Technologies all producing parts for the J41.

First flight was in September 1991 and deliveries commenced in late 1992. First American customer, in May 1993, was Washington-based Atlantic Coast Airlines who flew the J41s on behalf of United Express and once had the world's largest J41 fleet with 33. In June 2004, this airline was re-born as a low-cost airline called Independence Air who have announced that they now plan an all-jet fleet and their J31s and J41s will be sold. The largest fleet of J41s outside of the USA belongs to Eastern Airways in the UK.

Early versions had slightly lower powered TPE331s, but since 1994 the type has benefited from higher weights and longer-range capabilities due to uprated engines. Corporate and Combi/QC versions of the Jetstream were also offered.

From 1996 to 1998, the design was marketed, produced and supported by Aero International (Régional) or AI(R). This was a combination of the regional airliner activities of BAe (Avro) and the Franco-Italian ATR Company. Since 1999 the type has been supported by BAe Systems Regional Aircraft at Prestwick in Scotland.

Details

Span: 18.29m (60ft 0in)
Length: 19.25m (63ft 2in)
Engines: Two 1,230kW (1,650shp) AlliedSignal TPE331-14GR/HR turboprops.
Cruise speed: 547km/h (295kt) max
Accommodation: 29 maximum.

First service: Loganair and Manx Airlines, November 1992.
Number built: 104
Number in service: 62, mostly in USA

Current Operators

Africa: Airlink Swaziland, Airlink Zimbabwe, MEX Mozambique EXpresso, South African Airlink.
Asia: Government Flying Service.
Australasia: Origin Pacific AW.
Europe: Eastern AW, Sun Air.
North America: Trans States AL.

Retired passenger ATPs have now found a new life as freighters in Sweden (West Air) and the UK (Emerald). (BAE SYSTEMS Regional Aircraft)

BAe ATP

BAE Systems Regional Aircraft
Woodford Aerodrome, Woodford
Cheshire, SK7 1QR, UK

In the early 1980s, British Aerospace decided to develop a stretched and improved version of their sturdy HS.748 twin-turboprop airliner. Designated ATP (Advanced TurboProp), the new design, announced in March 1984, retained very little of the 748's features, but did have the same fuselage cross section and basic wing structure.

The ATP was fitted with many advanced features, including a four-tube EFIS cockpit display, highly fuel-efficient 1,790kW (2,400shp) PW124 or 1,864kW (2,500shp) PW125 engines driving slow-turning six-blade composite propellers, carbon brakes and a new on-board environmental control system.

First flown in August 1986 from Woodford, the ATP attracted few orders. British Midland and Wings West Airlines did order the type but Wings West decided to stick with their Fairchild Metros, and cancelled their order. British Airways eventually acquired 15 and Air Wisconsin bought 10 for its United Express operations. Despite the ATP being the quietest aircraft in its class, and very economical to operate, most airlines in the market for a twin-prop regional airliner preferred the ATR 42/72 series. The ATP's relatively slow cruising speed, some early reliability problems and the types derogatory nickname of 'Skoda' certainly did not help the BAe sales department.

By the middle of 1994, all the ordered

aircraft had been delivered (by which time production and marketing had been moved to Prestwick), and the newly created Jetstream Aircraft division of BAe became desperate to revive sales. With the hope of gaining some market commonality with their very successful Jetstream 31/41 series, Jetstream Aircraft renamed the ATP and launched it as the Jetstream 61in April 1993. With more powerful PW127D engines, higher design weights and a new interior based on the J41, the J61 achieved certification in June 1995 but still failed to achieve commercial success. In 1996 marketing of the type was stopped in favour of the ATR72 after BAe Regional and the European manufacturer ATR agreed to merge their regional aircraft activities and create AI(R).

The last ATP was handed over to Seoul Air International in 1994 for services in Korea. At Prestwick, nine unfinished and unflown ATPs and the two completed J61s were later reduced to spares, some of them ending their days with the Prestwick fire service. However, in 1998 the last three unsold ATPs did find a home with British World (2) and Sun-Air of Scandinavia (1).

In mid 2000, BAe (now BAE Systems) teamed up with HS748 freighter operator West Air Sweden to develop an ATP freighter conversion programme. Two ATPs were initially converted but retained the standard doors. The first ATP

Freighter with a new large freight door first flew at Lidkoping on 10th July 2002. Two other freight conversion programmes exist. In June 2003 BAE Systems Regional Aircraft and Romaero announced theirs while in late 2004 Exeter-based European Aviation Services were already working on their first conversion. The first of 10 ATP Freighters modified with the Large Cargo Door built in Bucharest was delivered to West Air Sweden in 2004.

Details

Span: 30.63m (100ft 6in)
Length: 26.00m (85ft 4in)
Engines: ATP two 1,978kW (2,653shp) P&WC PW126A turboprops; J61 two 2,050kW (2,750shp) P&WC PW127D turboprops
Cruise speed: ATP 493km/h (266kt) max; J61 500km/h (270kt) max
Accommodation: 72 maximum

First service: May 1988, British Midland Airways
Number built: 65
Number in service: 28

Current Operators

Asia: Asian Spirit.
Europe: Emerald Aw, EuroAir, Loganair, SATA Air Azores, Sun Air, West Air Europe, West Air Sweden.

This colourful 48-seater HS.748 reflects the equally colourful island of Bali. Series 2B PK-IHV is one of four still serving Bali Air at Denpasar. (Avimage)

BAe (HS) 748 & HAL 748

British Aerospace, Woodford, Cheshire, UK
Hindustan Aeronautics Ltd, Chakeri, Kanpur, India

Having decided to re-enter the commercial market, Avro launched their 'DC-3 replacement' in the late 1950s. The 36-seater Avro 748 was a conventional low wing design, and like its rival the Fokker F.27 Friendship, it was powered by the remarkable Rolls-Royce Dart turboprop.

First flown from Woodford in June 1960, 18 Series 1 were initially built with 1,400kW (1,880ehp) Darts. In 1961, the second prototype Series 1 was converted into the first Series 2. This had more powerful Dart 531s and increased weights and range. In 1967, the 748 Series 2A was launched with a choice of two more powerful versions of the Dart.

A vigorous worldwide sales drive saw the 748 demonstrator touring Europe, Africa, India and the Far East in 1963, and the Caribbean, South America and Canada in 1964. Around this time, Hawker Siddeley absorbed the Avro company, thus re-naming the aircraft, the HS.748.

An agreement with the Indian government, saw the 748 assembled from British-built components by Hindustan Aircraft Ltd at Kanpur. After the first example flew in November 1961, a total of 89 were completed by 1984; all were either operated by the Indian Air Force or Indian Airlines.

A much modified 748, known as the Avro 780, was used by the RAF as the Andover C.1 from 1965. The Royal New

Zealand Air Force also bought them. They had a rear loading ramp, 'kneeling' undercarriage and additional structural strengthening to cope with the higher weights. After retirement from military service, a few of these well-maintained Andovers have found a new life as civilian freighters particularly in Africa.

By 1977, the 748 design had become part of the British Aerospace empire and was it further updated as the Series 2B, with more power, an increased wingspan and a modified tail. The last version produced was the Super 748. This first flew in July 1984 and was similar to the 2B, but had a completely updated flightdeck and cabin, and quieter engines. BAe later radically revised and rethought the HS.748 and it emerged as the ATP in 1986. The last HS.748 built was delivered to Makung International Airlines (later Uni Air) in January 1989.

The small airlines of Canada have always liked the 748 for its reliability and strength. Its ability to cope with airfields that would cause problems with some of today's turboprops means that today, nearly 30 of these veterans are still in service in Canada.

Details

Span: -2A 30.02m (98ft 6in);
   Super 31.23m (102ft 6in)
Length: (-2A and Super) 20.42m
   (67ft 0in)
Engines: Two 1,700kW (2,280ehp) Rolls-
   Royce Dart RDa.7 Mk.534-2, or 535-2,
   or 552-2 turboprops.
Cruise speed: 452km/h (244kt) max
Accommodation: 58 maximum

First service: Skyways Airways,
   December 1961
Number built: 382 (inc 89 built in India)
Number in service: 82 civil

Current Operators

Africa: 748 AS, Air Katanga (HS780), Airquarius Avn, ATO (HS780), Cameroon AL, Executive Aerospace, Malu Avn (HS780), Pelican AS, Waltair (HS780).

Asia: Air Fast, Bali Air, Best Air, Royal Nepal AL, Serendib AL.

Europe: Emerald AW, West Air Sweden.

North America: Air Creebec, Air Inuit, Air North, Calm Air, First Air, Wasaya AW, Westwind Avn.

South America: Atlantic AL de Honduras.

The third largest 'low-cost' airline in the UK is flybe. Their fleet of Dash 8s and BAe146 include this Series 300 G-JEBE seen here at Gatwick. (Author)

BAe 146

British Aerospace (BAe)
Hatfield Airfield
Hertfordshire, UK

Launched with the help of a government loan in 1973, the Hawker Siddeley HS 146 evolved from a 40-seater jet airliner, initially proposed in the 1960s, into a four-engined short-range airliner available in two versions, the 80-seat -100 and the 100-seat -200. Despite several years during which the design work was frozen due to financial problems, the 146 eventually emerged in 1978 under the banner of British Aerospace. The first BAe 146 flew at Hatfield in September 1981.

Key elements in the design were the use of four super-quiet, Avco Lycoming (now Honeywell) ALF502 powerplants and a high wing layout. Additional features included a spacious cabin with excellent passenger views, five or six abreast seating, large clamshell air-brakes on the rear fuselage and a sturdy, twin wheeled, undercarriage retracting into the fuselage.

The BAe 146 was initially built as a basic -100 and a stretched (2.39m/7ft 8in) -200. The further stretched -300 first flew in May 1987, entering service with Air Wisconsin in 1988.

All series of the BAe 146 were available in 'QT (Quiet Trader) guise. These had a large 3.33m x 1.93m (10ft 11in x 6ft 4in) outward-opening cargo door in the rear fuselage, a strengthened floor and a built-in cargo handling system. Dothan (USA)-based Pemco converted them from new-build passenger 146s. Other versions were the executive Statesman (similar to those used by the British Royal Flight), the 'QC (Quiet Convertible) and the unordered military STA (Small Tactical Airlifter).

The 146 series became the first of the 'quiet' jets to break down the barriers imposed by airport authorities that previously had banned all jets or had enforced a night-time curfew. Its remarkable ability to carry out 'steep' approaches onto short runways also allowed the 146 to be the first jet airliner to be allowed access to the London City Airport and also at other airports with difficult terrain or noise sensitive areas nearby.

From 1990 the type was subjected to a major redesign and improvement campaign which resulted in the BAe/AI(R) RJ series. The 146 is still popular with passengers, but as they are retired from front line services, their potential use as freighters becomes more viable. Pemco World Air Services in partnership with BAE Systems offer freight conversions of passenger 146s that take 90 days to complete and cost over $2m. In 2004, Hireplane Cargo Conversions and Cranfield Aerospace Ltd proposed another freighter conversion programme. In late 2004 an American aerial firefighting company obtained a BAe146-100 to investigate its potential as a water bomber.

Details

Span: (All series) 26.21m (86ft 0in)
Length: -100 26.20m (85ft 11in);
   -200 28.60m (93ft 10in);
   -300 30.99m (101ft 8in)
Engines: Four 30.0kN (6,700lb) or 31.0kN (6,970lb) Honeywell ALF502-R3 or -R5 turbofans. Late series -200 & -300 have LF-507-1H.
Cruise speed: 787km/h (425kt)
Accommodation: -100, 94 max;
   -200, 112 max; -300, 122 max.

First service: Dan-Air London, May 1983
Number built: -100, 34; -200, 115; -300, 70.
Number in service: 163 (all series) worldwide

Current Operators

Africa: Air Botswana, Air Zimbabwe.
Asia: Air Fast, China Eastern AL, Druk Air.
Australasia: Air Link, Australia Air Express, National Jet Systems.
Europe: Albanian AL, Atlantic AW, Axis AW, British AW Citi Express, City Jet (Air France), Club Air, Direct Flight, Eurowings, Flightline, Flybe, Hemus Air, Malmo Avn, Mistral Air, Pan Air, Skyways Express, SN Brussels AL, Titan AW, TNT AW, WDL.
North America: Air Canada Jazz, Air Wisconsin AL (United Express).

Until January 2004 Helsinki-based Blue 1 was known as Air Botnia. Their fleet includes RJ85 OH-SAO 'Oulujarvi'. (BAE SYSTEMS Regional Aircraft)

BAe RJ70/85/100/115/RJX

BAE Systems Regional Aircraft
Woodford Aerodrome, Woodford
Cheshire, SK7 1QR, UK

In 1990, British Aerospace, who at the time, were the manufacturers of the BAe 146, announced a major revision to the series. The 'new' 146 would have better engines, a new digital flightdeck and an all-round improvement in performance and range. In 1992, BAe launched the revised BAe146 family as a series of four Regional Jetliners, with the same wing/engine combinations but different fuselage lengths. Basically, each RJ was a direct replacement for the earlier BAe 146, with the RJ70 replacing the 146-100, the RJ85 replacing the 146-200, and the RJ100 and RJ115 replacing the 146-300. Externally, the RJs are virtually indistinguishable from the 146s.

Launch customers for the RJ family were Business Express, Crossair, Dan-Air and Meridiana Spain. The first RJ to fly in March 1992 (an RJ85) was the last aircraft ever to be built at the Hatfield factory before it closed, leaving all future production centred at Woodford, near Manchester.

Major features in the RJ series includes Category IIIA all weather landing capability, FMS and a four-screen EFIS. The RJ was then unique among regional jets in having FADEC on the LF507 engines. This device allows cooler starting, monitors engine speeds and controls the temperatures. The RJ Series was, like the BAe146, available in QT-Quiet Trader, QC-Quiet Convertible, and Combi layouts, but none of these variants were ordered.

By 1993, the RJ airliners were collectively called Avroliners, in recognition of the new company name Avro International Aerospace (Woodford having been the main production centre for the former Avro Company). In 1995, the AI(R) consortium was formed from ATR, Avro and Jetstream, allowing the RJs to be marketed alongside the J41, ATR 42 and ATR 72.

Yet another upgrade occurred in March 2000 when BAE (the AI(R) consortium having only lasted a couple of years) announced the RJX series. Powered by Honeywell AS977 engines, three versions were announced, the RJX70, 85 and 100. The RJX85 first flew in April 2001 followed by the RJX100 on 23rd September. Two months later, 52 years of continuous jetliner production in the UK ceased when BAE Systems announced the cancellation of the RJX programme due to poor sales prospects post 9/11. 14 orders were lost.

Details

Span: 26.34m (86ft 5in)
Length: RJ70 26.19m (85ft 10in),
   RJ85 28.55m (93ft 8in),
   RJ100 and 115 30.99m (101ft 8in)
Engines: Four 27.27kN (6,130lb) or
   31.15kN (7,000lb) Honeywell LF507
   turbofans
Cruise speed: 801km/h (432kt)
Accommodation: RJ70 82 max.
   RJ85 100 max. RJ100 112 max.
   RJ115 116 max.

First service: Crossair, April 1993
Number built: 170
Number in service: 163 worldwide

Current Operators

Asia: Pelita Air.
Australasia: National Jet Link.
Europe: Air Malta, Aegean AL, Blue 1, British AW Citi Express, Euromanx, Lufthansa Cityline, Malmo Avn, SN Brussels AL, Swiss Intl AL.
Middle East: Turkish AL.
Former Soviet Union: Air Baltic, Mesaba AL (Northwest Airlink), Uzbekistan AW.

This 19-seat Beechcraft 1900D N81533 is operated by Fort Lauderdale-based Gulfstream International Airways on behalf of Continental Express. (Raytheon)

BEECH 1900C & 1900D

Raytheon Aircraft
10511 E Central, PO Box 85
Wichita, Kansas 67201-0085 USA

Having had great success with their executive Queen Airs, King Airs and the 15-seater twin-prop commuter Beech 99, Beech decided to re-enter the regional airliner market in 1979.

Basing their design on the Model 200 Super King Air, the company stretched the fuselage to take 19 seats and, to enhance aerodynamic stability, added stabilons to the rear fuselage and tailets to the tailplane. The new model 1900C first flew in September 1982 and was granted FAA certification in 1983. Initially powered by PT6A-65 engines, the more powerful 820kW (1,100shp) -65B later became the standard on the 1900C. Sixty-six of the early 1900C model were built before production switched to the longer-range C-1 in 1987. 174 1900C-1 were built with the last one delivered to Flandres Air in 1991. The C/C1 found favour in the USA, with early orders from Cascade Airways, Bar Harbor Airlines and Brockway Air. In addition to the 66 1900C were 11 Model 1900C Exec-Liners.

Poor cabin height in the 1900C/C-1 was rectified with the announcement of the new 1900D model in March 1989. Built at Wichita, this had many improvements to the 1900C, principally the 0.36m (1ft 3in) taller fuselage which had 28% more internal volume allowing stand-up room inside. The windows and passenger entry door were larger and the whole aircraft was covered in stability 'aids', including winglets, finlets and large

strakes under the rear fuselage. The prototype 1900D was built using a 1900C aircraft and first flew in March 1990. The all freight version of the 1900D has a 2,500kg (5,500lb)-payload capacity.

Despite its somewhat ungainly appearance, the 1900D sold well, with New Mexico-based Mesa Airlines (a United Express carrier) receiving a total of 118. Like the 1900C, the 1900D was available in 12-seater Exec-Liner guise. Raytheon received the last order for a 1900D in June 2002 and the last was delivered a year later. Though production has stopped, Raytheon have said they can re-open the 1900 production line if a customer wants to buy a 'fleet'.

Details

Span: 'C 16.61m (54ft 6in);
   'D 17.67m (57ft 11in)
Length: 'C 17.63m (57ft 10in)
   'D 17.63m (57ft 10in)
Engines: 'C two 820kW (1,100shp)
   P&WC PT6A-65B; 'D two 955kW
   (1,279shp) P&WC PT6A-67D
Cruise speed: 'C 495km/h (267kt) max;
   'D 533km/h (288kt) maximum
Accommodation: ('C and 'D) 19 max

First service: 'C Bar Harbor Airlines Feb
   1984; 'D Mesa Airlines, 1991
Number built: 248 1900C; 438 1900D
Number in service: 168 1900C, 366
   1900D, most in USA

Current Operators

Africa: Air Affaires Gabon (D), Air Burundi (C), Air Express Algeria (D), Air Namibia (D), Air Tropiques (C), ALS (C), Avn Assistance Intl (C), Awesome Flight Services (D), Comav Avn (C/D), Compion AV (D), Equaflight Service (D), NAC Executive Charter (D), National AW Corporation (C/D), Norse AC (D), Overland AW (D), Regional AL (D), Rossair (C/D), Rossair Kenya (C/D), SAL Express (C/D), Sonair (D), Transairways (C), Zambian AW (D).

Asia: Air Shenpix (D), Asiatours (D), ASSL (C), Buddha Air (C/D), Indonesia AT (D), MHS Avn (D), Reliance Transport and Travel (D), Travira Air (D).

Australasia: Air Link (D), Eagle AW (D), Emu AW (C), GWA (C), PACAV (C), Pel-Air (D), Vincent Avn (C/D).

Europe: Airlinair (D), Alsair (D), Aria (C), Atlantique Air Assistance (C/D), Avanti Air (C/D), Avn Assistance (C), Aviator AW (D), Danish AT (C/D), Euromanx (D), Hahn Air (D), Hex Air (D), Naysa (C/D), Octavia AL (C), Pan Européenne AS (D), PGA Express (D), Private Wings (D), Regional (D), Rossair Europe (D), Swedline Express (D), Twin Jet (C/D), Wanair (D).

Middle East: Falcon Express Cargo AL (C).

N America: Air Alliance (D), Air Creebec (D), Air Labrador (C/D), Air Midwest (America West Express, Mesa AL, US AW Express) (D), Air-Serv Intl (C), Alaska Central Express (C), Alpine Air (D), Ameriflight (C), Autec Avn Services (D), Central Mountain Air (C/D), Colgan Air (US AW Express) (C/D), Commutair (Continental Connection) (D), Corporate Air (C), Frontier Flying Service (C), Georgian Express (C/D), Globemaster AC (C), Great Lakes AL (C/D), Gulfstream Intl AL (Continental Connection) (D), Hageland Avn Services (C), Knight-hawk Air Express (C), Mesa AL (America West Express) (D), North Cariboo Air (C), Northern Thunderbird Air (D), NT Air (C), Pacific Coastal AL (C), Prince Edward Air (C), Scenic AL (C), Skylink Express (D), Skyward Avn (D), Skyway AL (Midwest Connection) (D), Suburban Air Freight (C), TAB Express AL (C), Transwest Air (C), Vintage Props and Jets (C), Wasaya AW (D).

S America: Aerotaca Express (C), Aero Transporte (C), Air Santo Domingo (D), Alpine Air Express (C), Avior Express (D), Hawk de Mexico (C), Latina de Avn (C), SAEREO (C/D), SAP (C/D), SASCA (C), SEARCA (C), Servicios Aeronauticos Sucre (C), Skyking AL (C), Sky Unlimited (D), Vertical de Avn (C).

Possibly the last scheduled passenger services by Boeing 707 are carried out by Iranian airline SAHA using ex-Iranian military 707s from Tehran. (Mike Barth)

BOEING 707/720

Boeing Commercial Airplane Group
PO Box 3707, Seattle
Washington 98124-2207, USA

Conceived in the 1950s as a jet-powered military tanker for the USAF, but with a potential for production as an airliner, the Boeing Model 367-80, popularly known as the 'Dash Eighty', first flew in July 1954. This prototype became the Boeing 707, an airliner that became synonymous with jet air travel for the 1960s.

The first order for the 707, in October 1954, was for 29 of the military version known as the KC-135A Stratotanker (Boeing Model 717). Since then, the KC-135 family has grown and grown taking on a wide range of duties with a re-engining policy looking set to keep versions flying for many more years. The 707 airframe also has served the USAF and other air forces in several guises and it forms the basis of the E-3 AWACS, E-6 Mercury and E-8 J-STARS platforms.

The first civil order did not arrive until 1955, when Pan American ordered 20. Once Pan Am had taken this step towards a jet fleet, many other major airlines were compelled to keep up, and ordered huge numbers of 707s along with the similar rival, the Douglas DC-8.

Initial Boeing 707 variants were the basic 707-120 and the more powerful 707-220. Qantas of Australia ordered a special long-range version known as the 707-138. This had a short-fuselage similar in length to the Boeing 720. The stretched fuselage Intercontinental -320 first flew in January 1959, leading to the Rolls-Royce Conway-powered -420, and finally the highly successful turbofanned - 320B and 'C.

The 707-320C first flew in February 1963 and was a convertible passenger/cargo variant with a large freight door. It is the most common type of civilian 707 still flying today. The Boeing 720 was a short-to-medium range, 130-seater variant with a lightened structure and aerodynamic modifications to increase its cruise speed to Mach 0.9. In all, 154 Boeing 720s were built, the last airline to operate them being MEA in 1995.

After the Chapter 2 noise restriction legislation appeared in 1985, 707s without hushkits were banned in the USA and Europe. As an alternative to hushkits, various companies including Comtran and QNC offered re-engining programmes but unlike the civil DC-8s that have successfully been re-engined with the new generation CFM56 engines, all surviving civil 707s are still powered by JT3Ds. Only the USAF and the French Air Force has spent the $30 million or so per aircraft required to re-engine their KC-135s with CFM56s.

Virtually all the current 707 operators use the type as a freighter; however, in early 2004, Saha Airlines from Iran was still carrying passengers in its fleet of ex-military 707s. Perhaps the most famous 707 currently flying is the 707-138B owned by John Travolta and flown by him on goodwill tours in full Qantas Airlines colours.

Details

Span: -120 39.90m (130ft 10in);
   -320B 44.42m (145ft 9in)
Length: -120B 44.07m (144ft 6in);
   -320B 46.60m (152ft 11in)
Engines: -120B four 76.2kN (17,000lb) P&W JT3D-1; -320B four 80kN (18,000lb) P&W JT3D-3 or 84.4kN (19,000lb) P&W JT3D-7 turbofans.
Cruise speed: -120B 1,000km/h (540kt) max; -320B 974km/h (525kt) max
Accommodation: -120B 179 max
   -320B 219 max
Freighter payload: 40,000kg (88,900lb)

First service: Pan American World Airways, October 1958
Number built: 855 707, 154 720
Number in service: 70 B707s, mostly in Africa.

Current Operators

Africa: Air Leone, Air Memphis, Allied Air, Azza Transport, Cargoplus Avn, Enterprise World AW, Great Lakes AW, Hewa Bora AW, Interair South Africa, Johnsons Air, Kinshasa AW, Libyan Arab AL, Mahfooz Avn, Spirit of Africa AL, Sudan AW, Sudanese States Avn, Trans Arabia AT, Tristar Air, Wimbi Dira AW.
Asia: South East Asia AL.
Europe: Romavia.
Middle East: Saha Air.
South America: BETA Cargo, LADE, Skymaster AL, Transcontinental Sur.

Boeing 717-2CM EC-HOA of Aerolineas Baleares is seen here approaching Arrecife on Lanzarote. A superb place for aircraft photography. (Tony Best)

BOEING 717

Boeing Commercial Airplane Group
PO Box 3707, Seattle
Washington 98124-2207, USA

Although it had been first announced at the 1991 Paris Air Show, the actual launch of McDonnell Douglas MD-95 was not made until ValuJet (which became AirTran in 1997) ordered 50 plus 50 options in October 1995. Two versions were initially proposed, the base-line model MD-95-30 and the Extended Range -30(ER). In August 1997, the McDonnell Douglas company and Boeing were 'merged', with Boeing taking over the MD-95 design and renaming it the Boeing 717. Much discussion revolved around the re-use of this designation as it had been originally applied to the military C-135 in the early 1950s. Boeing stopped production of the MD-80 and MD-90 leaving the 717 as the only MD type to be marketed by Boeing after the takeover. It first flew in September 1998.

Last in the long-lived DC-9/MD-80/ MD-90 line, the 717 features Rolls-Royce (originally BMW Rolls-Royce) BR715 turbofans, a fully automatic Flight Management System and a six-screen Honeywell EFIS. The aircraft, assembled at Long Beach, was the first Boeing to be built on a moving line, similar to that used in the car industry. At least 12 other countries build components for the 717. The wings come from Canada, fuselage sections from Italy, the empennage and horizontal stabilisers from Taiwan and the cockpit section is built in Korea.

The original MD-95 was actually given the B717-200 designation in January 1998 at the same time as the 80-seat -100 and 129-seat -300 were announced. The -300 was to have had an additional rear service door and forward fuselage strakes but neither version has been built. In 2003, Boeing unveiled the 40-80 passenger B717 Business Express model for corporate use, with new auxiliary fuel tanks and a range of 3,700km.

Though its operators have clearly found the 717-200 to be a very efficient short-haul, high- frequency 100-seater that can compete very well with the A318 and the Embraer 195, by the end of 2004, the future sales prospects were poor. With only 30 outstanding orders to be completed and production running at one per month, the final blow for the 717 came when Pembroke Leasing cancelled 14 outstanding commitments. Not surprisingly, in January 2005 Boeing announced that the 717 line would be closed in mid-2006 along with the Long Beach plant, thereby ending airliner production at this historic site. The last 717s will be completed for AirTran, Midwest and Turkmenistan..

The largest current fleet is operated by AirTran in the USA who, as ValuJet, were the launch customer. The second customer, TWA, is now gone, and some of its fleet have been bought by AirTran. Only a dozen 717s are in service in Europe.

Details

Span: 28.44m (93ft 3in)
Length: 37.82m (124ft 0in)
Engines: two 82.3kN (18,500lb) to 93.4kN (21,000lb) Rolls-Royce BR715 A1-30 turbofans
Cruise speed: 811km/h (438kts)
Accommodation: 117 maximum

First service: AirTran, September 1999,
Number built (ordered): 137 (18)
Number in service: 137

Current Operators

Asia: Bangkok Air.
Australasia: Jetstar AW.
Europe: Aebal, Eurowings, Olympic AL.
Former Soviet Union: Turkmenistan AL.
North America: Air Tran AW, Hawaiian AL, Midwest

Brightly coloured Boeing 727-25C freighter S9-BAU is registered in Sao Tome & Principe but based in Angola. (Afavia-fotos.co.za)

BOEING 727-100

Boeing Commercial Airplane Group
PO Box 3707, Seattle
Washington 98124-2207, USA

Design studies for this medium to short-range partner for the Boeing 707 commenced around 1956. The original intention was to power it with three Allison-built, Rolls-Royce RB-163 Spey turbofans but this powerplant was rejected and JT8D engines specifically designed for the 727 and fitted with thrust reversers, were chosen instead.

As is still the case today, Boeing aimed for the maximum commonality with their other types in order to reduce initial costs and design delays. This manifested itself in the identical fuselage profile of the 707 from the cabin floor upward, and the very similar cockpit layout. The advanced new wing was the first on an airliner to have triple-slotted trailing edge flaps, and the APU (fitted in the starboard wheel well) was also a first for a Boeing airliner.

On 30th November 1960, United and Eastern Airlines both ordered 40 Boeing 727s, bringing the project to production status. The first 727 flew from Renton in February 1963, at which time Boeing had further orders for 131, including the first foreign order for 12 for Lufthansa. This airline flew its last 'Europa Jet 727' service in October 1992, 28 years after its first delivery.

In 1964, Boeing announced that Northwest Orient Airlines were the launch customer for a convertible passenger/cargo version known as the 727-100C. This version was later developed into the

727QC (Quick Change), which also had the large (3.4m x 2.18m/11ft 2in x 8ft 2in) forward freight door and first entered service with United Airlines in 1966.

To ensure their continued use in the western world, surviving 727-100s have either been re-engined or 'hushkitted' in order to conform to current noise restrictions. The Dee Howard Company of San Antonio, Texas, refitted 44 UPS Airlines 727-100s with Rolls-Royce Tay 651 engines and an updated EFIS cockpit, these are known as the 727QF (Quiet Freighter). Valsan's conversion used JT8D-217C or -219 engines in the outboard positions together with other noise reduction modifications. Hamilton Aviation in Tucson, Avborne Heavy Maintenance and Stambaugh Aviation were still offering 727-100 freighter conversions in 2003.

Currently, the 727-100 is popular in Africa with 8 airlines operating the type while the largest fleet is with UPS Airlines who have around 50 including their Tay-powered 727-100QFs.

Details

Span: 32.92m (108ft 0in)
Length: 40.59m (133ft 2in)
Engines: Three 62.3kN (1,400lb)
   Pratt & Whitney JT8D-7 turbofans
Cruise speed: 960km/h (518kt) max
Accommodation: 131 maximum

First service: Eastern Airlines, February 1964
Number built: 582
Number in service: 170, most in North & South America, with many now in Africa

Current Operators

Africa: Air Gemini, Angola AC, Hewa Bora AW, Inter Air South Africa, Miba Avn, Nationwide AL, Trans Air Congo, Wetrafa Airlift.

Asia: Intra Asia Air, Kam Air, UB Air.

Europe: Star Air.

North America: All Canada Express, Custom AT, Express.Net AL, FedEx, First Air, Kelowna Flightcraft, Morningstar Air Express, Northern AC, Planet AW, Ryan Intl AL, UPS AL.

South America: Aerosucre, Aviandina, LA Suramericanas, LAB, Nuevo Continente, Panavia Cargo AL, TAME, TAP, VARIG LOG, Vensecar Intl.

Note the winglets on Amerijet's Boeing 727-227 freighter N794AJ as it taxies out for departure at Grantley Adams International Airport on Barbados. (Author)

BOEING 727-200

Boeing Commercial Airplane Group
PO Box 3707, Seattle
Washington 98124-2207, USA

Announced in August 1965, the Series 200 Boeing 727 was created with minimum changes to the established Series 100, except for a 6.1m (20ft 0in) extension to the fuselage, made up from two equal length 'plugs' fore and aft of the wing. Launch customer, in August 1965, was Boston-based Northeast Airlines, who ordered six, closely followed by American Airlines with an order for 22. The first -200 flew in July 1967 leading to type certification that November.

Having the same fuel capacity as the smaller -100, the -200 suffered from reduced range; however, with support from Ansett ANA and Trans Australia Airlines, Boeing proposed the higher capacity, longer range -200 'Advanced' in 1970. This featured the JT8D-15 engine, higher weights and greater fuel capacity. First delivery was to Iberia in 1972.

In 1981, the all-freight version of the 200 Advanced, the -200F Advanced, was offered. This had all the windows removed, a stronger fuselage and a forward main-deck freight door. The last ever 727 built was a -200F Advanced delivered in September 1984 to Federal Express.

Conversions of passenger -200s to freighter status have also taken place. FLS Aerospace at London-Stansted joined the list of those offering the facility with their first conversion (for TNT Express, operated by Sterling) entering service in March 1997.

Like the -100, the -200 can also be converted to conform to Stage3/Chapter 3 noise requirements. The Valsan Company converted 21 aircraft by replacing the outer engines with JT8D-200s and acoustically treating the centre one. After Valsan went bust, this programme was taken over by Goodrich. More than 800 Stage 3 hushkit sets, made by FedEx Aviation Services, have also been supplied and fitted.

The number of active 727s declined rapidly following the US airline slump in late 2001. Almost half of the airworthy examples were grounded and few have been restored since then. One interesting use of a 727 involves the Zero-Gravity company in Los Angeles. In October 2004 they began flights for adventurous passengers wishing to experience weightlessness using a modified 727-200 operated by Amerijet International. The 27 passengers can float around during a 2 hour flight over the Gulf of Mexico, climbing at 45° nose up and then descending in a controlled parabolic curve.

Details

Span: 32.92m (108ft 0in)
Length: 46.69m (153ft 2in)
Engines: Three P&W JT8D turbofans. Variants from 64.4kN (14,500lb) to 72.95kN (17,400lb)
Cruise speed: 953km/h (515kt) max
Accommodation: 189 max

First service: Northeast Airlines, December 1967.
Number built: 1,260 (including 15 -200F Advanced)
Number in service: 560

Current Operators

Africa: Aero Africa, African Express AW, Afrik Air Links, Air Algérie, Air Gemini, Air Mauritanie, Airquarius Avn, Albarka Air, Allied Air, Angola AC, Buraq Air, Chanchangi AL, Dasab AL, Freedom AS, Hewa Bora AW, IRS AL, Jetline Inc, Kinshasa AW, Libyan Arab AL, Mahfooz Avn, Nationwide AL, Safair, Sonair, Sudan AW, Teebah AL, Transafrik Intl, Trans Sahara Air, West African AL, Wimbi Dira AW, Yemenia.

Asia: Aero Lanka, Air Macau, Ariana Afghan AL, Efata Papua AL, Indonesian AL, Intra Asia AL, Jatayu AL, Kam Air, Mandala AL, Merpati, Pacific East Asia Cargo, Serendib AL, Transair, Transmile AS.

Australasia: Asian Express AL, Australian Air Express, Heavylift Cargo AL, Jetex.

Europe: Air Contractors, Aviogenex, JAT, Swiftair.

Middle East: Iran Air, Iran Aseman, Palestinian AL, Rais Cargo, Syrianair.

Former Soviet Union: AZAL Azerbaijan AL.

North America: All Canada Express, Amerijet, Asia Pacific AL, Astar AC, Capitol Cargo Intl AL, Cargo Jet AW, Champion Air, Contract AC, Custom AT, Express.Net AL, Falcon Air Express, FedEx, First Air, Kalitta Air, Kelowna Flightcraft, Kitty Hawk AC, Miami Air, Morningstar Air Express, Pan Am, Planet AW, Ryan Intl AL, Starjet Canada, Sunworld Intl AL, Transmeridian AL, UPS AL, Westar Express.

South America: Aerogal, Aero Honduras, Aeromexpress, Aeropostal, Aerosucre, Aerosur Bolivia, Aviacsa, DHL Aero Expreso, LAB, LA Suramericanas, LAMCASA Carga, Santa Barbara AL, Sky AL, TAME, TOTAL LA, VARIG LOG, VASP, Vensecar Intl.

Abuja-based Albarka Air of Nigeria started jet operations with BAC 1-11s prior to buying Boeing 727s and this 737-200 5N-YMM. (Afavia-fotos.co.za)

BOEING 737-100/200

Boeing Commercial Airplane Group
PO Box 3707, Seattle
Washington 98124-2207, USA

Announced in November 1964 as a short-range twin-jet 60/85-seater, the new Boeing 737 became the first of a whole series of 737s that eventually outsold every other airliner in the world.

To save production costs and to give the airlines valuable commonality of parts, many systems and components of the Boeing 707, 720 and particularly the 727 were utilised, including passenger doors, cabin furnishings, the engines and significantly, the fuselage cross-section. Design features included wing-mounted (as opposed to pylon-mounted) engines that allowed for a shorter undercarriage and a built-in airstair.

By the time construction started in 1965, passenger capacity had been raised to 99 and orders had come from Mexicana, Western, Pacific, United and launch customer Lufthansa. The German airline ordered 21 Boeing 737-100s in February 1965. United's order was for 40 of the stretched -200, plus options on another 30.

First flight of the -100 prototype was in April 1967 at Boeing Field in Seattle. The first of 248 -200s flew in August, and both sub-types were granted FAA certification in December. The -100 proved unpopular in comparison with the -200, and only 30 were built for Lufthansa, Malaysia-Singapore Airlines and Avianca.

In 1970, production moved to Renton and in 1971 the -200 was replaced by the -200 'Advanced' with a new brake system, more efficient thrust reversers,

longer engine nacelles and other improvements. Over 100 -200s were completed as 200C (Convertible) and 200QC (Quick Change) versions. These had a 2.18m (7ft 2in) by 3.40m (11ft 2in) cargo door, and a strengthened floor.

The 737-200 has also seen limited use with the military. Largest operator is the USAF who bought 19 T-43A for crew trainer and transport duties. The Indonesian Air Force operate three highly-modified 737-2X9 Surveillers for maritime reconnaissance and transport. A total of 865 of the -200 Advanced were delivered to operators all over the world. The last JT8D-powered 737 was delivered to CAAC of China in August 1988. There are still over 600 of the popular Advanced (or Adv) model in service, many of which have had their engines 'hushkitted' in order to conform to the Stage 3/Chapter 3 noise restrictions. Two US companies, Nordam and AvAero, have both developed Stage 3 hushkits for the 737's JT8D engines.

Details

Span: 28.35m (93ft 0in)
Length: -100 28.65m (94ft 0in);
  -200 30.48m (100ft 0in)
Engines: Two 62.7-77.4kN (14,000-
  17,400lb) P&W JT8D turbofans
Cruise speed: 917km/h (495kt)
Accommodation: -100 115; -200 130;
-200 Adv 125 max

First service: Lufthansa, Feb 1968
Number built: 1,144
Number in service: 680

Current Operators

Africa: ADC AL, Aero Africa, Air Algérie, Air Corridor, Air Gabon, Air Guinée Express, Air Madagascar, Air Namibia, Air Tanzania, Air Zimbabwe, Albarka AS, Bako Air, Bellview AL, Benin Golf Air, Comair, Dasab AL, EAS AL, East African AL, Ethiopian AL, Flair Afrique, Fresh Air, Hewa Bora AW, Interair South Africa, Kenya AW, Kulula.com, LAM, Lignes Aériennes Congolaises, Nationwide AL, Regional Air, Royal Air Maroc, Safair, Slok Air, South African AW, Space World Intl AL, Sudan AW, TAAG Angola AL, Teebah AL, Tuninter, VSA Avn, Yemenia.

Asia: Aero Asia, Air Fast, Air Philippines, Air Sahara, Alliance Air, Bali Air, Batavia Air, Blue Dart Avn, Bouraq, Celebes Xpress Air, Efata Papua AL, Indian AL, Intra Asia AL, Iraqi AW, Jatayu AL, Kamair, Kartika AL, Mandala AL, Merpati, Pearl Air, Phuket AL, President AL, Royal Khmer AL, RPX AL, Seulawah Nad Air, Shaheen Air Intl, Sriwijaya Air, Star Air, Transmile AS, Tri-MG AL, Xpress Air.

Australasia: Airwork.

Europe: Air Mediterranée, Air One, Air Slovakia, Aviogenex, Europe Air Post, European Avn AC, Ryanair.

Middle East: AMC AL, Dolphin Air, Iran Air, Iraqi AW.

Former Soviet Union: Aerosvit, Lithuanian AL, Phoenix Avn, Ukraine Intl AL.

North America: Air North, Alaska AL, Aloha AL, America West AL, Ameristar AC, Canadian North, Canjet AL, Casino Express, Delta AL, Falconbridge, First Air, Hooters Air, Pace AL, Ryan Intl AL, Sierra Pacific AL, Southwest AL, Westjet.

South America: Aerolineas Argentinas, Aerosucre, Aerosur Bolivia, American Falcon, Austral, Aviacsa, Aviadina, Avior Express, Azteca AL, Bahamasair, Cayman AW, COPA AL, Estafeta Carga Aerea, LAN Chile, LAN Express, Magnicharters, Nuevo Continente, PLUNA, Rico LA, Rutaca AL, Sky AL, Southern Winds, TACA Intl AL, TANS, VASP.

Boeing 737-300 N773CT at Southend prior to delivery to Adam Air in Indonesia in September 2004. (Tony Best)

BOEING 737-300

Boeing Commercial Airplane Group
PO Box 3707, Seattle
Washington 98124-2207, USA

The 737 Series 300 was by far the most popular 'Classic' 737 powered by the CFM56 high-bypass turbofan. Originally envisaged as a simple stretch of the -200, the planned Stage 3/Chapter 3 noise restrictions and the availability of the quiet and efficient CFM56 engine prompted Boeing to change their high-selling design.

Boeing managed to retain 80% of the earlier 737-200 airframe parts in the revised design. The differences, apart from the engines and their pylons, include a 2.64m (8ft 8in) fuselage stretch that was created by inserting two 'plugs' fore and aft of the wing, a dorsal fin extension, new leading edge slats and longer wings and tailplanes. The nose undercarriage leg was also lenghtened to ensure ground clearance for the larger engines. The cockpit was also updated with an early version of an EFIS display comprising four all-colour Cathode Ray Tubes (CRT).

Boeing formally launched the new 737-300 in March 1981 with orders for ten each for USAir and Southwest Airlines. Only a few orders were received in 1982 but by the time the prototype was rolled out in January 1984, the order book stood at 50. After the first flight in February 1984, airlines gradually became more interested in the -300, especially as the new engines were excellent on fuel economy and its pilots could have a common rating for all the new series of 737s including the -400 and -500. Only one basic version, with a choice of engines, was built; however,

Boeing did sell a few in executive layout with a plush VIP interior.

No 737-300s were built by Boeing with main deck cargo capability; however, three companies offer freight or QC conversions, Bedek Aviation Group in Israel, Pemco World Air Services in Alabama, USA and a conglomerate led by ICAS of Taiwan assisted by Boeing and Flight Structures. Ten 737-300s will be converted to freighters in Indonesia by Bedek in association with Garuda's GMF Aero Asia company. Pemco modified some newly-built 737-300s straight from the factory.

The 1,500th CFM powered 737 was delivered in September 1994 and production was switched to the 'New Generation' 737-600/700/800/900 in 1998. The last 737-300 was delivered to Air New Zealand in December 1999 and the type, along with the -400 and -500 is now referred to as the '737 Classic'. With 1,113 built, the -300 has become one of the most common airliners in the Western world.

Details

Span: 28.88m (94ft 5in)
Length: 33.40m (109ft 7in)
Engines: Two 88.97-97.86kN (20,000-22,000lb) CFM International CFM56-3 turbofans
Cruise speed: 908km/h (491kt) max
Accommodation: 149 maximum

First service: Southwest Airlines, December 1984
Number built: 1,113
Number in service: 1,050 worldwide

Current Operators

Africa: Aerocontractors, Air Austral, Air Madagascar, Air Malawi, Comair, Karthago AL, Kenya AW, Precisionair, TACV, Tiko Air.

Asia: Air Asia, Air China, Air Sahara, China Eastern AL, China Postal AL, China Southern AL, China Southwest AL, China United, China Xinhua AL, China Xinjiang AL, China Yunnan AL, Citilink, Garuda Indonesia, Hainan AL, Merpati, Pakistan Intl AW, Philippines AL, Shandong AL, Shanghai AL, Shenzhen AL, Yangtze River Express AL.

Australasia: Air New Zealand, Air Vanuatu, Airwork, Freedom Air, Jet Connect, Palau Micronesia Air, Qantas Aw.

Europe: Aegean AL, Aigle Azur, Air France, Air Horizons, Air Malta, Air One, Air Plus Comet, Air Polonia, Astraeus, Axis AW, Blue Air, Bluebird Cargo, BMI Baby, British AW, Bulgaria Air, Channel Express, DBA, Easyjet AL, Euro Atlantic AW, Europe Air Post, Fischer Air, Flyglobespan, Flyme Sweden, Helios AW, Hola AL, Iceland Express, Ion Tiriac Air, Islandsflug, JAT, Jet 2, Lauda, LOT, Lufthansa, Malev, MAT-Macedonian AL, Norwegian Air Shuttle, Olympic AL, SATA Intl, Tarom, Titan AW.

Middle East: Fly Air, Jordanian Avn.

Former Soviet Union: Aerosvit, Transaero AL, Turkmenistan AL, Ukraine Intl AW.

North America: America West AL, Continental AL, Delta AL, Falcon Air Express, Frontier AL, Hooters Air, Pace AL, Southwest AL, United AL, US AW.

South America: Aero Honduras, BRA Transportes Aereos, Cayman AW, GOL Transportes Aereos, LA Azteca, LAB, Magnicharters, Nordeste, PLUNA, Rio Sul, VARIG, VASP.

OK-FAN is one of three 737-300s owned by Fischer Air. It flew its first service in April 1997 as a dedicated airline to the Fischer Travel Agency. (Author)

The fast growing Jet Airways from Mumbai in India has a large fleet of 737s including this Boeing 737-45R VT-JAT bought new in 1998. (Phil Camp)

Istanbul-based airline MNG Pax use 737-400s, MD-82s and an A300 for passenger services. The freight division have A300s with MNG Cargo titles. (Author)

BOEING 737-400

Boeing Commercial Airplane Group
PO Box 3707, Seattle
Washington 98124-2207, USA

Work on a stretched version of the CFM56-powered Boeing 737 series commenced in the early 1980s; however, Boeing's preoccupation with their '7-7' and '7J7' designs delayed the actual launch of the Boeing 737-400 until June 1986. The -400 was promoted as a 150 seat Boeing 727 replacement that, because of its 80% parts commonality could provide significant saving for operators of the existing 737-300 that were looking for a larger aircraft to add to their fleet. The -400 customers would also benefit from a common crew type rating for the -300/400.

Launch customer was North Carolina-based Piedmont Airlines, who in 1988 merged with USAir. In June 1986 they announced an order for 25 -400s with a further 30 on option. The first -400 was rolled out at Renton in January 1988, and first flew a month later.

Apart from the fuselage stretch, created by adding a 1.83m (6ft 0in) plug forward of the wing, and another 1.22m (4ft 0in) behind, the -400 differs little from its forebear. The wings and undercarriage had to be strengthened to cope with the aircraft's higher weight and because of the extra capacity, the -400 had to be supplied with two extra over-wing emergency exits. A tailskid under the rear fuselage was also installed to counter any temptation to over-rotate by pilots used to the take-off characteristics of the shorter -300.

Boeing also offered a version with higher gross weights. It had optional fuselage and wing strengthening, additional fuel tanks, new flaps and slats and a revised undercarriage. The basic model is also available in 'long-range' format with either one or two auxiliary fuel tanks in the rear cargo hold.

Like the -300, Boeing never built an all-freight version of the -400, but the same three companies that offer -300 conversions also offer -400 conversions, although none have been completed yet. These are Bedek Aviation in Israel, Pemco in Alabama and a consortium led by Inter Continental Aircraft Services from Taiwan assisted by Boeing and Flight Structures. The first ICAS/Boeing conversion for Alaska Airlines should start in early 2005. A blended winglet conversion programme for the 737-400 has been on offer by Aviation Partners since May 2003.

Having been replaced by the equivalent 'New Generation' 737-800, the last ever '737 Classic', a 737-400, was rolled out in December 1999 and delivered to CSA Czech Airlines in January 2000. The type is still in extensive use and the current largest fleets are operated by Malaysian, Alaska Airlines and US Air.

Details

Span: 28.88m (94ft 9in)
Length: 36.45m (119ft 7in)
Engines: Two 97.86-104.5kN (22,000-23,500lbst) CFM International CFM56-3C1 or -3B2 turbofans
Cruise speed: 912km/h (492kt) max
Accommodation: 189 maximum.

First service: Piedmont Airlines, October 1988.
Number built: 486
Number in service: 460, worldwide

Current Operators

Africa: Air Gabon, Atlas Blue, Comair, Royal Air Maroc, Safair.

Asia: Adamair, Air Nippon, Air Sahara, Asiana AL, Atlas Jet Intl, Batavia Air, China Xinhua AL, Garuda Indonesian, Hainan AL, JAL Express, Japan Trans Ocean Air, Jet AW, Lion AL, Malaysia AL, Mandala AL, Nok Air, Philippines AL, Skynet Asia AW, Thai AW.

Australasia: Air Nauru, Qantas AW.

Europe: Aer Lingus, Aegean AL, Air Berlin, Air Europa, Air One, Air Polonia, Axis AW, Blue Panorama, Braathens, British AW, Corsair, CSA, Futura, JAT, KLM, Lauda, LOT, Malev, Olympic AL, SATA Intl, Skynet AL, Travel Service, TUI AL Belgium, Virgin Express.

Middle East: Fly Air, MNG AL, Pegasus AL, Sky AL, Turkish AL.

Former Soviet Union: Aerosvit, Transaero AL, Ukraine Intl AW.

North America: Alaska AL, Ryan Intl AL, US AW.

South America: BRA Transportes Aereos, VARIG.

This shot of Aer Lingus' Boeing 737-548 EI-CDD was taken from the excellent viewing area beside the south runway at Manchester International Airport. (Author)

BOEING 737-500

Boeing Commercial Airplane Group
PO Box 3707, Seattle
Washington 98124-2207, USA

The short-bodied version of the second generation, CFM56-powered Boeing 737, is similar in length to the JT8D powered Boeing 737-200, and carries a similar passenger load, but, in comparison, its maximum range is increased by one third, and it uses up to 20% less fuel per passenger.

Boeing had planned to develop a 100-seater short fuselage version of the 737-300 series for some time, but they temporarily shelved the idea while promoting the stretched 737-400. Eventually, what became the 737-500 was given various designations including 737-Lite, 737-1000 and even 737-400! The engines proposed at that time included the CFM56-3, the RR Tay and the JT8D-400. It officially became the -500 when launched in May 1987 after orders and options were received from Braathens SAFE of Norway and Southwest Airlines from Texas. These were soon followed by further orders from Euralair of France and Maersk Air of Denmark.

The short body was achieved by removing two fuselage plugs from the -300 fuselage, one forward (1.07m/3ft 6in) and one aft (1.37m/4ft 6in) of the wing. Very little else was changed, thus ensuring the 85% commonality of airframe parts between the -300, -400 and the -500. Purists might like to know that the -500 has a new fairing at the wing/fuselage junction and new

nosewheel tyres! Boeing also offered the -500 as a HGW/Long-Range version with additional fuel capacity and more powerful engines.

The first 737-500 was rolled out at Renton on 3rd June 1989 and the first flight took place four weeks later. FAA certification was granted in February 1990. The 737-500 probably lost some sales because it was in competition with other Stage 3/Chapter 3 certificated types, such as the Fokker 100 and the BAe 146. Also, at that time, many operators preferred to keep their trusty 737-200s and fit 'hushkits' if necessary, rather than buy a new aircraft. The last of 389 series 500s was delivered to ANA-All Nippon Airways in Tokyo in July 1999.

Unlike the -300 and -400, the series 500 is not suitable for conversion to an all-freight layout. This is because the forward fuselage is too short to be fitted with a standard 3.56m x 2.29m (11ft 10in x 7ft 8in) cargo door without the forward projecting engine getting in the way of loading/unloading. The last of 389 series 500s was delivered to ANA-All Nippon Airways in Tokyo in July 1999.

Details

Span: 28.88m (94ft 9in)
Length: 31.01m (101ft 9in)
Engines: Two CFM International CFM56 turbofans, rated at 82.29-88.97kN (18,500-20,000lb)
Cruise speed: 911km/h (492kt)
Accommodation: 132 maximum

First service: Southwest Airlines, February 1990
Number built: 389
Number in service: 360 worldwide

Current Operators

Africa: Air Austral, Royal Air Maroc, Rwandair Express, Tunisair.

Asia: Adamair, Air Nippon, Asiana AL, China Southern AL, Garuda Indonesian, Xiamen AL.

Europe: Aer Lingus, Air Baltic, Air France, Air Mediterranée, BMI Baby, Braathens, British AW, CSA, DBA, Hapag Lloyd Express, LOT, Lufthansa, Luxair, Maersk Air, Sky Europe AL Hungary, Slovak AL, Smart Wings, Thomson Fly.

Middle East: Egyptair, Turkish AL.

Former Soviet Union: Aerosvit, Air Baltic, Belavia, Estonian Air, Georgian AW, Lithuanian AL, Ukraine Intl AW.

North America: Canjet AL, Continental AL, Pacific Sky AC, Southwest AL, United AL.

South America: Aerolineas Argentinas, Nordeste, Rio Sul.

Gleaming new wingletted 737-752 XA-CAM of Aeromexico taxies out at Los Angeles International in August 2004 bound for Mexico City. (Author)

BOEING 737-600/700

Boeing Commercial Airplane Group
PO Box 3707, Seattle
Washington 98124-2207, USA

The third series of the best selling Boeing 737 was originally given the designation 737-X, and included plans for a further fuselage stretch to boost capacity to 190. In the early 1990s, Boeing discussed their plans with more than 30 airlines and in 1993, they officially launched the 737-X after an order from Southwest Airlines for 63 '737-300Xs' (which became the 737-700).

The three aircraft in the 737-X series (later renamed -600, -700 and -800) are all slightly larger than the second generation 737s that they replace. The -600 has the same fuselage as the -500 and was called the -500X until it was officially launched in March 1995 after an order from SAS for up to 76 aircraft.

Features for all the aircraft in the series – which Boeing market as the Next-Generation 737 – included new, longer and wider wings (25% more area) to give greater fuel capacity and fuel efficiency, with a consequent increase in range and speed. The fin and horizontal stabiliser were increased in size and area and the cockpit and the external layout of doors and service hatches were unchanged from the -300/400/500 to maintain commonality.

The first of the Next-Generation 737s, -7H4 N737X, made its first flight from Renton on 9th February 1997 followed by the first -700 delivery to Southwest Airlines in December. Launch customer for the -600 was SAS; their first aircraft entered service in September 1998.

In November 2001, Boeing delivered the first 737-700C passenger/freighter convertible to Saudi Aramco. Launched with an order for two from the US Naval Reserve in September 1997, the -700C (known by the Navy as the C-40A Clipper) was the first freighter 737 offered by Boeing since 1966. It has a 3.4m x 2.1m side cargo door and an onboard freight handling system. Another military variant is the AEW&C Wedgetail that was ordered by the Royal Australian Air Force in December 2000. The first of six for the RAAF was flown in May 2004.

The BBJ1 (Boeing Business Jet) is based on the -700 but has the strengthened wing of the -800. It was certified in November 1998 and more than 60 BBJ1s have been delivered to date. The winglets on the BBJ1s are built by Aviation Partners in a joint venture with Boeing. The airline version of the -700 can also be fitted with winglets.

Unlike the high-selling -700, the -600 has found few buyers. Of the 56 in service, none are in operation in the USA while SAS remain the largest operator with 30 aircraft. The -700 is a different matter with over 850 either built or on order. Southwest Airlines will eventually have a fleet of 276.

Details

Span: 34.31m (112ft 7in)
Length: -600 31.24m (102ft 6in); -700 33.63m (110ft 4in)
Engines: Two 82.3-107.6kN (18,500-24,170lb) CFM International CFM56-7 turbofans
Cruise speed: 852km/h (460kt)
Max accommodation: -600 132; -700 144

First service: -600 SAS Sept 1998, -700 Hapag Lloyd April 1998
Number built (ordered): -600 56 (12), -700 590 (375)
Number in service: -600 56, -700 590.

Current Operators

Africa: Air Algérie (-600), Air Mauritanie, Air Senegal Intl, Air Seychelles, Ethiopian AL, Kenya AW, Royal Air Maroc, Tunisair (-600 & -700).

Asia: Air China (-600 & -700), Air Sahara, Changan AL, China Eastern AL, China Southern AL, China Southwest AL (-600), China United, China Xinjiang AL, Hainan AL, Jet AW, Shanghai AL, Shan Xi AL, Shenzhen AL, Xiamen AL.

Australasia: Air Pacific, Virgin Blue.

Europe: Air Berlin, Astraeus, Braathens, Easyjet AL, Fordair, Germania, Hamburg Intl AL, Hapag Lloyd Express, Kosova AL, Lauda (-600 & -700), Luxair, Maersk Air, Malev (-600 & -700), Privatair, SAS (-600 & -700), Tarom, Transavia AL.

Middle East: Oman Air, El Al.

Former Soviet Union: Air Astana, Transaero AL.

North America: Air Tran AW, Alaska AL, Aloha AL, Continental AL, Southwest AL, Westjet.

South America: Aeromexico, Azteca AL, COPA AL, GOL Transportes Aereos, Rio Sul.

The Caribbean airlines always manage to create great colour schemes. Boeing 737-8Q8 9Y-ANU displays its calypso oil drum colours in Miami. (Author)

BOEING 737-800/900

Boeing Commercial Airplane Group
PO Box 3707, Seattle
Washington 98124-2207, USA

The -800 and -900 Series of the Boeing 737 introduced further extended fuselage lengths from the -700 creating the longest Boeing 737 yet. The 42.11m (138ft 2in)-long Series 900 is 4.54m (14ft 11in) longer than the competing Airbus A320.

Features of the -800/-900 include the use of the same wing as the -600/-700 (25% larger than the Classic's), a six screen EFIS flightdeck and efficient CFM56-7B engines. By altering the display on the EFIS, cockpit instruments can be displayed in the same format as the Classic 737s, allowing both types to be flown by crew with a common type rating. Aviation Partners/Boeing blended winglets are offered on new build -800s and can also be retrofitted. They have yet to assess whether they would be useful on the -900. Despite the extra fuselage length of the -900, it is unable to carry more passengers than the -800's maximum of 189 because it has the same number of emergency exits.

Launched in September 1994, the 737-800 (originally referred to as the 737-400X) was first ordered by Hanover-based airline Hapag Lloyd with an order for 16 in November 1994. It first flew in July 1997 and the initial delivery was made in April 1998. In 2001, a Boeing Business Jet based on the fuselage of the -800 was launched as the BBJ2. Nine BBJ2s had been sold by September 2003.

Launch customer for the -900 was Alaska Airlines. The prototype was rolled out at Renton in July 2000 and first flew that September. The flight test programme was completed in April 2001 allowing the first production model to be handed over to Alaska Airlines the following month.

In mid 2004, Boeing proudly announced that they had won the contract to replace the US Navy's P-3 Orions with their B737-800ERX 'Multi Mission Maritime Aircraft'. The first should be ready in 2006 and the design may even become the basis for a new longer-range and heavier 737-800 variant. The MMMA deal could involve up to 108 aircraft worth $20 billion.

Boeing has proposed a longer-range 737-900X with a strengthened undercarriage and adjacent structure. If extra emergency exits were fitted aft of the wing, it could carry up to 220 passengers.

Boeing unveiled a short-field performance enhancement kit in 2004. Using aerodynamic, structural and instrumentation mods, the modification package was initially designed for the -800/-900. The kit has been ordered by the Brazilian carrier GOL and their first modified -800 should be delivered in late 2006.

Details

Span: 34.31m (117ft 2in)
Length: -800 39.50m (129ft 6in),
   -900 42.11m (138ft 2in)
Engines: Two 107.6kN (24,170lb) to
   121kN (27,300lb) CFM56-7B turbofans
Cruise speed: Mach 0.785 (530mph)
Accommodation: 189 maximum

First service: -800 April 1998 Hapag
   Lloyd -900 Alaska Airlines May 2001.
Number built (ordered): -800 799 (340),
   -900 47 (8)
Number in service: -800 799, -900 44

Current operators

Africa: Air Algérie, Royal Air Maroc, South African AW, Yemenia.

Asia: Air China, Air Sahara, China AL, China Eastern AL, China Southern AL, China Southwest AL, China Xinhua AL, Hainan AL, Jet AW (-800 & -900), Korean AL (-800 & -900), Mandarin AL, MIAT Mongolian AL, Shanghai AL, Shenzhen AL.

Australasia: Air Pacific, Pacific Blue AL, Polynesian, Qantas AW, Virgin Blue.

Europe: Air Berlin, Air Europa, Air Horizons, Britannia AW AB, Eurocypria AL, Excel AW, Futura, Hapag Lloyd, Helios AW, KLM (-800 & -900), Lauda, Malev, Neos, Novair, Ryanair, SAS, Sterling European AL, Transavia AL, Travel Service, TUI AL Belgium, Visig.

Middle East: El Al, Inter AL, KTHY, Oman Air, Pegasus AL, Sky AL, Sun Express, Turkish AL.

Former Soviet Union: Air Astana, Belavia.

North America: Alaska AL (-900), American AL, ATA AL, Continental AL (-800 & -900), Delta AL, Miami Air, Ryan Intl AL, Sun Country AL.

S America: BWIA, GOL Transportes Aereos, VARIG.

Air Atlanta Icelandic painted this B747-243B TF-ARO in these special Olympic markings for a month-long world tour prior to the 2004 games. (Tony Best)

BOEING 747-100/200

Boeing Commercial Airplane Group
PO Box 3707, Seattle
Washington 98124-2207, USA

Probably the most significant aircraft of the 1970s and beyond, the 'Jumbo Jet' brought affordable long-range travel to the world's airline passengers. The original Boeing 747 was designed in the mid-1960s, based on Boeing's work on a large logistics transport for the US military (the CX-HLS requirement which gave rise to the Lockheed C-5A Galaxy).

The resulting 747 was essentially an overgrown 707 with four engines widely spaced along the wing leading edge and a fuselage with a single passenger deck with two aisles seating ten across. The cockpit is positioned above this deck with a small cabin lounge area behind.

Prior to the official launch, in July 1966 Pan American World Airways made the world's biggest airliner order when it ordered 25 Boeing 747s. When further orders arrived from JAL and Lufthansa, Boeing went ahead with production.

By the time the prototype first flew at Everett, in February 1969, the 747 had won orders for 160 aircraft from 27 airlines. FAA Type Approval was granted in December 1969, and PanAm flew the first trans-Atlantic 747 service in January 1970.

The heavier and longer range 747B was announced in November 1967. This had extra fuel and a revised undercarriage for greater weights, and was later given the designation 747-200, leaving the original as the -100. The -200 was available with a choice of three engines, the CF6-50E, the JT9D-7 or the Rolls-Royce RB211.

Although a pure cargo 747 was planned from the start, a 747F did not appear until Lufthansa's first example flew in November 1971. This had a hinged nose that swings upwards to permit direct entry/exit of pallets or freight. The 747C 'Convertible' (also with the hinged nose) first flew in March 1973 and was first delivered to World Airways. The 747 'Combi' was normally built without the hinged nose, and was fitted with a large rear cargo door. The first Combi was delivered to Sabena in 1974.

In 1973, Boeing introduced the B747SR designed specifically for the high density, short haul market in Japan. Japan Air Lines still have a few -100SRs which are configured for over 560 passengers while All Nippon Airways' 747SRs only carry 528! KLM had some of their -200s modified by Boeing to have the Stretched Upper Deck that was designed for the -300.

The type is now being withdrawn from front line service; however, a new life for the 747-200 may come from a strange direction. In spring 2004, Evergreen International Aviation were testing a series 200F water bomber. This 'Supertanker' can carry 91,000 litres (24,000US Gal) of fire retardant in the main deck tanks and can dump the whole lot in 10 seconds!

Details (Specifications for 747-200)

Span: 59.64m (195ft 8in)
Length: 70.66m (231ft 10in)
Engines: Four 243kN (54,750lb) P&W JT-9D or 233.5kN (52,500lb) GE CF6-50 or 236kN (53,000lb) RR RB211-524 turbofans
Cruise speed: 905km/h (490kt)
Accommodation: 500 max (10 abreast)

First service: Pan American, Jan 1970
Number built: -100 167; -100B 9; -100SR 27; -200B 224; -200C 13; -200F 73; -200M 77
Number in service: 330 worldwide

Current Operators

Africa: Air Gabon, Air Universal, Kabo Air (-100 & -200), MK AL, Northeast AL, Royal Air Maroc.

Asia: Air China, Air Hong Kong, Air India, ANA (-100 & -200), Cathay Pacific, Dragonair, Garuda Indonesia, Indonesian AL, JAL Intl (-100 & -200), JALways, Japan Asia AW, Korean AL, Malaysia AL, NCA (-100 & -200), Orient Thai AL (-100 & -200), Pakistan Intl AL, Phuket AL, Transmile AS.

Europe: Air Atlanta Europe, Air Atlanta Iceland, Air France, Air Plus Comet, European Avn, Iberia, Lufthansa, Lufthansa Cargo, Martinair, Ocean AL, Pullmantur.

Middle East: Cargo AL, El Al, Iran Air (-100 & -200), Kuwait AW.

Former Soviet Union: Air Bridge Cargo, Volga-Dnepr AL.

North America: Atlas Air, Evergreen Intl AL (-100 & -200), Kalitta Air (-100 & -200), Northwest AL, Polar Air Cargo, Southern Air, UPS AL (-100 & -200).

South America: Aerolineas Argentinas.

With an easterly wind and a sunny day at Gatwick, great landing shots like this of 747-443 G-VROS can be had from a farmer's field. (Author)

BOEING 747-300/400

Boeing Commercial Airplane Group
PO Box 3707, Seattle
Washington 98124-2207, USA

In the quest to achieve the greatest capacity in an airliner without creating a monster that required larger runways, taxiways and parking areas, Boeing decided to launch a Series 200 of the 747 in 1980 with a 'Stretched Upper Deck' (SUD). This extension to the 'Jumbo's' top floor carried 44 more passengers and, by improving the aerodynamics of the fuselage, increased the cruise from Mach 0.84 to 0.85. The 747-SUD designation was changed to 747-300 after it was launched with an order for five by Swissair in June 1980.

Of the 81 -300s built, 21 were 'Combi' versions with a port side maindeck cargo door behind the wing. The new model -300 first flew in October 1982 and the first -300 delivery was a 'Combi' delivered to Swissair in March 1983.

The -300 naturally led to another variant and this became the most successful 747 ever, the 747-400. First offered to the airlines in May 1985, the 747-400 was initially ordered by Northwest Airlines, Singapore Airlines, KLM and Cathay Pacific. The -400 has the same fuselage as the -300 but has longer, lighter and more aerodynamic wings and is easily recognisable by the 1.83m (6ft 0in) high, drag-reducing winglets. Other features include a two-crew EFIS cockpit, more advanced engines and greater fuel capacity and range. Versions include the -400 'Combi' and the -400F freighter that first flew in May 1993. This has the -200F fuselage with the short upper deck, an

upward-opening nose cargo door and an optional port side rear cargo door.

The 'odd' one in the -400 family is the 568-seater 747-400D (Domestic). This short-range development was announced in October 1989 specifically for the Japanese internal market where huge numbers of passengers rely on the 'Jumbo' for short flights, often only one hour long. It dispenses with the wingtip extensions and winglets because of the minimal advantages that they provide over short distances. The 747-400ER is an extended-range higher weight version with extra fuel capacity. It first entered service as a passenger liner with Qantas and as a freighter with Air France in 2002.

In 2004, it was announced that KAL Aerospace at Gimhae would convert 19 Boeing 747-400s to 747-400SF (Special Freighter) configuration between 2006 and 2012. Other companies carrying out conversion to -400SF are IAI Bedek, Singapore Engineering and TAECO in China. A 'Guppy'-style special freighter conversion known as the 747 LCF (Large Cargo Freighter) is being designed by Boeing to carry outsize 787 components.

Details (Specifications for B747-400)

Span: 64.44m (211ft 5in)
Length: 70.66m (231ft 10in)
Engines: Four 252-280kN (56,750-63,000lb) turbofans. Either P&W PW4056 or '4062, GE CF6-80 or Rolls-Royce RB211-524

Cruise speed: 939km/h (507kt) max
Accommodation: 568 (-400D)

First service: (-300) Swissair, March 1983; (-400) Northwest Airlines, Feb 1989
Number built (ordered): 81 747-300 (production stopped 1990); 628 (33) 747-400
Number in service: 70 -300, 607 -400

Current Operators

Africa: Cameroon AL (-300), Namibia AL (-300), Royal Air Maroc (-400), South African AW (-300, -400), TAAG Angola AL (-300).

Asia: Air China (-400), Air India (-300, -400), All Nippon AW (-400), Asiana AL (-400), Cathay Pacific (-400), China AL (-400), China Southern AL (-400), Dragonair (-300), EVA Air (-400), Garuda Indonesia (-400), JALways (-300), JAL Intl (-400), Japan Asia AW (-300), Korean Air (-300, -400), Malaysian AL System (-400), Mandarin AL (-400), Orient Thai AL (-300), Pakistan Intl AL (-300), Philippine AL (-400), Phuket AL (-300), Singapore AL (-400), Singapore Cargo AL (-400), Thai AW Intl (-400).

Australasia: Air New Zealand (-400), Air Pacific (-400), Qantas (-300, -400).

Europe: Air Atlanta Iceland (-300 & -400), Air France (-300 & -400), British AW (-400), British Asia AW (-400), Cargolux (-400), Condor Flugdienst (-400), Corsair (-300), Global Supply Systems (-400), Iberia (-300), KLM (-400), KLM Asia (-400), Lufthansa (-400), Pullmantur (-300), Sabena (-300), Swissair (-300), Virgin Atlantic AW (-400)

Middle East: Egyptair (-300), El Al (-400), Emirates (-400), Kuwait AW (-400), Saudi Arabian (-300, -400)

North America: Air Canada (-400), Atlas Air (-300 & -400), Canadian AL Intl (-400), Northwest AL (-400), Polar Air Cargo (-300 & 400), United AL (-400)

South America: Aerolineas Argentinas (-400), Surinam AW (-300), Varig (-300).

Ex-KLM Boeing 747-306 PH-BUW is pictured prior to delivery to Surinam Airways in the summer of 2004. It is now registered PZ-TCM. (Paul Zethof)

TAAG Angola Airlines operate two 747-300s on international services from Luanda including this 747-312(M) D2-TEA 'Cidade de Kuito'. (Author's collection)

One of the few airlines to operate the Boeing 747SP is Syrianair. Both their aircraft were delivered new in 1976. (Mike Barth)

BOEING 747SP

Boeing Commercial Airplane Group
PO Box 3707, Seattle
Washington 98124-2207, USA

With the advent of the long-range Airbuses and Boeings, the Boeing 747SP is now a rare sight with only 15 or so in current airline use. Designed for use on very long-range services or on routes whose traffic levels could not justify the use of the standard high capacity 747-100, the 747SP (Special Performance) was launched in August 1973. With around 100 less passengers than a standard 747, the SP had a greater rate of climb, a higher maximum cruising altitude, a higher cruise speed and an incredible range, for the time, of 6,000nm.

Pan American were the launch customer in September 1973 when they ordered a fleet of ten. Further orders soon followed from Iranair and South African Airways. Remarkably, Iranair still operate the same four 747SPs that they received from Boeing in the late 1970s. SAA had earlier encouraged Boeing to develop the 747SP because of their need to fly non-stop from South Africa to Europe around the 'bulge' of Africa. This was necessary because much of Africa had then refused overflight rights to the South Africans. On 24th March 1976, SAA's first 'SP created a new distance record for a commercial aircraft when it flew on delivery from Paine Field, Washington to Cape Town, 16,510km (10,290 miles) in 17 hours, 22 minutes.

The first flight was made on the 4th of July 1975 followed by certification flights

using the first four SPs over a seven-month test programme. Certification was granted in February 1976 followed by the first delivery to Pan American during the next month. Their first scheduled service with the SP was between Los Angeles and Tokyo on 25th April.

With its 14.35m (47ft 1in) reduction in overall length and a 1.52m (5ft 0in) fin extension, the 747SP is easily distinguished from every other version of 747. However, the SP in not merely a shortened 747; significant changes had to be incorporated in the fuselage centre section to allow use of the same upper deck cabin and the rear fuselage was altered to achieve a more rapid reduction in width. Other perhaps less noticable changes included a lighter wing with different trailing edge flaps, a double hinged rudder and an extended and lowered tailplane.

After only 44 had been sold, Boeing closed down production of the SP in 1982. However one further example was built. A VIP version, which first flew in March 1987, stayed with Boeing for a while until it was eventually delivered to the United Arab Emirates Government in December 1989.

Of the 45 747SPs built, 39 were powered by Pratt & Whitney JT9D engines and six with Rolls-Royce RB.211s. Original customers included Qantas, TWA, Iranair, CAAC, Braniff, Syrianair, China Airlines, Korean Airlines

and SAA. By the 1990s the type had become popular with the governments of Middle Eastern countries (Oman, UAE and Saudi Arabia) for use as a long-range biz-jet.

Details

Span: 59.64m (195ft 8in)
Length: 56.31m (184ft 9in)
Engines: Four P&WC JT9D-7A or Rolls-Royce RB211-52B2, 524C2, 524D4 turbofans of 205.7-236.32kN (46,250-53,110lb)
Cruise speed: 939km/h (507kt)
Accommodation: 360 maximum

First service: Pan American, April 1976
Number built: 45
Number in service: 15

Current operators

Africa: Yemenia.
Middle East: Iran Air, Syrianair.

The Britannia Airways name, dating back to 1962, will progressively be replaced by the Thomson brand. This 757 will probably carry Thomsonfly titles. (Author)

BOEING 757

Boeing Commercial Airplane Group
PO Box 3707, Seattle
Washington 98124-2207, USA

Boeing's 'new generation' 757 airliner got off to a slow start but eventually became a huge success with sales over 1,000 to 55 customers. Initial planning work commenced in the early 1970s and the 757 evolved through a variety of designs ending up looking like a stretched T-tailed B727 with two 'new technology' engines. Even though Boeing had received firm orders for this format from British Airways and Eastern Airlines, in 1979 they decided once more to radically alter the layout. The 'T' tail was replaced by a more conventional design and the nose section was revised to accept a two-crew, six-screen EFIS flightdeck. This would closely match the cockpit of the Boeing 767, allowing the use of a common crew rating. The prototype 757 first flew in February 1982 with Rolls-Royce RB.211-535C engines. It was later converted to P&W power, flying again with their engines in March 1984.

The 757-200 (the -100 was not built) was the standard passenger version normally seating 186 to 220 passengers. The first cargo version was the windowless -200PF 'Package Freighter' that was developed for UPS. It had a large cargo door, a new crew door and a 9g barrier net behind the cockpit. A single 757-200M Combi was built for Royal Nepal Airlines. It was delivered in 1988 and is still in service. The stretched (7.10m/23ft 3in) and strengthened -300 which can seat up to 279 was launched

at the 1996 Farnborough Airshow after an order for 12 was received from Condor Flugdienst.

By October 2003, Boeing had only 12 aircraft on order and they announced that the 757 line at Renton would be closed in late 2004. Although the last two 757s were completed in November 2004, Shanghai airlines will delay their delivery until April and June 2005.

Between 2000 and 2003, DHL received 34 B757 Special Freighters. Boeing had converted these from passenger aircraft at a cost of $1 billion. Independently-developed freighter conversions are also offered by Pemco, Precision Conversions and Alcoa Aerospace/SIE. Continental Airlines are the launch customer for the Aviation Partners winglet programme. With the promise of a 5 to 10% reduction in fuel burn, they plan to modify at least 11 of their 757-200s with the winglets. Service entry is expected in summer 2005.

Details

Span: 38.05m (124ft 10in)
Length: 47.32m (155ft 3in)
Engines: Two 166.4-185.5kN (37,400-41,700lb) turbofans. Either Rolls-Royce RB211-535C/535E4, or Pratt & Whitney PW2037, or '2040
Cruise speed: 914km/h (493kt) max
Accommodation: 239 maximum
Payload: (-200PF) 36,220kg (79,830lb) max

First service: Eastern Airlines, Jan 1983
Number built: 1,050
Number in service: 1,030

Current Operators

Africa: Ethiopian AL, Royal Air Maroc, TACV.

Asia: Air China, Cebu Pacific, China Southern AL, China Southwest AL, China Xinjiang AL, Far Eastern AT, Kampuchea AL, Orient Thai AL, Phuket AL, Royal Brunei AL, Royal Nepal AL, Shanghai AL, Xiamen AL.

Europe: Air Atlanta Iceland, Air Finland, Air Greenland, Air Scotland, Air Slovakia, Belair, Bluebird Cargo, Britannia AW, British AW, Condor Flugdienst, DHL Air, Dutchbird, European AT, Excel AW, Finnair, First Choice AW, Flyjet, Greece AW, Hola AL, Iberia, Icelandair, Icelandair Cargo, Monarch AL, My Travel (UK), Privatair, Star Air, Thomas Cook AL, Titan AW.

Middle East: Arkia, Atlas Jet, El Al, Israir, Sun D'or Intl AL.

Former Soviet Union: Air Astana, AZAL Azerbaijan AL, Turkmenistan AL, Uzbekistan AL, VIM AL.

North America: American AL, America West AL, ATA AL, Continental AL, Delta Al, Harmony AW, Hooters Air, North American AL, Northwest AL, Omni Air Intl, Pace AL, Primaris AL, Ryan Intl AL, Sky Service AL, Song, Transmeridian AL, United, UPS AL, US AW.

South America: Aeromexico, Avianca, Mexicana, PLUNA, VARIG.

A unique aircraft! 9N-ACB 'Gandaki' is the world's only Boeing 757-200 Combi. It was delivered new to Kathmandu in 1988. (Author)

Zoom Airlines' 767-300s will fly to Gatwick from seven cities in summer 2005; Toronto, Vancouver, Ottawa, Halifax, Edmonton, Montreal and Calgary. (Author)

Only Continental and Delta operate the 767-400. The appropriately registered prototype N76400 was at the 2000 Farnborough Air Show. (Richard Hunt)

BOEING 767

Boeing Commercial Airplane Group
PO Box 3707, Seattle
Washington 98124-2207, USA

With the provisional designation '7X7', Boeing launched their ideas for a 200-seater wide-bodied airliner in 1972. Over the next few years, several designs were considered, including some with three engines, but by 1978 the layout was firm enough for Boeing to name their wide-body twin as the Model 767.

United Airlines gave Boeing the launch order for 30 767-200s in July 1978. Not long after, Boeing also offered the smaller, narrow-bodied Boeing 757 to the airline industry. The two types would have many common systems and parts; indeed, Boeing stated that about half the parts of the 757 and 767 would be inter-changeable. Significant for the airlines ordering both the 757 and 767 would be the similarity in cockpit layout, permitting a common flight-crew type rating.

First flown in September 1981, the 767 was from the start, offered with a multiple choice of engine makes and performance. The basic -200 (the smaller -100 was cancelled) was followed by the -200ER (Extended Range) in 1982. As more powerful engines became available, the -200ER was improved with further fuel capacity and an increase in MTOW. This version was first delivered to Ethiopian Airlines in May 1984.

Japan Air Lines were the launch customer for the stretched (6.42m/21ft 1in) -300 which was announced in 1983. Like the -200, this was soon followed by an 'ER' version and also a freighter

(300ERF) which is in service with All Nippon, Asiana, ABSA Cargo, Florida West, Lan Chile and UPS.

Design work on the further stretched (6.4m/21ft 1in) and much modified 767-400ER commenced in 1996. The launch customer was Delta Airlines who ordered 21 in January 1997. It has longer wings with raked wingtips, a taller undercarriage, aerodynamic improvements and an upgraded flightdeck. It first flew in October 1999 and entered service in August 2000 with Continental and Delta.

Freighter conversions for the -200 are available from IAI Bedek and Aeronavali. Military versions include four freighter/tankers for the Italian Air Force and four E-767 AWACS for Japan. After a damaging acquisition scandal, the USAF is still considering whether to buy 100 KC-767 tankers. In late 2005 however, they will receive a single 767-400ER as a testbed for the future E-10A Multi-sensor Command and Control aircraft.

Details

Span: -200/300 47.57m (156ft 1in), -400ER 51.92m (170ft 4in)
Length: -200/200ER 48.51m (159ft 2in); -300/300ER 54.94m (180ft 3in); -400ER 61.36m (201ft 4in)
Engines: Two 213.5-282.5kN (48,000-63,500lb) turbofans. Engines include General Electric CF6-80, Pratt & Whitney JT9D-7R4, PW4050/52/62.

Rolls-Royce RB.211-524G
Cruise speed: 914km/h (492kt) max
Accommodation: -200, 216; -200ER, 174; -300, 261; -300ER, 210, -400ER, 375.

First service: United Airlines, Aug 1982
Number built (ordered): 922 (24)
Number in service: 846 civil worldwide

Current Operators

Africa: Air Algérie, Air Gabon, Air Madagascar, Air Mauritius, Air Seychelles, Air Zimbabwe, Cameroon AL, East African, Eritrean AL, Ethiopian AL, Kenya AW, Nationwide AL, Royal Air Maroc.

Asia: Air China, Air Do, ANA, Asiana AL, China Eastern, Eva Air, Hainan AL, JAL Intl, Japan Asia AW, NCA, Royal Brunei AL, Shanghai AL, Skymark AL, Vietnam AL.

Australasia: Air New Zealand, Air Nuigini, Air Pacific, Australian AL, Qantas AW.

Europe: Air Atlanta Europe, Air Atlanta Iceland, Air Europa, Alitalia, Belair, Belgium Exel, Blue Panorama, Britannia AW, British AW, Condor Flugdienst, Euro Atlantic AW, Excel AW, First Choice AW, Holland Exel, Icelandair, KLM, Lauda Italy, LOT, Lufthansa, Malev, Martinair, My Travel (UK), SAS, Slovak AL, Swefly, TUI Belgium AL.

Middle East: El Al, Etihad AW, Gulf Air, Gulf Traveller.

Former Soviet Union: Aeroflot, Aerosvit, Kras Air, Phoenix Avn, Transaero AL, Turkmenistan AL, Uzbekistan AW.

North America: ABX Air, Air Canada, American AL, Continental AL, Delta AL, Florida West Intl AW, Hawaiian AL, North American AL, United AL, UPS AL, US AW, Zoom AL.

South America: ABSA, Aeromexico, Avianca, BRA TA, LAB, LAN Chile, MAS Air, Mexicana, PLUNA, Southern Winds, TAMPA, Universal AL, VARIG.

This is B777-224 (ER) N78001 landing at Gatwick in 2003. Note the size of the GE90 engine cowlings, almost as wide as a 737 fuselage! (Author)

BOEING 777

Boeing Commercial Airplane Group
PO Box 3707, Seattle
Washington 98124-2207, USA

Conceived originally as a stretched 767 to fill the product gap between the 767 and the 747, the Boeing 777 was first identified as the '7J7', and later the '767-X'. The 777 that emerged owed little other than format to the 767; it was an altogether larger and wider aircraft with dimensions much more in the 747 league. The programme was formally launched in October 1990 after United Airlines had ordered 34 aircraft.

Until the 787 appears, the 777 is Boeing's most advanced airliner, incorporating fly-by-wire technology and the latest, flat-panel liquid crystal displays in the two-pilot, award winning cockpit. The 777 also had the world's largest airliner landing gear until it was beaten by the A380. Weight saving innovations included the use of lightweight composite materials particularly in the tail and wing structure, these accounting for almost 9% of the total airframe weight. At the time, the wing aerofoil was claimed by Boeing to be the most efficient on a subsonic airliner. Although no airline has taken the option, the 777 is also available with folding wingtips to reduce the span to 47.3m (155ft) – about the same as the 767. This would allow the 777 to operate at airports with restricted gate widths.

First flown in June 1994, the 777 was soon awarded the full 180 minute ETOPS clearance, allowing it to operate on long overwater routes without the requirement

for nearby alternate airfields. The GE90-powered 777 commenced its ETOPS trials in February 1996.

Versions available included the basic 777-200 and the long-range 777-200ER. The -200ER (initially known as the 'B Market' and later the -200IGW Increased Gross Weight) carries an extra 62,280 litres (13,700 gals) of fuel giving a range of 13,389km (8,320 miles). The 777-200LR (Longer Range) was formally launched in February 2000. This 17,000km (9,100nm)-range airliner was ordered by Pakistan International and EVA Air. First delivery is due in 2006.

Announced at the 1995 Paris Air Show, the 10.13m (33ft 3in) stretched -300 version is more than 3m (9ft 10in) longer than a 747. The first -300 was delivered to Cathay Pacific in May 1998. The extended range 777-300ER has 2m (6ft 6in) raked wingtips, semilevered landing gear and a TSP (Tail-strike protection) system. First flown in February 2003, certification of this version by the FAA and EASA in 2004 followed a three aircraft flight-test programme lasting nearly 1,500 hours. The first 777-300ER was delivered to Air France in April 2004.

In 2004, Boeing revealed details of a 777 Freighter design based on the series 200LR. With an overall payload capacity of 110,000kg, the 777-200LRXF would carry more than an MD-11F. No commitment has yet been given to this version.

Details

Span: -200ER/300 60.93m (199ft 11in); -200LR/300ER 64.80m (212ft 6in)
Length: -200/200LR 63.73m (209ft 1in). -300/300ER 73.86m (242ft 4in)
Engines: Two 412kN (93,000lb) to 511kN (115,000lb) turbofans. Engines include PW4074/84/90/98, GE GE90 and RR Trent 884/892/895.
Cruise speed: 925km/h (499kt) max
Accommodation: 440 maximum (-200). 550 maximum (-300)

First service: United, June 1995
Number built (ordered): 490 (152)
Number in service: 480

Current Operators

Africa: Air Austral, Kenya AW.
Asia: Air China, Air India, ANA, Asiana AL, Cathay Pacific, China Southern AL, JAL Domestic, JAL Intl, Korean AL, Malaysia AL, Pakistan Intl AL, Singapore AL, Vietnam AL.
Europe: Air France, Alitalia, British AW, KLM, Lauda.
Middle East: Egyptair, El Al, Emirates, Kuwait AW.
Former Soviet Union: Aeroflot.
North America: American AL, Continental AL, Delta AL, United AL.
South America: VARIG.

This is a computer mock-up of a Blue Panorama Boeing 787. This Italian airline has ordered four 787s for delivery in 2008 (Boeing)

BOEING 787

Boeing Commercial Airplane Group
PO Box 3707, Seattle
Washington 98124-2207, USA

With Airbus stealing the limelight with their A380 twin-deck airliner, Boeing re-captured the public's interest when they revealed their Sonic Cruiser project in 2001. However, the Sonic Cruiser didn't really gain much interest from the airlines so Boeing switched back to a more conventional design, one that would be ultra efficient and with a bigger and better cabin than their current narrow bodied designs. This became the Boeing 7E7 (E = Efficiency).

Boeing formally launched their 11th commercial aircraft project, the 7E7, in April 2004 after the announcement of a record-breaking $6bn order for 50 aircraft from All Nippon Airways (ANA). Unusually for Boeing, it was given a name 'Dreamliner', but this name may now be dropped following the change of designation from 7E7 to 787 in January 2005.

As with many major projects like this, Boeing has to 'work share' major structures in order to reduce costs. Japan will be responsible for 35% of the structure, mainly the wings and the wing centre box. Vought Aircraft Industries of Dallas and Alenia from Italy will build the centre and rear fuselage sections while Boeing will be responsible for the final assembly (at Everett, Washington) and the manufacture of 35% of parts. Large pre-built sections of the 787 will be delivered to Everett in at least three modified 747-400 Special Freighters saving 20 to 40%

on delivery costs compared to conventional delivery systems.

Engine choice will be between the RR Trent 1000 and the GE90-based GEN-X. Engine/pylon interface for both engines will be identical allowing either to be used on the same aircraft.

Three sub types are planned using a new simplified designation system. The 217-seat base-line model will be the 787-8, the 289-seater short-range version will be the 787-3 and the stretched version seating 257 will be known as the 787-9. Assembly will start in 2006 with a planned first flight in late summer 2007 and service entry for the -8 in 2008, the -3 in 2010 and the -9 in 2012.

Design features include an extremely light and hightech structure made up of 57% composite material by weight. This will reportedly save as much as 15 to 20% in fuel compared to current types. The cabin will certainly be something new with sweeping arches, electronic LCD window shades over large windows, and a simulated sky effect on the ceiling produced by LEDs that change colour and brightness. The passengers will also be more comfortable because of the increased cabin pressure that will be set to the equivalent of 1,830m (6,000ft) altitude allowing for higher humidity. The distinctive tail design in the concept images may well change when the final configuration and shape is decided in mid 2005.

The first ANA 787s will be delivered in 2008. It was also announced in January 2005 that a group of Chinese airlines intend to take a total of 60 787s with deliveries commencing before the Beijing Olympic Games in August 2008; most of these will be long-range 787-8s.

Details

Span: 787-8 & -9, 58.80m (193ft 0in); 787-3, 51.80m (170ft 0in)
Length: 787-3 & -8 56.00m (182ft 0in); 787-9, 62.00m (202ft 0in)
Engines: Two Rolls-Royce Trent 1000 or General Electric GEN-X
Cruise speed: Mach 0.85
Accommodation: -3 289; -8 217; -9 257

First service: Planned for 2008

Current orders

Asia: Air China (15), ANA (50), China Eastern (15), China Southern (13), Hainan AL (8), Shanghai AL (9).
Australasia: Air New Zealand (2).
Europe: Blue Panorama (4), First Choice AW (6).
North America: Primaris AL (20).

Cimber Air celebrated its 50th Anniversary in August 2000. Bombardier CRJ200LR OY-MAV is seen landing at Basle inbound from Copenhagen. (Author)

BOMBARDIER CRJ 100/200

Bombardier Aerospace Regional Aircraft
123 Garratt Blvd, Downsview, Ontario
Canada, M3K 1Y5

The concept of creating a regional jet by using the basic design of a business jet was a new idea in the late 1980s. Canadair's 'wide-bodied' CL-600/601 Challenger biz-jet had been designed from the start for four-abreast seating with the potential for commuter airline work, but they had to wait some time before thorough market research revealed a demand for a stretched 50-seater.

The Regional Jet programme was officially launched in March 1989, after Canadair had received 'commitments' for over 50 aircraft, including six firm orders from DLT in Germany. The type was originally referred to as the Canadair Regional Jet, CRJ or Canadair Jet, but since the airliner is now sold under the Bombardier banner, it is only referred to as the CRJ.

Apart from the obvious fuselage stretch (6.09m/20ft) of the Challenger design, the airliner differs from its predecessor by having a longer and more advanced 'transonic' wing with extra strength for airline operations, a revised undercarriage, new engine nacelles, an extra starboard-side service-door/emergency-exit, and more fuel capacity.

The first CRJ was rolled out at the Dorval factory in May 1991, and first flew four days later. In October 1991, Comair, the Cincinnati-based airline, announced an order for 20 CRJs with a further 20 on

option. Canadian certification was awarded in July 1992 followed by the first delivery to Lufthansa Cityline (the new name for DLT after March 1992).

The standard -100 version was followed by the extended range -100ER. This can either have an additional 2,800-litre (740-US gal) centre-section fuel tank for the extra range, or a bigger galley. In March 1994, the -100LR (Long Range), with the extra tank and higher weights, was launched with an order from Lauda Air of Austria. The -200 designation was introduced in late 1995 for CRJs fitted with the improved CF34-3B1 engine.

Also available are a corporate version seating 18-30, now named the Challenger 800, and a SE (Special Edition) trans-Atlantic biz-jet. In December 2003 a real milestone was passed when the 1,000th CRJ was delivered (a CRJ700 to Comair/Delta Connection). This is only the eighth passenger jet type to have passed this figure. The largest CRJ fleet is operated by Delta Connection who have 259.

Seventy-five special 44-seat versions known as the CRJ440 were developed and built for Northwest Airlines starting in 2001. The aircraft is visually identical to the CRJ200 but it is available with fewer weight options.

Details

Span: 21.21m (69ft 7in)
Length: 26.77m (87ft 10in)
Engines: Two 41.01kN (9,220lb) General Electric CF34-3AI turbofans. -200 has CF34-3B1
Cruise speed: 786km/h (424kt)
Accommodation: 52 maximum

First service: Lufthansa Cityline, November 1992.
Number built (ordered): 957 (125)
Number in service: 936, most in North America and Europe

Current Operators

Asia: Air Sahara, China United, China Yunnan AL, CR AW, Fair, J-Air, Shandong AL, Shanghai AL.

Europe: Adria AW, Air Dolomiti, Air Nostrum (Iberia Regional), Austrian Arrows, Brit Air (Air France), Cimber Air, Eurolynx Avn, Eurowings, Lufthansa Cityline, Maersk Air, Malev Express.

North America: Air Canada, Air Canada Jazz, Air Wisconsin (United Express), Atlantic Southeast AL (Delta Connection), Comair (Delta Connection), Independence Air, Mesa AL (America West Express, United Express, US AW Express), Pinnacle AL (Northwest Airlink), PSA AL (US AW Express), Skywest AL (Delta Connection, United Express).

Atlantic Southeast Airlines operate a large fleet of CRJ200/700 regional jets on behalf of Delta Connection. N701EV is a CRJ700 series 701ER. (Bombardier)

BOMBARDIER CRJ 700/900

Bombardier Aerospace Regional Aircraft
123 Garratt Blvd, Downsview, Ontario
Canada, M3K 1Y5

After two years of development work, the stretched and refined 70-seat CRJ-X was launched in February 1997 under the new designation CRJ700.

To adapt the CRJ100/200 design, two fuselage plugs were fitted, one forward and one aft of the wing, creating a fuselage that was 4.72m (15ft 6in) longer. Although the interior length was actually increased by an additional 1.3m (4ft 3in) by moving the rear pressure bulkhead. The wings were extended by the addition of wing root plugs, leading-edge slats were fitted, the APU was moved and the undercarriage was modified with taller legs and new wheels. Other changes inside included higher windows, a new forward lower baggage compartment, new overhead lockers and floor and ceiling modifications to allow greater headroom. To allow for greater standardisation, the 30kg-heavier CRJ900 wing was fitted to the CRJ700 (now marketed as the CRJ700 Series 701) from 2003 and the use of the CRJ900 undercarriage and rear fuselage are also being considered. Field Aviation is completing five corporate shuttle versions.

First flight was made at Downsview on 27th May 1999 and since the first service with French airline Brit Air in early 2001, the 700 has suffered with some reliability problems necessitating various modifications to both the aircraft and the customer's operations and maintenance.

The further stretched (3.86m/12ft 7in) CRJ900 was launched at Farnborough 2000 and first flew in February 2001. Launch customer was the Mesa Air Group who ordered 25. Compared to the early 700s it had more powerful engines, extra emergency exits, lower rear fuselage strakes and a stronger wing, undercarriage and rear fuselage. An optional rear service door is also available. Additional variants are the heavier/longer range CRJ900ER and CRJ900LR. The CRJ900's GE CF34-8 engine was tested in GE's Boeing 747 flying testbed as a fifth engine.

A reconfigured version of the CRJ900 is the 74-seater CRJ700 Series 705. Its launch order from US Airways had to be cancelled after the pilots refused to fly it because of the US seating/MTOW scope clause restrictions causing the US Airways order to be switched to the lower capacity CRJ700 Series 701. Air Canada will receive the first Series 705s in 2005. A heavier/longer range CRJ700 Series 705ER is also available.

In a special ceremony at Downsview, Bombardier handed over its 1,000th CRJ, a Comair (Delta Connection) CRJ700, in December 2003. Delta Connection, who were the first airline to commence regional jet services in North America in 1993, currently have the world's largest CRJ fleet with over 250 CRJ200s and CRJ700s in service.

Details

Span: 23.24m (76ft 3in)
Length: 700, 32.51m (106ft 8in);
  900, 36.37m (119ft 4in)
Engines: Two 61.3kN (13,790lb) to
  63.4kN (14,255lb) GE CF34-8
  turbofans
Cruise speed: 827km/h (447kts)

Number built (ordered): CRJ700, 169 (91);
  CRJ900, 25 (21)
Number in service: 193

Current Operators

Asia: Shandong AL.

Europe: Brit Air (Air France), Lufthansa Cityline.

North America: American Eagle, Atlantic Southeast AL (Delta Connection), Comair (Delta Connection), Frontier Jet Express, Horizon Air, Mesa AL (America West Express, United Express), Mid Atlantic AW (US AW Express), PSA AL (US AW Express), Skywest AL (United Express).

Most of Aurigny's Trislanders display special colours sponsored by finance companies. G-RLON advertises Royal London Asset Management. (Frank McMeiken)

BRITTEN-NORMAN TRISLANDER

B-N Group Ltd
Bembridge Airport, Isle of Wight
PO35 5PR. UK

In the late 1960s, market research by Isle of Wight-based Britten-Norman revealed a demand for a larger capacity version of their successful twin-engined eight-seater BN-2 Islander. A stretched 14-seat BN-2S was built, but development was abandoned in favour of a more radical proposition. The novel and unique approach, was to combine a 2.29m (7ft 6in) fuselage stretch with the addition of a third Lycoming engine mounted on to a much-modified and strengthened tail fin. BN hoped that commonality of engine type with the Islander, and the consequent simplification of maintenance and reduction in spares holdings, would prove attractive to customers.

The No 2 BN-2 Islander prototype was converted at Bembridge to the new configuration and first flew as the Islander Mk.III on 11th September 1970. That afternoon it appeared at the Farnborough Airshow as the first Trislander.

Produced at Gosselies in Belgium from 1973, the only major variant was the BN-2A Mk.III-2. Extra baggage space was provided by fitting the same nose as the 'long nose' Islander. To assist take-off, the addition of a 1.56kN (350lbst) auxiliary rocket motor was proposed, but not taken up.

Trislander production ceased in 1981, but since then, several companies have tried to revive the design utilising uncompleted Trislander production sets. In 1982, an unsuccessful venture by the

International Aviation Corp of Homestead, Florida saw them buy production rights, unsold aircraft and eleven uncompleted sets for onward sale as the TriCommutair. In the late 1990s two of these sets re-appeared in Guernsey, where one was used in the rebuild of a Trislander for Aurigny Airlines. Audrey Promotions eventually shipped some of these sets to Australia for construction, but none were flown, and once again a Florida-based company then stated their intention to complete all the remaining sets.

In the late 1990s, Pilatus Britten-Norman were discussing license production of new Trislanders with the Shenzen General Aircraft Co of China but nothing was finalised. FLY BN Ltd (a subsidiary of the B-N Group Ltd) have 're-manufactured' a second-hand Trislander by stripping it back to bare metal and then rebuilding it with new parts. The aircraft, delivered to Rockhopper in March 2004, was the first 'new' Trislander in the Channel Islands for 20 years. In February 2003, sister company Britten-Norman Aircraft (BNA) announced at the Avalon Air Show that they were to restart manufacture of the Trislander because of the upsurge in interest in the aircraft, particularly in China. A 'Proof of Concept' aircraft was under construction in late 2004.

The type is hard to find because of the small numbers built. Aurigny Air Services

in Guernsey maintain an eight-strong fleet for their inter-island schedules in the Channel Islands. Despite their 1997 invitation to manufacturers to offer types to replace the Trislander 'in a couple of years time', there appears to be no direct replacement.

Details

Span: 16.15m (53ft 0in)
Length: 13.34m (43ft 9in); extended nose version 14.48m (47ft 6in)
Engines: Three 195kW (260hp) Lycoming O-540-E4C5 piston engines
Cruise speed: 290km/h (156kt)
Accommodation: 17 maximum

First service: October 1971, Aurigny Air Services
Number built: 83
Number in service: 25, the largest fleet is in Guernsey

Current Operators

Africa: United Air Services.
Australasia: Air Fiji, Great Barrier AL.
Europe: Aurigny AS, Lyddair, Rockhopper.
North America: Air Satellite, Vieques Air Link.
South America: Aerolamsa, El Sol de America, Transaven.

CASA C-212 'Big Joe' TN-AFD seen at Pointe Noire in the Congo is part of Aero Services fleet that includes Islanders, An-24s and a Yak-42. (Jacques Guillem)

CASA C.212 & IPTN NC-212 AVIOCAR

EADS CASA, Avenida de Aragon 404, 28022, Madrid, Spain
Indonesian Aerospace, Jalan Pajajaran 154, Bandung 40174, Indonesia

The CASA 212 Aviocar was designed in the late 1960s by the Spanish company Construcciones Aeronauticas SA (CASA) as a replacement for the C-47 Dakota, Junkers Ju-52/3m, and CASA-207 Azor piston transports operated by the Spanish Air Force. The prototypes were built to military specifications (including a rear-loading ramp) with the design being deliberately kept simple to ensure ruggedness and reliability. First flown in March 1971, initial deliveries were to the Spanish and Portuguese Air Forces in 1974. Commercial sales opportunities were not ignored and this simple design found early civilian buyers, particularly in Indonesia, where its strong fixed undercarriage, the rear loading ramp and reliable Garrett turboprops were an asset in underdeveloped regions.

The first civilian C.212CAs were powered by Garrett TPE-331-5s of 579kW (776ehp). Continuous improvements in the engine power saw various models offered including the C.212CB, C.212-5 and C.212-10. The -5 and -10 suffixes were later changed to Series 100 and 200. In 1979, the series 200 was launched with TPE-331-10s, stronger undercarriage and an increased MTOW. The first series 200 was built from an early prototype C.212 and was first flown in April 1978. The later series 300, identifiable by its longer nose and winglets, first flew in 1984 and was available as a 23/26 seater 'Airliner' with

an optional rear fuselage fairing instead of the rear loading ramp and in 'Utility' layout. The long nose has extra space for avionics and baggage. Other C.212-300 layouts included anti-submarine, Elint/ECM, and maritime patrol. A single demonstrator C.212-300P 'hot-and-high' version was built with PT6A-65 engines. Last variant is the C.212-400 which first flew in April 1997. This has more powerful TPE-331-12JR engines and a new cockpit layout featuring a four display EFIS.

From 1975, the C.212 was also assembled under licence in Djakarta, Indonesia, as the IPTN NC-212-100 and -200, for supply to customers in the Far East. Twenty-nine NC-212-100 were built for Indonesian domestic customers before assembly switched to the -200.

This remarkable little workhorse has sold well and by the end of 2004 it had achieved sales of 480 aircraft to 89 operators in 42 countries. Current use of the C.212 is mostly military, as the design is especially useful for parachute training and as a light transport. The largest civil fleet is currently in Indonesia with Merpati Nusantara.

Details

Span: 20.27m (66ft 7in)
Length: 16.15m (53ft 0in)
Engines: Two 670kW (900shp) AlliedSignal Garrett TPE-331-10R turboprops
Cruise speed: 370km/h (200kt) max
Accommodation: 26 maximum. Utility – 2,700kg (5,950lb)
(Details above are for Series 300)

First service: July 1975, Pelita Air Service
Number built: 480, more than half military
Number in service: 74 civil, most in Indonesia

Current Operators

Africa: Aero Service, AS Gabon, Kivu Air, Mozambique Expresso MEX.

Asia: Air Fast, Airmark, Dirgantara AS, Deraya Air Taxi, Merpati, Pelita Air, SMAC.

Australasia: Sky Traders.

Europe: Avi Trans Nordic, Med Avia.

North America: Arctic Transport Services, Bering Air, Bighorn AW, Boston-Maine AW, Evergreen Helicopters, F S AS, Murray Avn, Presidential AW, Village AC.

South America: DAP AW, SATENA.

Very rare Convair 240 N240HH is preserved at the Planes of Fame Museum in Chino, California in authentic Western Air Lines colours. (Jarrod Wilkening)

CONVAIR 240/340/440

Consolidated Vultee Aircraft
San Diego,
California, USA

In 1945, American Airlines asked the US aircraft manufacturers for a DC-3 replacement. Consolidated Vultee Aircraft, based in San Diego, offered their 30-passenger unpressurised Model 110. This attractive airliner made its first flight from San Diego in July 1946. Only one Model 110 was built, but the testing and studies of its economics paved the way for the bigger and better pressurised Model 240, (2 = number of engines, 40 = number of seats).

The Model 240 became the world's first pressurised twin-engined airliner and with an initial order from American Airlines for 75, the design was committed to production without the normal process of building a prototype. Around 1947, the company was given the shortened version of its name 'Convair' but surprisingly this name did not become official until 1954 when it became part of the General Dynamics Corporation. Thus the Model 240 later became the Convair-Liner.

Despite the huge numbers of former military C-47s available to the civil market, new models of the Convair 240 sold well, far better than its rival, the unpressurised Martin 202. Convair sold 171 Model 240s to five US carriers and nine foreign airlines while Martin only managed 43 Model 202/202As. In 1951, Convair produced the Model 340 by stretching the fuselage 1.37m (4ft 6in) and fitting more powerful engines (By this time the designation did not denote the number of engines!)

In 1955, prompted by the competition from the Vickers Viscount, Convair upgraded the 340 into the CV-440 and gave it the name Metropolitan. Standard interior was for 44 passengers; however, a 52-seat interior was optional, as was a nose-mounted weather radar. The 440 became very popular in Europe and gained significant orders from major airlines including Swissair, Sabena, SAS, Iberia, Alitalia and Lufthansa.

Both the 240 and 440 were also sold in large numbers to the USAF and USN for uses such as VIP transport, medical evacuation and as flying laboratories to test airborne electronic equipment. Military designations used included C-131, T-29 and R4Y. After their retirement, many of these well-maintained and inexpensive to buy ex-military aircraft were bought by civil airlines, mostly for operation as freighters.

Almost half of the total piston Convair-Liner production was converted to turboprop power between 1955 and 1967. These efficient turboprop-powered Convairs were much preferred to the radial-engined variety and many major US airlines, including Frontier, Lake Central, Allegheny and North Central had their piston Convair-Liner fleets converted.

The last piston-powered Convair-Liner was built as a VIP transport for the Superior Oil company in February 1958. There are now very few operational radial-engined Convairliners.

Details

Span: 32.12m (105ft 4in)
Length: 24.84m (81ft 6in)
Engines: Two 1,865kW (2,500hp)
  Pratt & Whitney R2800-CB16 or '17,
  Double Wasp radial piston
Cruise speed: 483km/h (261kt) max
Accommodation: 52 maximum
Payload (freighter): 5,820kg (12,836lb)
(Details above are for Convair 440)

First service: CV-240 June 1948,
  American Airlines; CV-340 March
  1952, United Airlines; CV-440 March
  1956, Continental AL
Number built: 176 CV-240; 311 CV-340
  (inc military versions), 199 CV-440
Number in service: 37

Current Operators

Africa: Rovos Air.

North America: Air Tahoma, BCCMCD, Coastal AT, Dodita AC, Four Star AC, Fresh Air, Geo Air, Miami Air Lease, Southwind AL, Starflite Intl Corporation, Trans Fair, Trans Florida AL, Tiger Contract Cargo, Tolair Services.

South America: Aerocedros, Aeroejecutivos, Aeronaves TSM, California Aeroservicios, NACIF Transportes Aereos, SAP,

Despite their title, CHC Helicopters (formally Court Helicopters) have a couple of immaculate Convair 580s including ZS-LYL. (Author's collection)

CONVAIR 540/580/600/640/5800

All originally built by Convair and converted by D Napier and Sons, Canadair, PacAero or Convair.

Early work on converting the Convair-Liner to turboprop power commenced in 1949, when the prototype Convair 240 was fitted with Allison T-38s and christened the Turbo-Liner. The result was not satisfactory due to the engine's lack of development, but this work provided data for the later conversions using more advanced Allison T-56s. The US military flew an Allison 501-D powered YC-131C in 1954, but declined to order the type in quantity for the USAF.

The British company, D Napier and Son, converted a CV-340 with their 2,280kW (3,000hp) NEl.1 Eland and first flew it at Luton, UK, in February 1956. This became the CV-540, which in turn was built in small numbers by Canadair for the Royal Canadian Air Force as the CL-66 (RCAF CC-109).

An agreement by Convair with PacAero Engineering Corp of Santa Monica in California produced the most popular conversion, the Allison-powered Convair CV-340 (and later CV-440) which first flew in January 1960. The designation CV-580 for these conversions did not appear until the type entered airline service. The largest fleet of 580s in Europe (9) is currently flown on behalf of DHL by the Spanish company Swiftair while in Canada, Kelowna Flightcraft have a dozen.

Convair's own efforts at converting their piston-powered airliners used the Rolls-Royce Dart 542-4 turboprop. Convair CV-240s with Darts became CV-600s, and CV-340s and 440s became CV-640s. The largest current fleet (7) of Dart-powered Convairliners can be found operating freight services with C & M Airways at El Paso in Texas.

The final, and most radical conversion, involved a fuselage stretch of a Convair 580 by the Kelowna Flightcraft Company in British Columbia, Canada. The resulting CV-5800 first flew in February 1992 and is 4.25m (13ft 11in) longer than the standard Convair-Liner. It is powered by two Allison 501-D22G (Series III) turboprops rated at 4,300 TSHP and has Honeywell EFIS instruments. It can cruise at 325mph and can seat up to 78 passengers, but the five built are currently in use as 21,500lb (9,700kg)-payload freighters with Contract Air Cargo, Air Freight NZ and Kelowna Flightcraft.

Details

Span: 32.12m (105ft 4in)
Length: 24.84m (81ft 6in)
Engines: Two 2,800kW (3,750shp) Allison 501-D13H turboprops
Cruise speed: 550kmh (297kt)
Accommodation: 56
(Data above is for the CV-580)

First service: Frontier, June 1964
Number built:
  175 Convair 580 (ex-340/440)
   39 Convair 600 (ex-240)
   28 Convair 640 (ex-340/440)
   17 CV/Canadair 540 (ex-340/440)
    5 Convair 5800 (ex-580)
Number in service: 76, mostly in North America

Current operators

Africa: CHC Helicopters.

Australasia: Air Chathams, Air Freight New Zealand (+CV5800), Pionair.

Europe: European AT, Swiftair.

Middle East: DHL Avn.

North America: Air Tahoma, C+M AW, Coastal AT, Conair Avn, Contract AC (+CV5800), Corporate Express, ERA Avn, Geo Air, Kelowna Flightcraft (+CV5800), Nolinor Avn, Rhoades Avn.

South America: Aeronaves TSM, Aeroperlas.

Evert Air Fuel's Curtiss C-46F Commando N1822M 'Salmon Ella' is pictured against some formidable scenery at Palmer Airport in Alaska. (Michael S Prophet)

CURTISS C-46 COMMANDO

Curtiss-Wright Corporation
St Louis
Missouri, USA

Originally envisaged in 1936 by Curtiss-Wright as a 24/34-seat pressurised airliner, the CW-20 (later known as the C-46 Commando in US military service) was intended to compete with the Douglas DC-3. The prototype took three years to complete before it first flew at St Louis in March 1940. Originally fitted with twin tailfins, the R-2600 Wright Cyclone-powered prototype revealed some aerodynamic problems; however these were rectified within a year after the aircraft was modified with a conventional single fin. The distinctive 'double-bubble' fuselage cross section was designed to allow pressurisation; however no production CW-20 was built with this equipment.

The Second World War ensured that the C-46 was produced in huge numbers to fulfil USAAF transport requirements. No civil airliner version was produced until after the war, when surplus aircraft were converted into freighters or passenger transports. In 1945, Eastern Air Lines ordered the CW-20E airliner version, but the availability of cheap former military C-46s and C-47s caused Eastern to cancel, and Curtiss never built a civil production CW-20.

Post-war, large numbers of retired USAAF Commandos were bought by airlines in the USA, particularly those operating non-scheduled freight services. US airlines like Riddle, Zantop, Capitol, Slick, AAXICO and The Flying Tiger Line

had huge fleets of C-46s in the 1950s and 1960s. Elsewhere in the world, the cavernous fuselage and large freight door of the big 'Charlie' was much in demand. Up until the 1990s, significant numbers were still flying in Bolivia, Brazil, Colombia, China and Venezuela and its popularity was such that several C-46s were rebuilt after major accidents, utilising parts from derelict examples held in store for just such occasions.

Several C-46 versions were built, but they were all outwardly similar, except for the C-46E which had a single cargo door and an old fashioned 'stepped' windshield. In 1952, a C-46F was modified with the addition of two 1.55kN (350lb) thrust Turboméca Palas turbojets under the wings, to boost take-off performance. Until 1960, Commandos were still being converted to Super C-46 status, with more powerful engines and increased weights.

The Commando is now mostly a museum exhibit, but in some places, its special characteristics ensure that a few still survive to carry general freight, fresh fish, fuel drums and the occasional passenger into dirt, gravel or grass strips that would otherwise cause problems to today's delicate turboprops. Around 30 survive in museums while perhaps another 20 are stored or derelict. Everts in Alaska has the world's largest active fleet of four.

Details

Span: 32.92m (108ft 0in)
Length: 23.27m (76ft 4in)
Engines: Two 1,495kw (2,000hp)
   Pratt & Whitney R-2800 piston
   radial engines
Cruise speed: 300km/h (169kt)
Accommodation: 65 maximum
Payload: 5,265kg (11,630lb)

First service: Summer 1942, USAAF
Number built: 3,181
Number in service: 11, mostly in Alaska

Current Operators

North America: Buffalo AW, Everts AC, Everts Air Fuel, First Nations Transport.
South America: Camba Transportes Aero, LA Canedo, NEBA.

AirSea Lines commenced floatplane ops in September 2004. Twin Otter HB-LSY flew from a lake by Corfu airport on delivery to Gouvia Marina. (Author)

DH CANADA TWIN OTTER

de Havilland Canada
Downsview, Ontario,
Canada

Recognising the need for a 20-seater twin-turboprop with STOL characteristics, de Havilland Canada began design work on their DHC-6 in 1964. By using several parts from their DHC-3 Otter design, the resulting Twin Otter was quickly built, and first flew in May 1965. The type has become synonymous with operations in difficult terrain and although production stopped in December 1988, the Twin Otter is still much in demand.

US FAA certification was achieved in May 1966 and first to operate the type was Trans-Australian The initial -100 variant can be identified by its short nose in comparison to the longer-nosed -200 and -300. Altogether, 115 examples of both the -100 and the -200 were built before the improved -300 first appeared in 1969 with more powerful engines and greater baggage capacity. The -300 became the most popular Twin Otter model with 614 completed when production finished in December 1988.

The modified 11-seater DHC-6-300S first flew in February 1973, with upper wing spoilers, improved braking and avionics. Only six were built for use by Airtransit Canada in an inter-urban STOL demonstration service.

The Twin Otter, often called the 'Twotter' is in use with several armed forces, particularly in South America, where Chile and Peru have the largest fleets. In Canada, four CC-138s are employed for search and rescue while

nine UV-18A/Bs are operated by the USAF and the US Army for transport and parachute training.

The Twin Otter can be adapted for skis or floats. When float mounted, the Twotter is usually fitted with the -100 short nose fuselage for two reasons. The first and most important is that the long nose is surplus weight and the second is that the baggage area in the long nose version cannot be accessed, unless you can walk on water! Float-equipped Twotters have extra finlets on the tailplane.

In Las Vegas, Twin Otter International converts series 300s to 'Vistaliners'. Mods include large panoramic cabin windows, a 19-seat air-conditioned interior and 4-blade props. These, along with the high wing and slow speeds (down to 90kts) of the Vistaliner make it a popular mount for sightseeing flights, such as to the Grand Canyon. Another modification available involves the fitting of a ventral pannier for 272kg (600lb) of freight/luggage.

Details

Span: 19.81m (65ft 0in)
Length: -100 15.09m (49ft 6in) -300 15.77m (51ft 9in)
Engines: -100, two 431kW (578shp) P&WC PT6A-20; -300 two 460kW (620shp) P&WC PT6A-27 turboprops
Cruise speed: -100 297km/h (160kt) max; -300 338km/h (182kt) max
Accommodation: 20

First service: Trans-Australian Airlines,1966
Number built: 844
Number in service: 416

Current operators

Africa: Aerocontractors, Air Burundi, Air Kenya, Air Madagascar, Air Sao Tome & Principe, Air Seychelles, AS Gabon, Ethiopian AL, Kivu Air, Libyan Arab AL, Regional AS, Rossair, Rossair Kenya, Schreiner AW Cameroon, Skytrail, Sonair, Star AV, TACV, TMK Air Commuter, Tunisavia, Yemenia.

Asia: Air Fast, Air Regional, China Flying Dragon Avn, Corporate Air, GT Air, Kenari Air, Malaysia AL, Maldivian Air Taxi, Merpati, MHS Avn, Pacificair, Pakistan Intl AL, Royal Nepal AL, Shangri-La Air, Skyline AW, Trans Maldivan AW, Trigana AS, Yeti AL.

Australasia: Aero Pelican, Air Calin, Air Fiji, Air Moorea, Air Tahiti, AL of PNG, Aviazur, Hevi Lift, Inland Pacific Air, MAF Papua New Guinee, Polynesian AL, Regional Air, Regional Pacific AL, Solomon AL, Southwest Air, Sun Air, Vanair, Whitaker AC.

Europe: Air Greenland, AirSea Lines, Business Wings, Finnair Cargo, Flugfelag Islands, Isles of Scilly Sky Bus, Loganair, Zimex Avn.

Middle East: Ayeet Avn, Iranian AT.

North America: Air Inuit, Air Labrador, Air Tindi, AS Intl, Aldair Avn, Artic Sunwest Charters, Caribbean Sun AL, Carson Helicopters, Continental Avn Services, Corporate Air, ERA Avn, First Air, Grand Canyon AL, Harbour Air, Innu Mikun AL, Katmai Air, Kenn Borek Air, Liard Air, Nakina Outposts Camps & AS, North Cariboo Air, North Wright AW, Ontario MNR AS, Osprey Wing, Provincial AL, Scenic AL, Seaborne Air, South Nahanni AW, Transwest Air, Unaalik Avn, Walkers Avn, Walsten AS, West Coast Air, Wiggins Avn.

South America: ADA, Aeroperlas, Air Guyane Express, AVCOM, Aviones Taxi, British Antarctic Survey, Carib Avn, Cayman AW, DAP AW, Dutch Caribbean AL, Helicargo, Inter Island AW, Island Air, LADE, Natureair, SAP, SAPSA, Surinam AW, SVG Air, TAPSA, Winair.

Air Greenland operate six Dash 7s from Nuuk. OY-CBT 'Papikkaaq' was bought in 1979 when the airline was called Greenlandair. (Robbie Shaw)

DH CANADA DASH 7

de Havilland Canada
Downsview, Ontario,
Canada

Famous for their excellent short take-off and landing (STOL) aircraft such as the Caribou, Buffalo and Twin Otter, de Havilland Canada started their Dash 7 project in 1972 after extensive customer surveys had established a need for a 50-seat STOL airliner. Airlines that operated into short runways or utilised 'hot and high' airfields could at last order an aircraft dedicated to the task.

Additionally, the decision to build STOL strips at major airports and 'downtown' locations could also provide future Dash 7 customers. Instead of using a conventional aircraft from these airfields, often with a subsequent reduction in payload and/or fuel uplift, the Dash 7 could fly 50 passengers from 800m (2,500ft) strips and descend on 6.2° glidepaths into airports surrounded by high ground or city buildings.

To achieve STOL performance, a high lift profile wing and a large 'T' tailplane were incorporated. The wing's advanced design included powerful double slotted flaps placed partly in the slipstream of the engines. Much attention was given to making the Dash 7 as quiet as possible, including ejecting the exhaust gases from the engines over the top wing surface and the use of slow-turning four-bladed propellers.

Initial production started in 1977 with the -100 and the all-freight -101, the higher weight/longer range -150 and -151 followed in 1986. Boeing's buy-out

of DHC in 1986 may have helped the sales of the Dash 8, but unfortunately it failed to boost prospects for the Dash 7. Airlines found that operating a four-engined airliner was expensive and that the Dash 8 could often do the same service at less cost and more speed. Since it first entered service in February 1978, it has sold only in very small numbers. However, even though production stopped in 1988, in many places it is still the definitive STOL airliner and at one time it made the headlines when it became the only type allowed to operate from the new London City Airport.

One highly modified Ranger version was built for the Canadian Government at a cost of $38m equipped with side-mounted radar and an observer's position above the cockpit. It is used for surveying ice floes and other environmental work. The US Army employs 13 Dash 7s as the RC-7/RC-7B on drug surveillance and electronic observation work. These civilian registered spyplanes are expected to remain in service until 2017.

Currently, Arkia of Israel operate the world's largest fleet of Dash 7s with 9 aircraft employed on domestic services.

Details

Span: 28.30m (93ft 0in)
Length: 24.60m (80ft 8in)
Engines: Four 835kW (1,120shp) P&WC
PT6A-50 turboprops
Cruise speed: 420km/h (230kt)
Accommodation: 50 maximum

First service: Rocky Mountain Airways,
February 1978
Number built: 113
Number in service: 56, worldwide

Current operators

Africa: Air Kenya, Yemenia.
Asia: Asian Spirit, Berjaya Air, Pelita Air.
Europe: Air Greenland.
Middle East: Arkia, Petroleum AS.
North America: Air Tindi, First Air, Trans Capital Air, Voyageur AW.
South America: AVCOM, British Antarctic Survey, DAP AW, Lineas Turistica Aerotuy.

Airsouthwest have three Dash 8 Series 300s. G-WOWA is seen at the Gatwick holding point about to depart for Newquay and Plymouth. (Author)

DH CANADA DASH 8

Bombardier Regional Aircraft Division
123 Garratt Boulevard, MS N42-43, Downsview
Ontario, Canada MK3 1Y5

The limited sales of their Dash 7 STOL airliner convinced de Havilland Canada that the market required a regional airliner that was faster, more fuel efficient and far less complicated to maintain, but still retaining STOL capability. The resultant Dash 8 design used a high wing and 'T' tail layout similar to the Dash 7, but with only two P&WC PW120 family turboprops. These give almost as much power as the four PT6A engines on the Dash 7, but burn much less fuel.

Although the Dash 8 is still referred to as a DHC product, from 1986 to 1992 it was built by a division of Boeing, and currently the design is jointly owned by Bombardier and the Ontario government.

First flown as the -100 in June 1983, in 1985 it was given a 3.43m (11ft 3in) fuselage stretch, more powerful PW123 engines and other mods to create the -300. The first -300s were delivered to Zhejiang Airlines and Time Air in 1989. In 1990, the further stretched 70-seater Dash 8-400 with PW150 engines was launched by Boeing in partnership with Mitsubishi Heavy Industries. There were originally two versions of the -400, the -400A was a 70-seater specifically designed for North America, and the -400B seated 74-78. In March 1992, the intermediate-sized 37-seater -200 was launched with a 25-ship order by the Mesa Air Group. Other versions included the high gross weight -100, a -300A, 'B and 'E, and the CT-142 for the Canadian Armed Forces.

The Q suffix (Quiet) first appeared with the Dash 8Q (first delivered to Mesa Air) in 1996. Since then, every Dash 8 has been delivered with a computer controlled noise and vibration suppression system. Since 1998, all Dash 8s have been known by the new, simplified designations, Q100, Q200, Q300 and Q400.

In late 2002, SAT Airlines (Sakhalinskie Aviatrassy) became the first airline in the FSU to operate the Dash 8 – a single second-hand Series 100. Since then they have acquired two more. In 2004, two Q400s were being modified as water bombers by Cascade Aerospace in Abbotsford, Canada for delivery to the French government in 2005.

By mid 2004 DHC/Bombardier had built 299 Series 100s, 95 Series 200s and 208 Series 300s. Currently the most popular version is the Q400 with around 86 delivered and about 30 on order.

Details

Span: Q100, 25.91m (85ft 0in)
Q300, 27.43m (90ft 0in)
Q400 28.42m (93ft 3in)
Length: Q100, 22.25m (73ft 0in)
Q300, 25.68m (84ft 3in)
Q400 28.42m (93ft 3in)
Engines: Two P&WC turboprops:
Q100, 1,490kW (2,000shp) PW120A
Q200, 1,605kW (2,150shp) PW123D
Q300, 1,865kW (2,500shp) PW123B
Q400, 3,778kW (5,071shp) PW150A

Cruise speed: (Q400) 667km/h (360kt)
Accommodation: Q100/200, 40 max;
Q300, 56 max; Q400, 78 max

First service: NorOntair, Dec 1984
Number built (ordered): 689 (31)
Number in service: 608 worldwide

Current Operators

Africa: Aerocontractors, Air Senegal Intl, Air Tanzania, AS Gabon, Midroc Avn, Schreiner AW Cameroon, South African Express AW, Trans-Nation AW, Trident Enterprises.

Asia: A-net Air Nippon Network (ANA), Changan AL, GMG AL, Island AS, Japan Air Commuter, Oriental Air Bridge, Ryukyu Air Commuter, Uni Air, Wings Air.

Australasia: Air Marshall Islands, Air National, Air Niugini, AL of PNG, Asia Pacific AL, Eastern Australia AL (Qantaslink), National Jet Systems, Polynesian AL, Queensland Regional AL, Skippers Avn, Sunstate AL (Qantaslink), Solomon AL.

Europe: Air Nostrum (Iberia Regional), Air Southwest, Augsburg AW, Austrian Arrows, Cirrus AL, Citi Express (British Airways), Denim Air, Fly Baboo, Flybe, Intersky, Olympic AL, SAS Commuter, Schreiner AW, Wideroe.

Middle East: Abu Dhabi Avn, Palestinian AL, Petroleum AS, Royal Wings.

Former Soviet Union: SAT AL.

North America: Air Canada Jazz, Air Creebec, Air Inuit, Air Labrador, Allegheny AL (US AW Express), Arctic Sunwest Charters, Caribbean Sun AL, ERA Avn, Hawkair AS, Horizon Air, Hydro Quebec, Island Air, Mesa AL (America West Express, United Express), Piedmont AL (US AW Express), Provincial AL, Regional 1 AL, Voyageur AW, Westpoint AL.

South America: Aires, Air Jamaica Express, Bahamasair, BWIA, Caribbean Star AL, Inter, LADE, LIAT, Magenta Air, Tobago Express.

Based at North Las Vegas Airport, 19-seater Dornier 228-202 N405VA of Vision Air flies scenic flights to the Grand Canyon. (Kevin Irwin)

DORNIER Do 228 & HAL Do 228

Hindustan Aeronautics Ltd
Transport Aircraft Division, PO Box 225
Chakeri, Kanpur 208008, India

Following on from their series of STOL light transports, Dornier utilised the same fuselage cross section as the Do 28 and Do 128 in their new commuter airliner, the Dornier 228.

Built at Oberpfaffenhofen, the aircraft is a conventional high-wing, retractable undercarriage design, but has an unconventional wing. This has a TNT supercritical aerofoil cross-section with an 8° sweep on the leading edge of the outer wing panels, and sharply raked wingtips finishing at a point. There are two baggage holds fore and aft and the passenger door has built-in steps allowing independence from ground services.

First flown in March 1981, the prototype was a 15-seat short-bodied -100. The first -200 flew in May 1981 and successful flight trials culminated in UK and US certification in 1984. In November 1983, a contract was signed with Hindustan Aeronautics Ltd, of Kanpur in India. It allowed HAL to license build up to 150 Do 228s over 10 years. One pattern aircraft was sent from Germany to India and phased construction commenced using kits from Dornier. The first Indian-built HAL-Dornier 228 flew in January 1986, and over 80 have been completed. The 228-202 is an upgraded and strengthened version built in India for their Light Transport Aircraft requirement. The Indian Navy's Maritime Surveillance 228s can stay airborne for

up to 8 hours and can be fitted with a huge variety of extras including 7.62mm guns, pollution control pods and a 360° radar with a scanning range of 475km.

German-built versions include the original -100, the -101 with stronger airframe and undercarriage, the long-bodied -200 and the similarly strengthened -201. Production of these models ceased in Germany in 1993. The further upgraded Dornier 228-212, identified by the under-fuselage strakes, was available from 1989. This version has a lower empty weight allowing more payload, revised avionics, better STOL performance and a stronger structure. The Do 228 sold well and was delivered to 80 customers in over 40 countries.

Apart from its roles as a commuter airliner and small freighter, the Do 228 is an extremely versatile mount for various non-airline operations equipped with a multitude of sensor/photographic devices for coast guard, maritime patrol, pollution surveillance, photogrammetry/geophysical survey or military multi-purpose missions.

In 1996, the Dornier company was taken over by Fairchild of San Antonio, Texas, who continued to market the Do 228 alongside their Metro and the Do 328 until production in Germany ceased in 1999. The 228 is still in production in India and HAL now have sole rights to market the type.

Details

Span: 16.97m (55ft 8in)
Length: 16.56m (54ft 4in)
Engines: Two 578.7kW (776shp) AlliedSignal TPE331-5-252D turboprops
Cruise speed: 433km/h (234kt) max
Accommodation: 19 maximum
(Details above are for -212)

First service: August 1982
Number built: 244 by Dornier (including kits sent to India):
80+ by HAL.
Number in service: 104 worldwide

Current Operators

Africa: Air Tanzania, Business Avn, DANA, Kaskazi Avn, VSA Avn.

Asia: A.Soriano Avn, Corporate Air, Cosmic Air, Gorkha AL, Hornbill Skyways, Indian AL, Island AS, Island Transvoyager, Jagson AL, Mandarin AL, New Central Avn, Sita Air, Skyline AW, Star Air Avn, Uni Air.

Australasia: Air Caledonie, Air Marshall Islands, Air Tahiti.

Europe: Aerocondor, Air Wales, Arcus Air, Business Wings, Islands Flug, Kato AL, LGW, Luft Transport, SATA Air Azores.

Middle East: Iran Aseman.

North America: Alta Flights, Inter Island Air, Summit AC, Vision Air.

South America: Aerocardal, Air Caraïbes, American Jet, LASSA, SAPSA.

Photographed at Geneva, Berne-based Sky Work Airlines' only aircraft is this Dornier 328-100 HB-AES. (Tony Best)

DORNIER Do 328

AvCraft Aviation
803 Sycolin Road, Suite 204, Leesburg, VA
20197, USA

In 1987, the famous German aircraft company Dornier commenced design work on a twin turboprop 30-seater commuter airliner and in August 1988 the programme was officially launched as the Dornier 328. Designed as a high-speed pressurised airliner, able to operate from STOLports and unprepared airstrips, it was to be built using a significant amount of composite materials (23% by weight) and with the latest EFIS cockpit. Normal cruising altitude was proposed as 7,620m (25,000ft) or 9,145m (30,000ft) with a high performance kit, while the cruising speed was set at a very respectable 620km/h (335kts).

The basic supercritical wing profile of the Do 228, with its distinctive cut-off wingtips, was given new flaps and an additional large centre-section housing extra fuel tanks. Other features included the sleek circular-section fuselage that seats three across and the all-new T tail design.

Launch customer Contact Air of Stuttgart ordered four in May 1989 and after some delays, the first of three development Do 328s flew from Oberpfaffenhofen in December 1991. European certification was granted in October 1993 followed by FAA certification that November.

Aermacchi built the main fuselage from sub-assemblies manufactured by Daewoo Heavy Industries in South Korea, and the wings, rear fuselage and tail came from DASA. British company Westland Aerostructures built the engine nacelles and doors. The component parts were all assembled, painted and first flown at Oberpfaffenhofen. Series production commenced in February 1993 and after Contact Air had decided to cancel their order, the Berne-based Swiss airline Air Engiadina became the first to receive a Do 328 in October that year. The major customer was Horizon Air in the USA who ordered 20 with options on a further 40. They actually received a total of 12.

Despite its major selling points of a high cruising speed, an outstanding cockpit design and a comfortable cabin with more seat width than a Boeing 737, the Do 328 suffered poor sales and only 110 were completed by 2004.

Do 328 versions originally included the standard -100, the longer range/higher weight -110, and the -120 with short field performance and various aerodynamic modifications including larger dorsal and ventral fins. Dornier were planning a 48-seat stretched 328 but in 1996, Dornier's parent company DASA sold 80% of the company to Fairchild. Since April 2003, the 328 design has come under the AvCraft banner but they have no plans to re-launch the turboprop version. Until late 2004, the largest operator was PSA (USAirways) with 24, but these were all withdrawn and placed in storage.

Details

Span: 20.98m (68ft 10in)
Length: 21.28m (69ft 10in)
Engines: Two 1,625kW (2,180shp) P&WC
  PW119B Turboprops.
  (Do 328-120 has PW119C)
Cruise speed: 620km/h (335kt) max
Accommodation: 33 maximum

First service: Air Engiadina, Oct 1993.
Number built: 110
Number in service: 31

Current Operators

Africa: Bristow Helicopters (Nigeria), DANA.
Europe: Air Alps Avn, Bonair, Cirrus AL, Lions Air, Private Wings, Scot AW, Skywork AL.
Sun Air, Welcome Air.
South America: SATENA, VIP.

Hainan Airlines have the world's largest fleet of Dornier 328Jets. Thirty-two-seater B-3960 was one of the first delivered in 1999. (Colin Ballantine)

DORNIER 328 JET

AvCraft Aviation
803 Sycolin Road, Suite 204, Leesburg, VA
20197, USA

Fairchild Dornier abandoned the proposed stretched 328 turboprop in favour of a PW306B turbofan-powered Do 328Jet in mid 1996. Officially launched in June 1997 with orders from Aspen Mountain Air and Proteus Airlines, the 328Jet was designed to fit between the 19-seat turboprops and the 50-seat regional jets.

First flown in January 1998, the 328Jet had minimum changes from its turboprop-powered brother. These included a fuselage strengthened where the wings and undercarriage were attached, modified flaps, stronger undercarriage and better brakes. It also has an advanced cockpit fitted with the all glass Honeywell PRIMUS 2000 Integrated Avionics System. FAA and JAA Certification was granted in July 1999 followed by the first deliveries in August that year.

With large sums of money invested in their new 728Jet, Fairchild Dornier struggled to make ends meet causing them to ask for court protection from their creditors; however, in April 2002 Fairchild Dornier was declared insolvent.

All production work had stopped at Oberpfaffenhofen in March 2002 but it was restarted in late 2004 by AvCraft Aviation who had acquired the production rights for the bankrupt Fairchild Dornier 328, 328Jet, Envoy and the larger 428Jet programme in 2003. The transaction included the purchase of

18 complete and five partially complete 328Jets which were very quickly sold. The standard price for a 328Jet is $11.5m and AvCraft boast that the 328Jet has the most space per passenger than any other regional jet, along with the widest aisle, ample shoulder and legroom and large overhead and underseat storage. They also claim that a turnround time of less than 20 minutes is possible. AvCraft are hoping to build 18 per year and the future looks good for the 328Jet/Envoy with reported interest for 275 aircraft from 51 customers including 13 airlines.

The Corporate version of the 328Jet is called the Envoy. This is available as a 12-passenger 'Executive', a 22-passenger 'Executive Shuttle' or a 14-18 seater 'Convertible'. Other 328Jet variants include aerial survey, airways calibration, fisheries patrol, search and rescue and air ambulance. Indeed, the 328Jet has found a niche market in civilian medevac work with operators such as ADAC of Germany and Tyrolean Jet Service.

The largest fleet of 328Jets is operated by Hainan Airlines, the largest independent airline in China. In 2004, they increased their fleet of 19 by purchasing an additional 8 aircraft from AvCraft, some of which will be operated by subsidiary airlines. The also have signed up for another 20 aircraft, the first five of which were delivered before the start of 2005.

Details

Span: 20.98m (68ft 10in)
Length: 21.28m (69ft 10in)
Engines: Two 26.9kN (6,050lb) P&W
  Canada PW306B turbofans
Cruise speed: 740km/h (405kts)
Accommodation: 31 to 33

First Service: August 1999
Number built (ordered): 109 (8)
Number in service: 55 (excl Envoys)

Current operators

Africa: Bristow Helicopters (Nigeria).
Asia: Hainan AL.
Australasia: Wanair.
Europe: Aero Dienst, Air Vallée, Bonair, Cirrus, Grossman AS, Private Wings, Tyrolean Jet Service, Welcome Air.
North America: Skyway AL (Midwest Connect).

Pretoria-based Rovos Air is a division of Rovos Rail Tours. They fly high quality tourist flights in two Convairliners and DC-3C ZS-CRV. (Rovos Air)

DOUGLAS DC-3

Douglas Aircraft Company
Santa Monica,
California, USA

In August 1932, the vice president of Transcontinental and Western Air (TWA) wrote to several manufacturers announcing their interest in acquiring ten or more 12-seater tri-motor aircraft. This letter inspired Douglas to build the one and only twin-engined 12-passenger DC-1 in 1933. This all-metal design evolved into the 14-seater DC-2, of which a total of 198 were built, proving the basic layout and providing Douglas with its first commercial success.

When, in 1934, American Airlines asked Douglas for a bigger DC-2 that could be used on sleeper services, the resulting Douglas DST (Douglas Sleeper Transport) that had beds for 14 or seats for 28 was, to all intents and purposes, the DC-3.

The Second World War brought orders for 10,000 military DC-3s, known as the C-47 Skytrain and C-53 Skytrooper (among other designations) by the US military. These were built by Douglas in Santa Monica, Long Beach and Oklahoma City. In addition, more than 2,500 were completed by other US companies under license. Nearly 5,000 were also built under license in the USSR as the Lisunov Li-2. The last Li-2 was built in 1954.

During the war, the adaptability, ruggedness and simplicity of the Dakota/Skytrain allowed it to be operated in all theatres and all conditions. It could be operated on skis in the winter and some were even operated on floats. The Royal Air Force received more than

1,900 Dakotas with many of these being passed to the Commonwealth air forces. At war's end, the thousands of surviving DC-3/C-47's were to form the backbone of worldwide civil and military air transport for many years.

In the 21st century, the Dakota still flies on a variety of tasks including scheduled and unscheduled passenger and freight services, skydiver transport, anti-mosquito spraying, rain cloud seeding, pollution control, aerial surveying, enthusiast and nostalgia trips and humanitarian relief work; it is also still operated by a few air forces. The type has remarkably outlived many of the so-called 'DC-3 replacements' that appeared from the 1950s onwards.

Most surviving DC-3/C-47s appear to be in the hands of preservationists; however several have been given life extensions by being converted to turboprop power while dozens of unconverted and unwanted examples sit engineless all over the world, waiting for expensive reconditioned Twin Wasps, or the scrapman's axe.

Details (Specifications for C-47A)

Span: 29.11m (95ft 6in)
Length: 19.43m (63ft 9in)
Engines: Two 895kW (1,200hp) P&W
   Twin Wasp R-1830 piston radial engines
Cruise speed: 266km/h (143kt)
Accommodation: 32 maximum

First service: American Airlines, May 1936
Number built: 10,654
Number in service: 182

Current operators

Africa: Air Kasai, Air Katanga, Airquarius Avn, Business Avn, Naturelink Charter, Nelair Charter, Phoebus Apollo Avn, Rossair, Rovos Air, Skyways Kenya, South African Historic Flight, Springbok Classic Air, Springbok Flying Safaris, Virunga AC, Wimbi Dira AW.

Asia: Victoria Air.

Australasia: Air Nostalgia, Flight 2000, Hardy Avn, HARS, Pionair, Qantas AW, Shortstop Jet Charter.

Europe: Air Atlantique, Air Service Berlin, Air Umbria, Dakota & Cie, Dakota Norway, DC-3 Vennerne, DC-Yhdistys, Dutch Dakota Association, Editions Stevens, Flygande Veteraner, Ju Air, Vallentuna Avn Club.

North America: Aero Freight, Airborne Support, AL History Museum, Air Pony Express, Air Tejas, Atlantic AC, Borinquen Air, Boyington Avn, Brooks Avn, Buffalo AW, Carolinas Avn Museum, Cascade Air, Catalina Flying Boats, Champlain Air, Clay Lacy Avn, Dakota Avn Museum, Delta AT Heritage Museum, Desert Air, Dream Flight, Dynamic Avn, Enterprise Air, Evergreen Vintage AL, First Flight Out, Florida AC, Fly One, Four Star AC, Gateway AL, Howe Bros Enterprise, Intl AS, Jim Hankins AS, Kenn Borek Air, Miami Valley Avn, Midline Air Freight, Missionair, Missionary Flights Intl, Nordair Quebec 2000, Nord Avn, Plummers Sioux AW, Prairie Avn Museum, Remote Area Medical, Southwind AL, Super Three, Tolair Services, Trans Northern.

South America: ADES, Aeroclub do RGS, Aeroejecutivos, Aero JBR, Aerolineas de La Paz, Aero MTLA, Aerosur Bolivia, Aerotaxi, Aerovanguardia, Air Colombia, Aliansa, El Sol de America, Latina de Aviacion, LA Canedo, SADELCA, SETCO, VIARCO.

Converted to turbine power by Professional Aviation in South Africa. ZS-MFY is owned by Rossair and flown on humanitarian flights. (Afavia-fotos.co.za)

DOUGLAS DC-3 TURBOPROP

Basler Turbo Conversions, 255 West 35th Ave, PO Box 2305, Oshkosh, WI 54903-2305, USA.
PAS, Lanseria Airport, PO Box 3171, Johannesburg, RSA

The first conversion of the C-47/DC-3 to turboprop power was completed in the UK in the late 1940s. This conversion was not intended as a DC-3 'replacement', but as an airborne test-bed for new engines. In August 1949, the world's first turbine-powered C-47 (powered by two Armstrong Siddeley ASMa.3 Mambas) was test flown by the RAF. The next year the RAF also flew a Dakota powered by the new Rolls-Royce Dart engine. In 1951, Field Aircraft Services fitted two Dakotas with Darts as part of the engine development programme associated with the Vickers Viscount. Between 1951 and 1953, these two were operated by British European Airways on scheduled freight services, allowing BEA the claim that they were the world's first airline to use turbine engines on revenue earning services. All these early conversions were later re-fitted with conventional piston engines.

Conroy Inc of Santa Barbara, California, converted a Dakota to Dart power in the early 1960s, using engines from a Vickers Viscount, and named it the Turbo Three. In 1977 this aircraft re-appeared with three Pratt & Whitney PT6 turboprops (one fitted to the nose) to become the Tri-Turbo Three. Another conversion using the PT6 engine was called the Turbo-Express. One was completed by USAC at Van Nuys, California, in 1982, and certificated in March 1984.

The current Basler conversion (currently costing around $4.2m) uses the popular PT6A engine to replace the original Twin Wasps, lengthening the fuselage 2.54m (8ft 4in) forward of the wing to maintain the position of the centre of gravity, extending and reshaping of the outer wings and the upgrading of the hydraulic and electric systems. It is identifiable from the other conversions by its round cabin windows. The Basler Turbo 67 was certificated in December 1990 and has sold mostly to the military. The USAF and the air forces of Thailand, Colombia, Guatemala, Bolivia, Mali, Mauretania and El Salvador all operate BT-67s.

The South African Air Force converted more than 30 C-47s to C-47TP Super Dakota configuration at a cost of $1.7 million each. Their conversion, based upon the US AMI rework that was marketed by Professional Aviation of Johannesburg involved a 1.00m (3ft 3in) fuselage extension, PT6A-65AR engines, various aerodynamic modifications and a new cockpit. The civil version was known as the Jet Prop DC-3 AMI.

Currently there are very few civilian operators of this modification. By far, the largest number of DC-3Ts can be found operating in South Africa with both the civil and military.

Details

Span: 28.96m (95ft 0in)
Length: 20.67m (67ft 9in)
Engines: Two 1,062kW (1,424shp) P&WC PT6A-67R turboprops
Cruise speed: 389km/h (208kt)
Accommodation: 38.
Payload: Five LD3 containers
(Details above for Basler Turbo 67)

First service: Unknown
Number converted: 40+
Number in service: 12 civil

Current Operators

Africa: Anglo AC, Kivu Air, Rossair Kenya, Spectrem Air Surveys.
North America: Aerocontractors, Basler AL, Enterprise Air, Missionary Flights Intl, Rhoades Avn, US Forestry Service.

Preserved in authentic South African Airways colours, South African Historic Flight DC-4 ZS-AUB has visited airshows in Europe and the USA. (Chris Mak)

DOUGLAS DC-4 SKYMASTER

Douglas Aircraft Company
Santa Monica,
California, USA

In 1935, the Douglas Aircraft Company responded to a request from United Air Lines for a four-engined long-range airliner. However, at that time, Douglas could not afford to commit its factories to such an expensive project without financial help. Because he was convinced that the new design was essential, the President of UAL then convinced the other four major US airlines (Pan American, Eastern, American and TWA) to each give Douglas $100,000 to finance the design and building of a prototype. The result was the DC-4 (later to be known as the DC-4E E=Experimental), a very advanced triple-tailed design that sadly proved to be far too complex and expensive. The only one built first flew in June 1938 and was sold in Japan in 1939.

Encouraged by the airlines, Douglas then simplified the design, leading to the first flight of the definitive DC-4 in February 1942. Initially offered with either 1,000hp Wright Cyclone or 1,050hp Pratt & Whitney Twin Wasp radial engines and with an interior that could seat 40 in ten rows of four, the DC-4 started to gain airline orders. By the time America entered the Second World War, 61 DC-4s had been ordered, but these, and all future DC-4 production was requisitioned by the US military and given the designation C-54 Skymaster.

After the war, hundreds of surplus

military transport aircraft, including C-54s, were sold to the world's airlines. This proved to be a serious problem for Douglas, who struggled to find buyers for its new aircraft. Only 78 DC-4s were built post-war for civil orders.

In 1945 the Canadair company, based at Cartierville, Canada, commenced production of the DC-4 under license from Douglas. Seventy of these Rolls-Royce Merlin-powered versions were built as the Canadair C-4 North Star (known by BOAC as the Argonaut). Only one survives in a museum.

A much later DC-4 variant was the Aviation Traders ATL 98 Carvair, 21 conversions being made in the UK between 1961 and 1968. Modified with an elevated flightdeck, extended fin and huge nose doors, motor vehicles or long freight items could be loaded directly into the fuselage.

After retirement from commercial freight or military service, many Skymasters in the USA were converted to fire-bombers. Their fuselages were stripped of all unnecessary weight and huge tanks were fitted either in or under the fuselage to carry the fire retardant liquid. After a series of accidents in 2002 involving similar aged types involved in fire bombing, the US Forestry Service cancelled their contracts early in 2004 and since then the DC-4 fire bombers have remained grounded. The few that do still fly are mostly freighters; however

two ex-South African Air Force examples have been restored to their former passenger glory and are flown on tourist charters and aerial safaris by the South African Historic Flight.

Details

Span: 35.81m (117ft 6in)
Length: 28.60m (93ft 10in)
Engines: Four 1,080kW (1,450shp) Pratt & Whitney R-2000-2SD-BG Twin Wasp radial piston engines
Cruise speed: 365km/h (197kt)
Accommodation: 86 maximum
Freighter payload: 14,742kg (32,500lb)

First service: American Overseas Airlines, October 1945.
Number built: 1,315
Number in service: 27, most in USA

Current Operators

Africa: Phoebus Apollo Avn, South African Historic Flight, Springbok Classic air.
Europe: Dutch Dakota Association.
North America: Aeroflite, Aero Union, Airborne Support, Ardco, Berlin Airlift Historical Foundation, Brooks Fuel, Buffalo AW, Skymaster Avn, TBM.

Undoubtedly the most highly polished classic airliner flying in 2005 is this DC-6B N996DM now flown by the Flying Bulls. (Bernhard Muller)

DOUGLAS DC-6

Douglas Aircraft Company,
Santa Monica,
California, USA.

Conceived as a stretched and pressurised upgrade of the DC-4, the DC-6 found many airline and military buyers worldwide and proved to be a remarkably long-lived machine. Its reliability, adaptability and low operating costs mean that as we approach its 60th birthday in 2006, there are still a handful of DC-6s gainfully employed around the world, while its original rival, the Lockheed Constellation, is relegated to museums and preservation groups.

The DC-6 used the DC-4's wing, but with more powerful engines and a pressurised DC-4 fuselage stretched by 2.06m (81in). The oval windows of the DC-4 were also replaced by 'modern' rectangular items. The three crewmembers were provided with latest radio and navigation equipment, and all the airframe leading edges had a highly efficient de-icing system to cope with the higher cruising altitudes.

More than a year before the first flight of the prototype DC-6 from Santa Monica in February 1946, American Airlines had ordered 50 DC-6s to compete with TWA's fleet of 'Connies' on US transcontinental services. Other early US operators included Panagra, United Air Lines, National Airlines, Delta and Braniff.

175 of the original DC-6 version were built before production was switched to the stretched DC-6A/B/C versions. The DC-6A had water/methanol-injected engines and was initially built as a pure freighter with

no cabin windows, a reinforced floor and two upward-opening main deck cargo doors. Some were later converted to passenger use while others were built as the DC-6C, which was an early example of the 'Quick Change' format.

The most numerous version built was the DC-6B. This pure passenger airliner was similar to the DC-6A but without the freight doors and strengthened floor. The DC-6B saw service worldwide with many major airlines particularly in Europe and the USA. The US military forces bought a total of 167 DC-6s (designated C-118 or R6D) for troop carrying, freighting or MEDEVAC missions. Various unofficial designations – 'DC-6AB', 'DC-6AC', 'DC-6A[C'], 'DC-6BF' were applied to DC-6s modified to freighters after withdrawal from front line passenger service. Two aircraft were also converted to swing-tail freighter configuration by Sabena in Belgium.

All of the 704 DC-6s/C-118s/R6Ds were built at Santa Monica and production stopped in 1958 after the DC-6 had evolved once again into the DC-7. The last ever DC-6, which was delivered to Jugoslovenski Aerotransport (JAT) in Yugoslavia, was still airworthy in 2004. Current DC-6 use is mostly freight, with a significant fleet to be found hauling general goods and fuel in Alaska. Other DC-6s are used for aerial sightseeing tours, while Conair use theirs for water bombing in Canada.

Details

Span: DC-6, 6A, 6B, 6C 35.81m (117ft 6in)
Length: DC-6 30.66m (100ft 7in); DC-6A, 6B, 6C 32.18m (105ft 7in)
Engines: Four 1,340-1,685kW (1,800-2,500hp) Pratt & Whitney R-2800 Double Wasp radial piston
Cruise speed: 501km/h (270kt)
Accommodation: DC-6 86 max; DC-6B 102 max; DC-6A payload 12,786kg (28,188lb)

First service: American Airlines, April 1947
Number built: 174 DC-6, 74 DC-6A, 288 DC-6B, 167 C-118.
Number in service: 35, mostly in USA, especially Alaska

Current Operators

Africa: NCA Namibia Commercial Avn, South Africa Historic Flight.
Europe: Air Atlantique, Flying Bull.
North America: Conair Avn, Everts AC, Everts Air Fuel, Florida AT, Nord Star AL, Northern AC, Northern Air Fuel, TBM, Universal AL.
South America: Air Colombia.

African International's DC-8s are registered in South Africa and Swaziland. DC-8-54 3D-AFR displays the company website in April 2004. (Afavia-fotos.co.za)

DOUGLAS DC-8-10/20/30/40/50

Douglas Aircraft Company
3855 Lakewood Boulevard, Long Beach
California 90846, USA

Having originally declared that the market for turbojet-powered airliners was too limited for Douglas to get involved, they waited until more than a year after the Boeing 707 prototype (the 'Dash 80') had been rolled out, before announcing plans for a jet-powered replacement for their piston-powered DC-7. The delay in getting their DC-8 design in the air probably cost Douglas some sales but despite the lead-time that was held by Boeing, the Douglas team were able to get their DC-8 in service only 11 months after the 707.

The initial order for 25 DC-8 Series 30s came from Pan American Airways in September 1955. PanAm were obviously hedging their bets because they ordered 20 Boeing 707s at the same time! By the end of the year Douglas had orders for 98 aircraft from seven airlines.

In February 1957, construction of the first DC-8 (built to Series 10 standard) commenced at the new factory at Long Beach. In front of an audience of over 95,000, 'Ship One' made its first flight on 30th May 1958. After its test flying was finished, Douglas leased it to National Airlines in 1961, having converted it to a Series 51 in 1960. This long-lived aircraft later flew with Trans International, Lufthansa, Canadian Pacific, Delta and Aeromexico. It was still flying in the early 1980s but was eventually scrapped in Arizona in 2001.

Altogether, ten DC-8s of various marks were used in flight tests and FAA certification trials. 'Ship One' was granted its FAA certificate in August 1959 and the first airline deliveries were made to Delta and United the following month.

Standard length DC-8s were produced in five series sub-divided into 16 models. They include the -10 for domestic services, the -20 with more powerful JT4A engines for hot-and-high airports, and the -30 with more fuel capacity, JT4A engines, and much heavier weights for intercontinental services. The -40 was similar to the -30 but had Rolls-Royce Conway engines, and the -50 had the new turbofan JT3D engines. The convertible -50CF had a strengthened floor and a large cargo door, while the -50AF was a windowless freighter built originally for United Airlines.

With the mid-1980s introduction of more rigorous noise restrictions in the West, many early DC-8s were withdrawn from use. However thanks to hushkits designed by some US companies, the low-houred Series 50s were able to be converted allowing them to conform to Chapter 2/Stage 2 and later Chapter 3/Stage 3 restrictions. At least 66 Series 50 DC-8s were hushkitted. Current use of the short fuselage DC-8 is confined to Series 50 aircraft in freight operations in Africa and South America.

Details

Span: 43.41m (142ft 5in)
Length: 45.87m (150ft 6in)
Engines: -10, -20, -30 four 55.3-77.8kN (12,500-17,500lb) Pratt & Whitney JT3C or JT4A turbojets; -40 four 77.9kN (17,500lb) Rolls-Royce Conway RCo 12 turbojets; -50 four 80.6kN (18,000lb) JT3D turbofans
Cruise speed: -10 900km/h (490kt); -50 933km/h (504kt)
Accommodation: -10, -20, -30, -40, 176 max; -50, 189 max

First service: United Airlines & Delta Airlines, September 1959
Number built: -10, 28; -20, 34; -30, 57; -40, 32; -50, 143; total 294
Number in service: 19 (-30 and -50)

Current Operators

Africa: African Intl AW, Kinshasa AW, Lignes Aériennes Congolaises, MK AL, Northeast AL, Waltair.
South America: Transportes Charter do Brasil.

Seen prior to delivery in August 2004 from Lasham airfield in Hampshire is Stage 3 compliant DC-8-62AF ST-UAA. (Tony Best)

DOUGLAS DC-8-60

Douglas Aircraft Company
3855 Lakewood Boulevard, Long Beach
California, 90846, USA

Launched in April 1965, the DC-8 Series 60 came in three versions, -61, -62 and -63, and these became known as the Super Sixty Series. In the same month, orders were announced for five -61s for United and four for Eastern Air Lines.

The original DC-8 was designed from the outset to accept fuselage plugs in order to stretch the aircraft to gain extra capacity. To create the stretch, an extra 6.10m (20ft) cabin section was built into the forward fuselage, and a further 5.08m (16ft 8in) section was added behind the wing, creating what is now commonly called the 'stretched' DC-8. The first version, the -61, was basically a JT3D-3B-powered -50 with the fuselage extensions, but retaining the -50 wing and engine pylons. It was first flown in March 1966.

The -62 was the ultra long-range version able to fly against prevailing winds from central Europe, non-stop to the US West coast. This had a longer wing span containing more fuel, but only a 2.03m (6ft 8in) two-section fuselage extension in comparison to the standard -50. First -62 flight was in August 1966 followed by first delivery to SAS in May 1967.

By combining the long fuselage from the -61 with the engines and wings of the -62, Douglas created the Super -63 in 1967. This was to become Douglas' last DC-8 version and the 556th and final DC-8 (a series 63 for SAS) was delivered in May 1972.

Freighter and 'Combi' versions include the -61F/CF, -62F/CF/AF, and -63F/CF/PF/AF. A total of 73 -60CF and 13 -60AF were delivered.

Proposed noise restrictions in the 1970s prompted the conversion of many DC-8-60s to quieter CFM56 engines, these became the -70s. Passenger operations with the DC-8-60 series have now finished and all the remaining airworthy aircraft are in use as freighters, mostly in North America.

Details

Span: -61, 43.41m (142ft 5in);
 -62, -63, 45.23m (148ft 5in)
Length: -61, -63, 57.12m (187ft 5in);
 -62, 47.98m (157ft 5in)
Engines: Four 80.6kN (18,000lb) P&W
 JT3D-3B turbofans; -63 mostly had
 85.1kN (19,000lb) JT3D-7s
Cruise speed: 965km/h (521kt) max
Accommodation: -61 and -63 259 max;
 -62 189 max

First service: United Airlines, Feb 1967
Number built: -61, 88; -62, 67; -63, 107.
 Total 262 (110 later modified to -70)
Number in service: 60, mostly in North
 America.

Current Operators

Africa: African Intl AW, Al-Dawood Air, Cargoplus Avn, Jetline Inc, Johnsons Air, MK AL, Silver Back Cargo Freighters, United Arabian.
Europe: Cygnus Air.
North America: ABX Air, Arrow Air, ATI, Murray Air.
South America: ABSA, Aeropostal, Skymaster Al.

TAMPA, Transportes Aereos Mercantiles Panamericanos, have just started to retire their fleet of colourful DC-8-71Fs. (Eddy Gual-Aviation Photos of Miami)

DOUGLAS DC-8-70

Douglas Aircraft Company, 3855 Lakewood Boulevard, Long Beach, California, USA
Cammacorp, El Segundo, Florida, USA.

In the late 1970s, with impending US noise restrictions looming, the future for all the 'first generation' jet transports depended on their ability to accept 'hushkitting' or new, quieter engines. In 1977, a group of former Douglas executives resurrected a 1965 proposal that had originally been rejected by Douglas to re-engine the stretched DC-8 series with new engines. They decided that the 262 DC-8 Series 60s built between 1966 and 1972 were ideal for re-engining with either the CFM International CFM56 high-bypass-ratio turbofans or the P&W JT8D-209, which was a re-fanned JT-8D.

The resulting Cammacorp company was set up in 1977 at El Segundo in Florida to oversee and market the conversions and the first order (30 conversions) came from United Airlines in 1979 for its fleet of DC-8-61s. This was soon followed by further commitments from Flying Tigers and Delta Air Lines. As United Airlines had selected the CFM engine for their conversions, Cammacorp decided to drop the P&W engine option and concentrate on a single power source.

The first flight of the Cammacorp DC-8 Super 70 was at Tulsa in August 1981 and after FAA certification trials it was delivered to United Airlines in April 1982. All -70 conversions retain their previous sub-series numbers; ie a converted DC-8-62 became a DC-8-72 and so on.

Modification work to convert these aircraft involved some wing strengthening as well as fitting the new engines, new pylons and the Grumman-designed nacelles. The conversion of the Series 61 aircraft was more complex and involved additional work because of the need to rebuild segments of the leading edge of the wing to cope with the new pylons.

In addition to the Cammacorp converted examples, Douglas completed 44; Delta Air Lines did 48 in Atlanta and nine each were produced by UTA France and Air Canada.

By the end of 1987, the small package carrier UPS had obtained a total of 42 -70s, while non-airline operators included the French Air Force, the Sultan of Oman and NASA. Currently, all -70s are freighters, and freight airlines like UPS and Air Transport International utilise the type's Stage 3/Chapter 3 noise compliance to allow round-the-clock operations particularly for their overnight and next-day delivery services.

Details

Span: 45.20m (148ft 5in)
Length: 57.12m (187ft 5in)
Engines: Four 97.9kN (22,000lb) CFM
   International CFM56-2C turbofans.
Cruise speed: 887km/h (479kt) max
Accommodation: 269 max, 209 typical
Maximum Payload: (-73AF) 50,650kg
   (111,800lb)

First service: United Airlines, April 1982
Number converted: 110
Number in service: 78, mostly in USA

Current Operators

Europe: Cygnus Air
North America: Astar AC, ATI, UPS AL.
South America: Promodal Transportes Aereo,
Tampa Colombia.

Laser of Venezuela operate this single 1966 DC-9-14 YV-977C 'Aldebaran' alongside three DC-9-32s for services out of Caracas. (Andy Marsh/Alpha Mike Tours)

DOUGLAS DC-9-10/20

Douglas Aircraft Company
3855 Lakewood Boulevard, Long Beach
CA 90801. USA

Just like its rival the Boeing 737, the DC-9 was initially powered by the Pratt & Whitney JT8D engine. Over the years, the two types have seen continuous development and competition, but the Boeing 737 always managed to stay ahead in the sales race. The main difference between the two types, for the passenger, is the seating arrangement; the Boeing seats six-across, while the DC-9 with its narrower fuselage can manage only five.

Proposed in the early 1960s as the Douglas Model 2086, the decision to go ahead with the design was given in April 1963 when Delta Airlines became the launch customer with an order for 15.

The prototype was constructed at Long Beach and first flew in February 1965. Like the DC-8, the DC-9 was designed from the beginning to accept fuselage stretches, enabling Douglas to adapt the basic layout for individual customer requirements. No actual DC9-10 or DC9-20 were certificated as these were terms used by Douglas to describe the basic design. The sub-series, ie DC-9-14 was used instead.

Competition for the DC-9 came initially from the British-built BAC 1-11 that had already achieved some airline sales in the USA, particularly with Braniff Airways. However, after a slow start, the DC-9-10 series soon overtook the BAC 1-11 with large orders from TWA, Air Canada, KLM, Eastern Airlines and Swissair.

The DC9 Series 20 was created following a request from Scandinavian Airlines for a DC-9 with better short field performance. This version first appeared in February 1966, and had more powerful engines, the longer wings from the DC-9-30 but the same fuselage as the -10. Only ten were built for SAS as DC-9-21s.

Currently the largest operator of the 'short' DC-9 is the Mexican airline, Aero California. Based in La Paz, their 10 hard-worked Series 14s and 15s are fitted with 85 seats. All these aircraft are now nearly 40 years old.

Details

Span: -10, 27.25m (89ft 5in);
  -20 28.47m (93ft 4in)
Length: -10, -20, 31.82m (104ft 5in)
Engines: -10, two 54.5-62.3kN (12,250-14,000lb) Pratt & Whitney JT8D-1/-5/-7 turbofans;
  -20, 66.7kN (15,000lb) JT8D-11
Cruise speed: 903km/h (487kt) max
Accommodation: 109 max

First service: Delta Airlines, Dec 1965
Number built: -10, 137; -20, 10
Number in service: 50, mostly in North and South America

Current Operators

Africa: East African Express.

North America: ABX Air, Ameristar AW, C+M AW, Evergreen Intl AL, Kalitta Charters, Northwest AL, Skyway, USA Jet AL.

South America: Aerocalifornia, Aeropostal, Inter, Lineas Aereas Suramericanas, LASER.

Low cost carrier '1 Time Aero' base this DC-9-32 ZS-NRA 'Azikho lo Nonsense' at Johannesburg for flights to Cape Town and Durban. (Afavia-fotos.co.za)

DOUGLAS DC-9-30/40/50

Douglas Aircraft Company
3855 Lakewood Boulevard, Long Beach
California, 90846. USA

After Boeing had revealed their revolutionary 737 design in 1964, the Douglas Aircraft Company, who had always planned to offer longer/heavier versions, were prompted to make public their stretched DC-9. This 'Advanced' DC-9 logically became the Series 30, which outsold all the other series of DC-9s, with eight airlines ordering 20 or more.

Initially powered by two JT8D-7 turbofans, the -30 had an increased wing span (1.22m/4ft), full span leading edge slats and double slotted flaps. The fuselage was stretched by 4.57m (15ft) allowing an extra 5 rows of seats for a maximum capacity 115. Eastern Air Lines, who had been involved in the pre-production discussions, ordered 24 Series 30s in February 1965 and the first -30 flew in August 1966.

The Series 30 was also developed for the military. In total, 41 military DC-9s were built as the C-9A Nightingale for aeromedical evacuation, the C-9B Skytrain II Navy/Marines transport, the VC-9C for VIP duties and the C-9K (a modified DC-9-32CF) for Kuwait. The Series 30 remained in production for 16 years and the last one was delivered to USAir in April 1982.

In 1966, the joint Danish, Swedish and Norwegian airline, SAS, asked Douglas to produce a further stretched DC-9 with greater capacity for short-range/high-capacity routes. The resulting -40 was

1.88m (6ft 2in) longer than the -30 and carried 125 in a high-density configuration. It first flew in November 1967 and because it had a shorter range than the -30, it found only one other customer, Toa Domestic Airlines of Japan.

When the higher thrust JT8D-17 became available in 1973, McDonnell Douglas added a further stretch of 2.44m (8ft 0in) and created the 139-seater DC-9-50 series. Launch customer was Swissair with an order for ten. The -50 also had modified thrust reversers, acoustically quietened nacelles, an improved anti-skid brake system and a revised cabin interior. The -50 is the only DC-9 to have small 'strakes' on either side of the forward fuselage.

The DC-9-30 was also available as -32LWF (Light Weight Freight), -32CF, -33CF and -34CF (Convertible Freighter), -32AF and -33AF (All Freight) and -33RC (Rapid Change). The last of 976 actual DC-9s, (not MD-80s), was a -32 (C-9) for the US Navy delivered in October 1982.

Around 1988, the ABS Partnership developed a hushkit for all versions of the JT8D engine allowing them to conform with the Stage 3/Chapter 3 noise restrictions. They have sold over 500 kits to operators including Airborne Express, Evergreen, Kitty Hawk, Reliant, SAS and USA Jet. Although several DC-9 re-engining programmes were started, none have been completed.

Details

Span: -30, -40, -50 28.47m (93ft 5in)
Length: -30 36.37m (119ft 4in);
-40 38.28m (125ft 7in); -50 72.00m
(133ft 7in)
Engines: Two Pratt & Whitney JT8D
turbofans rated from 64.5-71.2kN
(14,500-16,000lb)
Cruise speed: 907km/h (490kt) max
Accommodation: -30, 115; -40, 125;
-50, 139

First service: -30 Eastern Air Lines,
February 1967; -40 SAS, March 1968;
-50 Swissair, Aug 1975
Number built: -30, 662; -40, 71; -50, 96
Number in service: 400

Current Operators

Africa: 1 Time, African Express AW, Afrinat Intl AL, Air Gemini, Executive Aerospace, Ghana AW, Sosoliso AL, STA Toumai Air Tchad, Trans African AL, Wetrafa Airlift, Wimbi Dira AW.

Asia: Aero Asia, Cebu Pacific, World Avn.

Europe: JAT.

Middle East: Air Memphis.

Former Soviet Union: Khors Air Company, Um Air.

North America: ABX Air, Evergreen Intl AL, Midwest AL, Northwest AL, USA Jet AL.

South America: Aerocalifornia, Aerocaribe, Aeromexico, Aeropostal, Aerorepublica, Aserca AL, Dutch Caribbean AL, Inter, LASER, Tikal Jets AL.

Crawley-based Das Air Cargo's boss Captain Joe Roy has had fun with the registrations of his DC-10s. Two of them are 5X-JOE and 5X-ROY. (Author)

DOUGLAS DC-10

Douglas Aircraft Company
3855 Lakewood Boulevard, Long Beach
California 90846, USA

In 1966, American Airlines published their requirements for a 250-seater twin-engined, short/medium-range airliner. Douglas reasoned that a larger, three-engined layout would have greater appeal than a twin, and by Autumn 1967 they had offered American their DC-10 design. The Lockheed TriStar also evolved from the same airline's request, but in 1968, the suitability of the Douglas design was confirmed when American Airlines placed an order for 25 DC-10s Series 10 plus options for a further 25. The type was officially launched in April after orders and options for another 60 were received from United Airlines.

Prototype construction commenced at Long Beach in January 1969 followed by the first flight in August 1970. By this time, nearly 250 DC-10s had been ordered by 14 airlines.

The initial DC-10-10 was very similar in performance to the TriStar 1 and was primarily used in the US domestic market. The -15 first flew in January 1981 and was designed for hot-and-high operations with Aeromexico and Mexicana. The most popular DC-10 was the long-range -30. This type gained orders from several major European airlines including Swissair, Finnair and Alitalia who all later ordered the MD-11. The Pratt & Whitney powered -40 (originally the -20) was launched when Northwest Airlines ordered 22 in October 1968. All -30s and -40s, (apart from those

-40Ds delivered to Japan Air Lines), have longer wings and an extra main undercarriage leg under the centre fuselage. The -40 can be identified by the larger forward engine cowling on the centre engine.

The DC-10-10CF and DC-10-30CF are passenger/freight convertibles, while the -30AF is a pure freighter. These aircraft all have a large forward main deck freight door and associated freight handling gear. Since 1990, several passenger DC-10-10, -30 and -40 have been converted to freighters by Aeronavali in Italy. Encouraged by the freight airline FedEx, McDonnell Douglas (later Boeing) created the MD-10 two-crew/glass cockpit version of the DC-10-10 and -30. The project was launched in 1996 and the first MD-10 conversion flew in April 1999. FedEx plan up to 98 conversions by 2006.

The last DC-10 was built in 1989, and although the type suffered from a spate of disastrous accidents in the 1970s, the DC-10 remained a popular type worldwide and outsold the TriStar by almost two-to-one. However, with the advent of newer and more efficient types, both the DC-10 and TriStar are disappearing from passenger service and around 76 DC-10s are currently in storage.

Details

Span: -10, 47.34m (155ft 4in);
-20, -30, 50.40m (165ft 4in)
Length: 55.29m (181ft 5in)
Engines: Three 178-240.2kN (40,000-54,000lb) turbofans. Either GE CF-6 or Pratt & Whitney JT9D.
Cruise speed: 908km/h (490kt) max
Accommodation: 380 maximum
Maximum payload: -30AF 80,286kg (176,992lb)

First service: American Airlines, August 1971
Number built: -10, 131; -15, 7; -30, 206; -40, 42 (Plus 60 KC-10 for USAF)
Number in Service: 125

Current Operators

Africa: Avient AV, DAS AC.
Asia: Biman Bangladesh AL, JAL Intl, JALways, Japan Asia AW, Garuda Intl.
Europe: JAT, Sud AL.
Former Soviet Union: Aeroflot.
North America: Centurion AC, FedEx, Gemini AC, Northwest AL, Omni Air Intl, World AW.
South America: Cielos AL, Santa Barbara AL, South Winds Cargo, VARIG LOG.

The Bandeirante was once a common sight in the UK but type is now hard to find. G-TABS belongs to Norwich-based Skydrift. (Author)

EMBRAER EMB-110 BANDEIRANTE

Embraer
Av. Brigadeiro Faria Lima, 2170, 12227-90 –
São José dos Campos, São Paulo, Brazil

Created under the direction of French designer Max Holste, the Bandeirante was an indigenous response to a request from the Brazilian Ministry of Aeronautics for a light transport for both civil and military use. The aircraft was Embraer's first successful civil aircraft and it proved to be the forerunner of a long line of excellent commercial aircraft built in Brazil.

The first of three prototypes was flown in October 1968 with the Brazilian military designation YC-95 prior to all three being delivered to the Air Force in February 1973. Given the name 'Bandeirante' in memory of the early Brazilian explorers, it was put into production at Sao Paulo by the newly created Embraer (Empresa Brasileira de Aeronautica SA) organisation in 1969. After the first production version was flown in August 1972, early deliveries were made to Transbrasil and VASP, where the Bandeirante's sturdy design and modern comforts were well appreciated by those used to the rigours of the DC-3.

The multiple versions of this aircraft include the initial 15-seat commercial model EMB-110C, the EMB-110P with 18 seats for Brazilian internal services, the EMB-110E executive transport, the EMB-110F freighter and the EMB-110S survey aircraft. The EMB-110C was the first Embraer type to enter commercial service after it was delivered to TransBrasil in April 1973. The first

Bandeirante (110P) export order came from Provincetown-Boston Airways in 1981.

The EMB-111 maritime surveillance aircraft was produced at the request of the Comando Costeiro, the Brazilian Air Force Coastal Command. This has an extended nose, housing a search radar, and wingtip fuel tanks. It first flew in August 1977 and deliveries were made to Brazil (as the P-95) and Chile.

Of the later sub types, the most common civil version was the EMB-110P1, which was a convertible for passengers or freight with a large rear cargo door. The EMB-110P2 was stretched by 85cm (9in), increasing seating to 21. Other updates included a 10° tailplane dihedral on the 'P1A and 'P2A from 1983. The first P1A was delivered to Provincetown-Boston Airlines in December 1983 and 10 were built as C-95Cs for the Brazilian Air Force. Currently, the Força Aérea Brasileira has 100 C-95/EMB-111s in service.

Although production stopped in 1991, the 'Bandit' (as it is often colloquially called) is still popular worldwide and can be found in service from Fiji to Nigeria; however, most Bandeirantes are still serving their homeland in Brazil.

Details

Span: 15.32m (50ft 3in)
Length: 15.10m (49ft 7in)
Engines: Two 559kW (750shp) Pratt & Whitney Canada PT6A-34 turboprops
Cruise speed: 417km/h (225kt) max
Accommodation: 21 maximum

First service: Transbrasil, April 1973
Number built: 500
Number in service: 123, mostly in Brazil

Current Operators

Africa: Knight Avn, Naturelink Charter, Sky Power Express AW.

Australasia: Air Fiji, Airlink, Air National, Air Ngukurr, Air Rarotonga, Air South Charter, ASA, Australian East Coast Airports, Islands Nationair, King Island Air, Macair AL, Regional Air, Vanair.

Europe: Ada Air, Euroair, Keen AW, Scan Con Travel, Skydrift.

Middle East: Payam AS.

North America: Air Creebec, Air Now, Pacific Coastal Air, Royal Air Freight, Skyward Avn.

South America: ABATE LA, Aerotaxi, Aeromas, Air Class, APUI Taxi Aereo, Cat Island Air, Cruiser Taxi Aereo, GENSA, Leair Charter Services, Manaus Aero Taxi, META, PENTA, Rico LA, Rico Taxi Aereo, Rutaca AL, TAF LA, TAVAJ LA, Taxi Aereo Itaituba, Taxi Aereo Weiss.

Skywest Airlines operate dozens of Brasilias on behalf of United Express including EMB-120ER N560SW seen here at San Luis Obispo in August 2004. (Author)

EMBRAER EMB-120 BRASILIA

Embraer
Av. Brigadeiro Faria Lima, 2170, 12227-90 –
São José dos Campos, São Paulo, Brazil

The worldwide sales success that Embraer had enjoyed with their Bandeirante encouraged the company to design a faster, pressurised version, which had greater capacity. In 1979, design work commenced on the new aircraft based on a stretched version of the Embraer EMB-121 Xingu executive aircraft. The resulting EMB-120, which was originally to have been called the Araguaia, was later renamed the Brasilia, after the country's capital city. Manufacture began in May 1981 and the prototype first flew in July 1983, powered by PW115s. Three flying and three static pre-production aircraft were involved in a two-year certification programme leading to the Brazilian type certification being granted in May 1985.

In June 1985 at the Paris Air Show, the launch customer, Atlantic Southeast Airlines, based in Atlanta Georgia, took delivery of the first of 60 Brasilias to enter ASA service. Other early customers included DLT of Germany and Air Midwest from Wichita, Kansas, who flew schedules for American Eagle. The type was a great success as a commuterliner in the USA with Comair, Skywest, Texas Air and Westair all ordering large fleets.

The many versions of the EMB-120 included the -120C Cargo and 120QC Quick-Change, both of which had a payload of 3,500kg (7,715lb), and a corporate version fitted with a luxury interior. The -120ER (Extended Range)

first appeared in 1992, having an increased MTOW and greater range. In 1993, this was replaced by the 120ER Advanced, which had a bigger cargo capacity of 700kg (1,545lb), a quieter cabin and various wing modifications including improved flaps. The fuselage design of the Brasilia was used as the basis for the highly successful series of jet-powered aircraft, the ERJ 135, 145 and the Legacy business jet.

The Força Aérea Brasileira currently operate nine VC-97 Brasilias but they are being replaced by standard EMB-120s. The International Airline Support Group has bought 10 kits from Embraer to convert passenger Brasilias into EMB-120FC freighters; these all-freight Brasilias can carry 3,700kg (8,157lb) of bulk and containerised cargo.

Details

Span: 19.78m (64ft 10in)
Length: 20.00m (65ft 7in)
Engines: Two Pratt & Whitney Canada PW118 or '118A turboprops rated at 1,342kw (1,800shp)
Cruise speed: 574km/h (310kt)
Accommodation: 30 maximum

First service: Atlantic Southeast Airlines, October 1985
Number built: 352
Number in service: 184 (+ over 90 in storage)

Current Operators

Africa: Charlan AC, Capital AL, Diexim Expresso, LAM.

Asia: VASCO.

Australasia: Air Fiji, Air North, ASA, Network Avn Australia, Regional Pacific AL, Skippers Avn.

Europe: Air Exel, Amadeus Flugdienst, IBA, Ibertrans, Luxaviation, Octavia AL, Regional, Sky Europe AL, Swiftair.

Former Soviet Union: Air Moldova.

North America: Ameriflight, Corporate Air, Great lakes Avn, Lakeland AT, Players Air, Skywest AL (Continental Express, Delta Connection, United Express).

South America: Austro Aero, Avensa, Avioquintana, Avior Express, META, Oceanair LA, Passaredo, PENTA, Puma Air, Rico LA, SAEREO, SAP, TRIP.

ZS-OTM is a 37-seater ERJ-135LR operated by Johannesburg-based South African Airlink seen here at Bamako in Mali. (Jacques Guillem)

EMBRAER ERJ 135/140

Embraer
Av. Brigadeiro Faria Lima, 2170, 12227-90 –
São José dos Campos, São Paulo, Brazil

The 50-seat EMB-145 (see page 87) was achieving impressive sales when Embraer launched the short-bodied 37-seater version in September 1997. Two prototype ERJ 135s were constructed by modifying a couple of EMB-145s whose fuselages were shortened by removing two plugs totalling 3.50m (11ft 6in). No other major structural changes were required but with less weight to carry, AE 3007 engines de-rated by FADEC could be fitted. Various sections are 'imported' to Brazil including the rear and centre fuselage sections from Belgium, the fin and tailplane from Chile and the wings from Spain. The first flight was made in July 1998 followed by US, Brazilian and European type certification in July 1999 and the ERJ 135 entered service with Continental Express later that month.

The ERJ 135 is offered in two regional jet versions, the ERJ 135ER and 135LR. In October 2003 the ERJ 135 became only the third jet airliner permitted to fly the 5.5° glide path approach into the London City Airport. The others are the Fokker 70 and the BAe146/RJ series. JetMagic of Ireland flew ERJ 135 services to Cork from LCY for a short while before going bust. A corporate jet was also developed and is known as the Legacy ECJ135. The prototype Legacy fist flew on 31st March 2001 and was certificated in 2002. All the ERJ 135/140/145s are built at the giant São José dos Campos site while the

specialist military versions and the Legacy bizjets are built at Gavião Piexoto.

The gap between the 135 and the 145 was filled by the mid-sized ERJ 140 which was launched at the European Regional Airlines Convention in Paris in September 1999. The main reason for the development of this sub-type was the complicated 'scope clause restrictions' in the USA. These involve the commuter airlines and their pilots arguing about how many 50-seater regional jets they could operate and how much the pilots should get paid for flying regional jets in comparison to the 'major' airlines.

Easily adapted from the 145/135 airframe, the 44-seat ERJ 140 was first flown in June 2000 and entered service with American Eagle (59 ordered) in 2002. The ERJ 140LR has a range of 3,056km (1,650nm). Other orders are from Midwest for 20 and Chautauqua Airlines for 15. The 135/140/145 types all have a common crew type-rating and considerable commonality of spare parts.

Details

Span: 135/140, 20.04m (65ft 9in)
Length: 135, 26.34m (86ft 5in);
  140, 28.45m (93ft 5in)
Engines: Two 33kN (7,426lb) Rolls-Royce
  AE3007-A1/3 turbofans
Cruise speed: 834km/h (450kts) max
Accommodation: 135, 37; 140, 44.

First service: ERJ 135 Continental
  Express, July 1999.
Number built (ordered):
  ERJ 135, 105 (19); ERJ 140, 74 (20)
Number in service: ERJ 135 105;
  ERJ 140 74.

Current operators

ERJ135
Africa: South African Airlink.
Europe: BMI Regional, City AL, Hex Air, Pan Européenne AS, Regional (Air France).
North America: American Eagle AL, Chautauqua AL (American Connection, Delta Connection), Express Jet AL (Continental Express).

ERJ 140
North America: American Eagle AL, Chautauqua AL

Regional operate a mixed fleet of small airliners from four hubs at Paris CDG, Lyon, Bordeaux and Clermont-Ferrand. This is ERJ-135 F-GOHB. (Author)

Seen at Fort Lauderdale in Florida is Embraer ERJ-145JR N837MJ, operated by Mesa Airlines on behalf of US Airways Express. (Author)

HB-JAN is an ERJ-145LU that still had its Crossair colours instead of SWISS when photographed at Basle in July 2004. (Author)

EMBRAER ERJ 145

Embraer, Av. Brigadeiro Faria Lima, 2170, 12227-90 –
São José dos Campos, São Paulo, Brazil
Harbin Embraer Aircraft Industry Co Ltd Harbin, Heilongjiang, China

At the Paris Air Show launch of the EMB-145 Amazon in 1989, the Embraer brochures revealed a reconfigured Brasilia with Allison GMA 3007 turbofans mounted over the wing, and a fuselage stretched to accommodate 45 passengers. As the design evolved, the Amazon name was dropped, and the engines were re-positioned beneath a new, supercritical 'wingletted' wing. The final EMB-145 layout, with rear mounted engines, was not launched until January 1992 because of delays caused by the privatisation of Embraer.

The EMB-145 design (marketed as the ERJ 145 since 1997) uses 30% of Brasilia parts including the entire nose and cabin cross-section, while the wing, based on the aerofoil of the cancelled CBA-123, is without winglets. The 9.2m (30ft) stretched Brasilia fuselage can seat 50 passengers in a two-plus-one layout.

The first order for the EMB-145 came from Trans Brasil in 1993, and the prototype first flew in August 1995. At the 1996 Farnborough Airshow, the aircraft was guaranteed success when Continental Express announced an order for 25, with a further 175 under option.

The standard ERJ 145 with a 1,480km (919nm) range was followed by the extended range 145ER and the longer range 145LR in 1998. Launched at Farnborough in 2000, the winghted Extra Long Range ERJ 145XR can fly up to 3,700km (2,230nm) and was granted

Brazilian certification in September 2002. Following US certification, the first one was delivered to Houston-based ExpressJet Airlines (Continental Express) in October 2002.

The Brazilian factory builds a dozen 145s per month and expects to deliver 170 ERJ/Legacy jets in 2005.

In 2002, a joint venture known as Harbin Embraer Aircraft Industry (HEAI) was started between Embraer and the China Aviation Industry Corp II (AVIC II) subsidiaries Harbin Aircraft Industry and Hafei Aviation Industry Co to license-build the 145 in China. Embraer have 51% of the venture and Harbin/Hafei 49%. HEAI flew their first locally assembled ERJ 145, built using an Embraer-manufactured forward and centre fuselage plug, on 16th December 2003. Planned production is one a month and the first order for 6 Chinese-built ERJ 145s came from China Southern and the first two were delivered in June 2004.

The Brazilian Air Force has chosen the EMB 145 AEW&C for their SIVAM surveillance system. It is equipped with the Ericsson Erieye radar system mounted above the fuselage. Other military versions are the EMB 145 RS/AGS with sensors mounted beneath the fuselage and the Embraer P 99, a 145-based multi-purpose armed version used for anti-submarine/surface and maritime patrol missions.

Details

Span: 20.04m (65ft 9in)
Length: 29.87m (98ft 0in)
Engines: Two 33.2kN (7,476lb) Allison AE3007A turbofans
Cruise speed: 797km/h (430kt)
Accommodation: 50 maximum

First service: Continental Express, January 1997
Number built (ordered): 774 (148)
Number in service: 603

Current Operators

Asia: China Southern AL, PB Air, Sichuan AL.

Europe: Air Exel, Alitalia Express, Austrian Arrows, BMI Regional, Cirrus AL, Citi Express (British AW), City AL, Eastern AW, Finncomm AL, LOT, Luxair, Portugalia AL, Regional (Air France), Skyways Express, Swiss Intl AL.

North America: American eagle AL, Chautauqua AL (Delta Connection, United Express), Express Jet AL (Continental Express), Mesa AL (US AW Express), Trans States AL (American Connection, United Express, US AW Express).

South America: Aerolitoral, Air Caraïbes, Rio Sul, SATENA.

Magnificent company-taken photo of three of the sleek new Embraer types, the ERJ-170, 190 and 195. (Embraer)

EMBRAER 170/175/190/195

Embraer
Av. Brigadeiro Faria Lima, 2170, 12227-90 –
São José dos Campos, São Paulo, Brazil

This latest and largest Embraer family of jets was launched in 1999 as the ERJ 170 and ERJ 190 with an $4.9 billion order (subsequently reduced) from Crossair for up to 160 aircraft. The competition in the 70-90-seat market came from Bombardier's CRJ 700/900, the Avro RJX and the Fairchild Dornier 728. However, Embraer saw the need for a much bigger RJ and their 70-108-seater 170/175/190/195 series introduced a spacious 4-abreast cabin that passengers would only normally find in a mainline airliner. Both the RJX and the Fairchild Dornier projects died leaving the new Embraer series as a market leader.

The **Embraer 170's** (the ERJ prefix was dropped in 2002) European launch customers were LOT and Alitalia Express while in North America the first orders came from US Airways with a $2.1 billion order for 85 aircraft with another fifty 170/175s on option. The first flight was made in February 2002 and four pre-production aircraft were used in test flights plus another two for static tests. Originally scheduled to enter service in December 2002, certification delays caused by avionics software problems and some flight test incidents meant it was not until early 2004 that it was given its Brazilian and FAA type certificate. It also became first new transport aircraft to be given a type certificate by the newly formed EASA (European Aviation Safety Agency). In March 2004 the first Embraer

170s were delivered to US Airways, Alitalia Express and to LOT. Sixty had been delivered by the end of 2004.

The first confirmed order for the stretched (1.77m/5ft 9in) **Embraer 175** came from Air Canada in November 2004 (they also ordered a large fleet of Embraer 190s). Because the 175 has a 95% commonality of parts with the 170, it was a straightforward programme and it first flew June 2003.

The first **Embraer 190** was rolled out at São José dos Campos on 9th February 2004. It first flew on 12th March and continued its test flying from Embraer's new airfield at Gavião Peixoto. By late 2004 it had gained 155 orders, of which 100 (plus 150 options) were for launch customer New York-based jetBlue. They specified the higher gross weight 190LR and their first is due for delivery in August 2005. In 2004 further orders came from Air Canada, COPA and TAME Ecuador.

The development of the **Embraer 195** (originally designated ERJ190-200) continues despite Swiss International suspending its first delivery (they had 15 on order) to August 2006. The single pre-series aircraft first flew on 7th December 2004 and certification is planned for mid 2006.

Advanced range versions, the 190AR and 195 AR are in development; when delivered all of jetBlue's aircraft will be to this specification.

Details

Span: 170/175, 26.00m (85ft 4in);
  190/195, 28.72m (94ft 3in)
Length: 170, 29.90m (98ft 1in);
  175, 31.68m (103ft 11in);
  190, 36.24m (118ft 11in);
  195, 38.65m (126ft 10in)
Engines: 170/175, two 62.3kN (14,200lb)
  GE CF34-8 turbofans;
  190/195, two 82.3kN (18,500lb)
  GE CF34-10E.
Cruise speed: 850km/h (460kts)
Accommodation: 170, 70; 175, 78;
  190, 98; 195, 108.

First service: LOT March 2004 (Embraer
  170)
Number built: 170, 36 (120), 175, 2 (10),
  190, (155), 195, 1 (0)
Number in service: 36 (all Embraer 170s)

Current Operators

Asia: Hong Kong Express.
Europe: Alitalia Express, LOT.
North America: Air Canada, Mid Atlantic AL
(US AW Express), Republic AL (United Express).
South America: TAME.

Very rare Fairchild F-27F HR-ATI of Atlantic Airlines de Honduras flies alongside a Fokker F.27 and a Fairchild FH-227. (Art Brett/Airteamimages)

FAIRCHILD F-27/FH-227

Fairchild Hiller Corporation
Germantown,
Maryland, USA

Fokker's F.27 Friendship was built and marketed under license by Fairchild at Hagerstown, Maryland, after agreement had been reached with Fokker in April 1956. Fairchild had quite correctly realised that the Friendship was a modern short-range turboprop airliner that they could build without the expense of the initial design and test work. Fairchild's hope that US domestic operators would place the initial orders was confirmed by orders from West Coast, Bonanza, Piedmont, and Northern Consolidated Airlines.

The first US-built Fairchild F-27 flew in April 1958. Slightly different from the Fokker built version, it had a longer nose housing a weather radar (later adopted by Fokker), more fuel capacity and standard seating for 40 passengers. FAA Type Approval of the Fairchild F-27 was granted in July 1958 and strangely it was a West Coast Airlines' Fairchild F-27 that flew the world's first 'Friendship' service on 27th September 1958, beating Aer Lingus's Fokker by three months. The other four US F-27 operators were able to start services over the next year allowing many of them to sell off their DC-3s.

Fairchild's versions included the F-27A and the F-27J (with uprated Darts) that was first operated by Allegheny in December 1966, the F-27B with a large forward cargo door, the F-27F corporate transport and the F-27M for hot-and-high operations.

When Fokker stretched the Friendship into the F.27 Mk.500, Fairchild Hiller (the new company name from 1966) followed suit with their stretched FH-227. This had a 1.83m (6ft 0in) forward fuselage plug allowing for an additional two rows of seats, plus various refinements especially for the US market. The FH-227 first flew in January 1966 and initial deliveries were to Mohawk Airlines who introduced their first FH-227 service on 1st July 1966. Ozark Airlines commenced their FH-227 operations that December followed soon after by Piedmont.

FH-227 versions included the 56-seat upgraded FH-227B, and the FH-227C, 'D and 'E with differing weights and engines. Only 79 FH-227s were built, with the majority being delivered to US commuter airlines. Second hand examples of the FH-227 found significant use in France as freighters in the 1980s but they all disappeared from service in the USA by the 1990s.

Currently only a handful of Fairchild F-27s and FH-227s can be found in Africa and South America, where the type still operates scheduled passenger services with some of the smaller airlines.

Details

Span: 29.00m (95ft 2in)
Length: F-27 23.50m (77ft 2in); FH-227 25.50m (83ft 8in)
Engines: F-27, two 1,282kW (1,720shp) RDa.6 Mk.511 Rolls-Royce Dart turboprops.
FH-227, two 1,700kW (2,250shp) RDa.7 Mk.532-7 Rolls-Royce Dart turboprops
Cruise speed: F-27 439km/h (237kt) max; FH-227 473km/h (255kt) max
Accommodation: F-27 44 max; FH-227 52 max

First service: West Coast, September 1958
Number built: F-27 128; FH-227 78
Number in service: F-27 6; FH-227, 3

Current Operators

Africa: Afrijet AL (F-27 & FH-227)
North America: Westex AL (F-27).
South America: Aerocaraibe (FH-227), Aerolineas Sosa (F-27), Atlantic AL de Honduras (F-27 & FH-227), CATA LA (F-27).

Key Lime Air use their Denver-based fleet of Metros, including Metro II N62Z, for charters in North America, Mexico and the Caribbean. (Author's collection)

FAIRCHILD METRO/EXPEDITER

Fairchild Dornier Aircraft
San Antonio
Texas, USA.

The successful series of Metro commuter airliners can trace their lineage back to the SA-26 Merlin I executive transport designed by Ed Swearingen in 1964. Built by Swearingen Aviation at San Antonio in Texas, this aircraft evolved into the Merlin IIA at the same time as a commuter version, the Swearingen SA-226TC Metro. The Metro first flew in August 1969 with accommodation for 19 passengers in a new pressurised circular section fuselage. FAA certification was granted in June 1970 followed by service entry in the US in 1973.

Fairchild Industries bought 90% of Swearingen Aviation in November 1971 and continued their designs, upgrading the Metro into the Metro II in 1974 with larger windows, reduced cabin noise and new cockpit seating. The heavier Metro IIA appeared in 1980, followed by the Series III with longer wings and more powerful engines. The IIIA version was designed to accept the very popular 746kW (1,000shp) PT6A-45R turboprops. This version first flew in December 1981.

Recognising the potential for its use as a small freighter, Fairchild built the Metro III-based Expediter with a large rear cargo door and a strengthened floor. First Expediter operator was local San Antonio-based SAT-Air in 1983.

The last variant built was the Metro 23, certificated in June 1990 with higher weights, more powerful engines and various improvements based on the

military C-26 Metro built for the USAF. An all-freight Expediter 23 was also available. In 1991 the Fairchild Corporation sold the Metro production plant at San Antonio and the new owners continued production under the name Fairchild Aircraft, later becoming Fairchild Aerospace. The very last Metro built was delivered to National Jet Aviation Services of Zelienople, PA in March 2001. In addition to its use by commuter and freight airlines, the Metro is in military operations with the US Air National Guard and the US Army as the C-26A and B. Its missions include MEDEVAC, freighting, counter-drug, aerial photography and other surveillance operations.

Many current operators seem to have small fleets of one or two Metros while the largest is California-based Ameriflight who have around 40 Metro/Expediters.

Details

Span: Metro II 14.10m (46ft 3in);
    Metro 23 17.37m (57ft 0in)
Length: 18.09m (59ft 4in)
Engines: Metro II, two 700kW (940shp) Garrett AiResearch TPE331-3UW-303G turboprops; Metro 23 – two 745kW (1,000shp) TPE331-11U-612G or 820kW (1,100shp) TPE331-12UAR turboprops
Cruise speed: Metro II 473km/h (255kt) max; Metro 23 542km/h (293kt) max
Accommodation: 20 maximum

First service: Commuter Airlines, 1973
Number built: 1,028
Number in service: 371 worldwide, mostly in the USA

Current operators

Africa: Charlan AC, Norse AC, Progress Air, Ryan Blake AC, Swazi Express AW, Wings Over Africa.

Asia: Serendib AL.

Australasia: Air Chathams, Air North, Air Tex AV, Airwork, Australia Air Express, Aviation Centre, Brindabella AL, Complete Aviation Services, Corporate Air, Hardy AV, Jetcraft AV, Macair AL, Pearl AV, Pel Air, Regional Express, Skippers AV, Sunshine Express AL, Transair.

Europe: Aeronova, Aireste, Artac Aviacion, Atlantic Express, Benair, BKS Air, Champagne AL, City Air, Euro Continental, Dynamicexel, European 2000 AL, European Air Express, FLM AV, Flugfelag Islands, IBA, Icaro, Malmo Air Taxi, Mediterranean Air Freight, North Flying, OLT, Regio Air, Südwestflug, Swiftair, Tadair, TAI, Top Fly, Ver-Avia, Zorex AT.

Middle East: DHL AV, Flying Carpet.

North America: Air One Express, Alta Flights, Ameriflight, Bearskin AL, Bellair, Berry AV, Big Sky AL, Bimini Island Air, Business AV, Carson Air, Castle AV, Corpjet, Flight Intl, F S AS, IBC AW, Key Lime Air, Lynx Air Intl, McNeely Charter Service, Merlin AW, National Jet AV Services, Nav AC, Norcanair AL, North Dene AW, Penair, Perimeter AL, Provincial AL, Quikair, Sierra West AL, Springfield Aircraft Charter, Starlink AV, Strong Arm AC, Sunwest Home AV, Superior AV, Western Air Express, Westex AL.

South America: Aero Costa Sol, Aerocuahonte, Aero Davinci Intl, Aeronaves, Aeropacifico, Airman, Air Tango, American Jet, All Borders AL, Baires Fly, DHL de Guatemala, Hawk Air, LC Busre, Transcarga Intl AW, Western Air.

Fokker F.27-500RF 4R-EXF in use by Expo Aviation for a twice-daily Colombo-Ratmalana to Jaffna service in November 2004. (Richard Vandervord)

FOKKER F.27 FRIENDSHIP

Fokker Aviation
PO Box 7600, 1117ZJ, Schiphol Oost
The Netherlands

Before the Airbus A320 appeared, the Fokker Friendship was the best-selling airliner designed in Western Europe with total Friendship production amounting to 786 built both by Fokker in Amsterdam and by Fairchild in the USA.

Fokker's 32-seat Project P.275 was one of many 'DC-3 replacements' proposed around 1950, but this one was a potential winner because it planned to use the best engine available at the time, the remarkable Rolls-Royce Dart. By 1952, Fokker had finalised the design, now called the F.27, which had a capacity for up to 40 passengers and a 483km (300nm) range. Fokker hoped that the F.27 could prove strong competition for the American designs and hopefully win them back the status that they had held between the two World Wars with their successful civil airliners.

The prototype first flew in 1955 and by the time the first production model (now given the name Friendship) flew in March 1958, American sales were boosted by the Fairchild Company who had commenced building the F.27 under license at Hagerstown, Maryland. Early deliveries from Fokker at Schiphol were to Aer Lingus, Braathens SAFE and Trans Australia Airlines.

Fokker variants included the initial Mk.100 with Dart 514s, the Mk.200 with the more powerful Dart 532 that first flew in September 1962, the Mk.300

Combiplane (similar to a -100 but with a large cargo door and strengthened floor) and the Mk.400 also with the 532 engines, but designed primarily for military use. A 1.5m (4ft 11in) fuselage stretch created the 52/60 seater Mk.500, while the quick-change Mk.600 had the -200 fuselage, the cargo door, and the stronger floor of the -300/-400.

The final Friendships produced in Amsterdam were a batch of F.27 Mk.500s for Air Wisconsin which were delivered in 1986, a remarkable 31 years after the F.27 first flew. The story continued however, with the similar-looking but totally redesigned Fokker 50.

Current passenger airline use is now diminishing, due to the strong sales of aircraft like the ATR 42 and Dash 8 and the rise of the regional jet; however, the type is still very common and often equipped to carry freight. The large fleet of Friendships currently operated under FedEx titles are due to be replaced by ATR 42s bought from American Airlines and Continental Airlines.

Details

Span: 29.00m (95ft 2in)
Length: Mk.500 25.06m (82ft 3in)
Engines: Two 1,279-1,730kW (1,715-2,320shp) Rolls-Royce Dart 514, '528, '532, '552, or '536 turboprops
Accommodation: 60 max, 52 standard
Cruise speed: 474km/h (256k)

First service: Aer Lingus, Dec 1958
Number built: 581
Number in service: 163 worldwide

Current Operators

Africa: Air Max Gabon, Air Tanzania, Air Tropiques, Libyan Arab AL, National AW Gabon, Sobel Air, Sonair, Sunu Air.

Asia: Asia Avia AL, Expo AV, GT Air, Merpati, Myanma AW, Pakistan Intl AL, Papua Air, President AL, Trigana AS.

Australasia: Aircruising Australia, Airwork, Executive AL.

Europe: Aba-Air, Air Contractors, Amerer Air, BAC Express, Channel Express, Farnair Hungary, Farnair Switzerland, Magic Blue AL, Miniliner, Sixcargo, Vuelos Mediterraneo, WDL.

Middle East: MNG AL.

North America: Mountain Air Cargo (FedEx), Westex AL.

South America: Aero Condor, Atlantic AL de Honduras, LAB, LADE, TAVAJ LA.

Fokker F28-4000 PK-GKZ, at Surabaya in June 2002, is flown on domestic low-cost services by the Citylink division of Garuda. (Richard Vandervord)

FOKKER F.28 FELLOWSHIP

Fokker Aviation
PO Box 7600, 1117ZJ, Schiphol Oost
The Netherlands

Initial design work on a jet-powered stablemate for the successful F.27 Friendship commenced in 1960. The F.28 was revealed to the public in 1962, and in order to start production, Fokker obtained a loan guaranteed by the Dutch government, repayable as a levy on sales.

The first order came from the German IT operator LTU in November 1965, followed by the F.28 first flight in May 1967. With the appropriate name Fellowship, final assembly of the aircraft was at Schiphol, with wings built by Shorts of Belfast and the rear fuselage and tail built by HFB and VFW in Germany. VFW later merged with Fokker in 1969 to create Fokker-VFW.

Initial version was the 65-seater Mk.1000; followed later in 1972 by the 79-seater stretched Mk.2000, first delivered to Nigeria Airways in October that year. In 1975, the -6000 appeared, this was based on the -2000, but with an increased wingspan and leading edge slats. Only two Mk.6000s were built but both were converted into Mk.4000s and ended their days with Air Mauritanie.

The most popular model was the 85-seater Mk.4000, basically a -2000 with the longer wings, it first flew in October 1976 and this type was the last to be completed in August 1987, 111 were built. In 1977 Garuda Indonesia were first to order the Mk.3000 which was based on the short-bodied -1000.

F.28 designations with a 'C' suffix denoted a forward freight door, and those with an 'R' had water-methanol injected engines for hot-and-high enhanced performance. All Fellowships have the familiar pair of large airbrakes that when closed, form the fuselage tailcone.

Because of its size, the F.28 was exempt from the Stage 3 noise restrictions in the USA. However, this did not apply in Europe. In April 1997, Fokker Aviation (the surviving element of the 1996 demise of the parent company) announced a re-engining scheme that would use the Rolls-Royce Tay 620 turbofan; the resulting conversion would be designated F.28RE. None were built.

The Tay-powered Fokker 70 and 100 replaced the Fellowship on the production line and since the arrival of the fuel-efficient Regional Jets, dozens of F.28s have been parked up awaiting their fate. Currently there are more than 40 in storage. Of the operational F.28s, the most significant fleets are currently with Merpati, Air Niugini and Airquarius Aviation in South Africa.

Details

Span: 25.07m (82ft 3in)
Length: 29.61m (97ft 2in)
Engines: Two 244kN (9,900lb) RR RB183 Spey Mk.555 turbofans
Cruise speed: 843km/h (455kt) max
Accommodation: 85 maximum
(Details above are for Mk.4000)

First service: LTU, March 1969.
Number built: 243
Number in service: 90

Current Operators

Africa: Air Burkina, Air Gabon, Air Ivoire, Air Mauritanie, Air One Nine, Airquarius AV, Avirex, Business AV, COAGE, East African Express, IRS AL, Libyan Arab AL, South African Airlink, South African Express AW.

Asia: Batavia Air, Biman Bangladesh AL, Citilink, Merpati, Myanma AW, Nurman Avia, Pelita Air, Post Ekspress Prima, President AL, Transwisata Air.

Australasia: Air Niugini, BTL.

Europe: Montenegro AL.

Middle East: Iran Aseman AL.

North America: ADI Charter Services, Canadian North.

South America: American Falcon, Icaro, LADE, LAER, Nuevo Continente, TAME.

Seen in front of a magnificent background at Molde Aaro airport in Norway in June 2003 is SAS Commuter's Fokker 50 LN-RNF. (Jonny Andersson)

FOKKER 50

Fokker Aviation
PO Box 7600, 1117ZJ, Schiphol Oost
The Netherlands

Designed as an enlarged and updated Fokker F.27 Friendship, the Fokker 50 was announced at the same time as the twin-turbofan Fokker 100 in November 1983.

Using F.27 fuselages, two prototypes were built, the first of which flew in December 1985. The F50, despite its outward similarity to the Friendship, contains 80% new or modified components, the most important being the PW125 engine with constant speed Dowty six-bladed propellers. Other major amendments include a four-screen EFIS cockpit, small winglets called 'Foklets', twin-wheel nose gear, more cabin windows and extensive cabin sound proofing. All these improvements combined to achieve an increase of 12% in cruise speed and a significant increase in fuel economy.

The first production model flew in February 1987 and Dutch certification was granted three months later. Early customers included DLT, Ansett Airlines, Austrian Air Services and Maersk Air.

Versions included the baseline model Fokker 50 which was supplied with either three or four doors, the Fokker 50 High Performance with more powerful engines (first ordered by Avianca), and the Fokker 50 Utility with a larger main door and strengthened cabin floor. A wide variety of mainly military variants were also put forward, but the only one to be built was the Fokker 60 Utility. Four of this stretched (1.62m/5ft 4in) version were built for the Royal Netherlands Air Force.

After the collapse of the Fokker concern in March 1996, outstanding orders on the Fokker 50 were slowly completed with the last two aircraft (for Ethiopian Airlines) being delivered in March and April 1997. These deliveries marked the end of an illustrious airliner type, going back to the very first Friendship of 1955.

Fokker Services have developed a freighter version for Swedish airline Aamapola Flyg and Aircraft Conversions Holding in Holland has teamed up with Composite Partners International BV to build two Fokker 50 Freighters with LCDs (Large Cargo Door). These will be delivered in early 2005 and will be the first Fokker 50s with an LCD. No Fokker 50s were ever sold in North America but the type is very common in Europe where Skyways of Sweden has the current largest fleet.

Details

Span: 29.00m (95ft 2in)
Length: 25.25m (82ft 10in)
Engines: Two P&WC turboprops, F50 1,864kW (2,500shp) PW125B; F50 'High Performance' 2,050kW (2,750shp) PW127B
Cruise speed: 532km/h (287kt) max
Accommodation: 58 maximum

First service: Lufthansa Cityline, August 1987.
Number built: 218
Number in service: 168, mostly in Europe, none in the USA

Current Operators

Africa: Blue Bird AV, Ethiopian AL, Mid AL, Sonair, Sudan AW.

Asia: Aero Mongolia, Air Andaman, Airmark, Indonesian AT, Malaysia AL, Mandarin AL, Nakanihon AL, Pelita Air, Riau AL, Transwisata Air.

Australasia: Skywest AL.

Europe: Aamapola Flyg, Air Nostrum (Iberia Regional), Contact Air, Denim Air, Denim AW Bavaria, Flugfelag Islands, K-Air, KLM City Hopper, Luxair, SAS, Skyways Express, Swe Fly, VLM AL.

Middle East: Aria Air, Iranian AT, Kish Air, Palestinian AL, Tafta AL.

Former Soviet Union: Air Astana, Air Baltic, Estonian Air.

South America: Aero Condor, Avianca, Oceanair LA, SAM.

Departing Manchester International for Lisbon as flight NI601in May 2004, Fokker 100 CS-TPA is one of six in the Portugalia fleet. (Author)

FOKKER 70/100

Fokker Aviation
PO Box 7600, 1117ZJ, Schiphol Oost
The Netherlands

In November 1983 Fokker launched the Fokker 100 at the same time as the Fokker 50 twin turboprop. Based on their F.28-4000 Fellowship, the F100 had a stretched fuselage allowing up to 122 seats, a new 30% more efficient wing, an EFIS glass cockpit and most importantly, it is powered by the Stage 3/Chapter 3 approved Rolls-Royce Tay turbofan.

Fokker joined forces with MBB (later DASA) and others to offset the construction costs. The wings were constructed in Northern Ireland by Shorts, some fuselage sections and the tail in Germany, and the engines and undercarriage in the UK.

The first airline to order the F100 was Swissair, who purchased ten in 1984. The F100 first flew in November 1986 followed by type certification a year later. Swissair's first example was delivered in February 1988. Later that year, 75 F100s (powered by the uprated Tay 650) were ordered by American Airlines, who also took options on another 75.

Other versions offered were the freight door-equipped F100QC Quick Change and the Fokker Executive Jet 100. This was a corporate version with seating for 20 to 40 passengers in airline style; the first example was delivered to the Ivory Coast Government in 1989.

Launched in November 1992, the Fokker 70 was basically a shorter version of the F100, the prototype being built by modifying one of the first F100s. Two

fuselage sections, one behind and one in front of the wing were removed creating a fuselage that was 4.62m (15ft 2in) shorter. This change was virtually the only difference between the types although the F70 had two less overwing exits. First flight in April 1993 was followed by certification in October 1994 and the first orders from Sempati Air and Pelita in Indonesia. At least three F70s were sold in the Fokker Executive Jet 70 layout. Other versions included the F70 for US carriers and an ER version with extra fuel capacity. Fokker also studied a stretched 130-seater Fokker 130 but this was abandoned after the company was declared bankrupt on 15th March 1996.

By the time production finished with the collapse of the company, the F100 and F70 combined had outsold their F.28 predecessors with 283 F100s and 48 F70s completed. In 1996, a company called Rekkof (Fokker spelt backwards) did try and restart F70/F100 production but was unsuccessful. In 2004 there was further talk of a new F70 production line being set up in Nanchang in China.

Details

Span: F100 & F70 28.08m (92ft 1in)
Length: F100 35.53m (116ft 7in);
  F70 30.91m (101ft 5in)
Engines: F100 & F70 two 261.6kN
  (13,850lb) Rolls-Royce Tay Mk.620-15,
  or F100 only, 267.2kN (15,100lb)
  Mk.650-15 turbofans
Cruise speed: 856km/h (462kt) max
Accommodation: F100 122; F70 80

First service: F100 Swissair, March 1988;
  F70 Sempati, March 1995
Number built: F70 48; F100 283
Number in service: F70 40; F100 202

Current Operators

Africa: IRS AL, LAM.

Asia: Cosmic Air, Korean AL, Mandarin AL, Merpati, Pelita Air, Transwisata Air, Vietnam AL (F70).

Australasia: Air Niugini, Alliance AL, Norfolk Jet Express, Skywest AL.

Europe: Air Vardar, Alpi Eagles, Aravaco, Austrian (F70), Austrian Arrows (F70 & 100), BMI, Brit Air (Air France), CCM AL, EU Jet, Germania, Gir Jet, Helvetic AW, KLM City Hopper (F70 & 100), Malev (F70) Montenegro AL, Portugalia AL, Regional (Air France) (F70 & 100), Slovak AL.

Middle East: Inter Express AL, Iran Air, Iran Aseman AL.

North America: Jetsgo.

South America: Mexicana, TAM LA, Uair.

Both the HS.748 and the rare Gulfstream 1 are regular sights in South Africa. Immaculate ZS-PHJ has been leased to Pelican Air Service. (Afavia-fotos.co.za)

GRUMMAN G.159 GULFSTREAM 1

Grumman Aircraft Engineering Corp
Bethpage, Long Island,
New York, USA

In the 1950s, Leroy Grumman saw the need for a purpose-built executive transport to replace the former military types in executive service such as the Lockheed Lodestar, B-25 Mitchell and DC-3/C-47 Dakota. The resulting G.159 design, although built for executive use, did later operate for various airlines.

Design work started in 1956, initially based on their piston-powered S2F Tracker and TF-1 Trader naval aircraft. However, the final design emerged as the largest aircraft of its time produced for the executive market. The low wing ten-seater was powered by two of the new Rolls-Royce Dart engines, and first flew as the G.159 Gulfstream in August 1958. FAA certification was granted in May 1959.

Design features included an APU for air conditioning and start-up and a forward airstair, both of which allow totally independent operations from remote sites. The large cabin windows were popular with passengers and have been retained, along with the basic fuselage dimensions, for the subsequent high-selling series of Gulfstream corporate jets.

Most Gulfstream 1s were supplied to US-based corporations as executive transports, but several were built as 19/24-seater commuter airliners. Military versions built included nine highly modified Gulfstream 1s supplied to the US Navy as the TC-4C Academe for training EA-6 navigators. A single VIP VC-4A was supplied to the United States Coastguard in March 1963 for use of the Washington-based Commandant of the Coast Guard. In 2001, this long-serving aircraft was replaced by another G.159!

Ten years after G.159 production finished in 1969, the then owner of the design, Gulfstream American Corporation, offered a 3.25m (10ft 8in) stretched conversion for use by commuter airlines. The 38-seater Gulfstream 1C first flew in October 1979 but failed to gain significant orders, and only five were built. First delivery was to Air North in Burlington, Vermont, followed by Air US of Denver, Colorado.

Although production ended with the 200th example in 1969, the G.159's (and the Rolls-Royce Dart's) longevity has meant that in 2004, there are still commercially operated examples, particularly in the USA.

Details

Span: 23.92m (78ft 6in)
Length: 19.43m (63ft 9in)
Engines: Two 1,485kW (1,990hp) Rolls-Royce Dart Mk.529-8X or 8E turboprops
Cruise speed: 560km/h (302kt) max
Accommodation: 24 maximum.
(Details above for G.159 Gulfstream 1)

First service: June 1959
Number built: 200 (5 converted to G-1C)
Number in service: 35

Current Operators

Africa: Air Inter Ivoire, East African Express, King AC, Nelair Charters, Tramon Air.
Asia: Post Ekspress Prima.
Europe: Stellair.
North America: Missionair, Phoenix Air, Propair, Riverside Intl AL.
South America: Global Air.

Laos, Mongolia, Nepal and Fiji have all bought the Y-12. The RDPL prefix on this Y-12 means 'République Démocratique Populaire Lao' (Author's collection)

HAMC Y-12

Harbin Aircraft Manufacturing
No 15 Youxie St, Pingfan District,
Harbin, 150066, China.

The HAMC Y-12 (Yunshuji 12 = Transport Aircraft No 12) is a 17-seat, short field utility aircraft, that has its origins in the eight-seater Y-11 that was built in small numbers from the mid-1970s.

In the early 1980s, an effort was made to improve the performance of the piston-powered Y-11. One example had its two Huosai engines replaced with 373kW (500shp) Chinese license-built Pratt & Whitney PT6A-10 turboprops, becoming the Y-11T1. The turboprop engine's greater power allowed HAMC to stretch the Y-11 fuselage and enlarge the cabin to accommodate 17 passengers, creating the first Y-12 I.

Other changes from the Y-11 included an increased wingspan and a new aerofoil section. The Y-12 I first flew in July 1982, and was followed by the Y-12 II, which had more powerful Chinese-built PT6A-27s. This first flew in August 1984 and was certificated in China in 1985. The Y-12 IV has a larger wing with winglets, a reinforced undercarriage with better brakes and a redesigned interior, seating 19. In April 1995, the Y-12 IV became the first aircraft designed and built in China to receive joint airworthiness certification from the American FAA and the Chinese CAAC. (The Y-12 II had already been certificated by the British CAA in June 1990). The Y-12E version is designed for operations at high altitudes. This has

more powerful engines with four-bladed props and new avionics. A version with pressurisation and a retractable undercarriage, the Y-12F, has also been studied. In 1998, the Canadian Aerospace Group was set up to sell the westernised version of the Y-12 IV Twin Panda. At one time they were confident of selling 15 to Brazil and reportedly had several more orders, but nothing seems to have come of this.

Other than carrying passengers and/or freight, the Y-12 is also operated in China on maritime survey missions and, when equipped with an airborne magnetometer, it is used on remote sensing operations. In addition to the many domestic sales of the Y-12, HAMC has exported civil and military examples to the Gabon, Eritrea, Tanzania, Iran, Laos, Mongolia, Sudan, Zambia, Zimbabwe, Mauritania, Fiji, Peru, Malaysia and Nepal. These sales have made the Y-12 the best selling aerospace export in China.

Details

Span: 17.24m (56ft 7in)
Length: 14.86m (48ft 9in)
Engines: Y-12 IV and II: two Chinese-built 500kW (680shp) P&WC PT6A-27 turboprops
Cruise speed: Y-12 II 292km/h (157kt)
Accommodation: Y-12 II 17 maximum; Y-12 IV 19 maximum

First service: 1983
Number built (ordered): 115+ (unknown)
Number in service: 24

Current Operators

Asia: China Flying Dragon AV, Lao AL, Shuangyang General AV, Xinjiang General AV, Zhongfei AL.
Australasia: Air Fiji.

The well-maintained IL-18s of Sharjah-based Phoenix Aviation are sadly now restricted by the UAE to carry freight only. (Author's collection)

ILYUSHIN IL-18

Ilyushin Design Bureau
Leningradsky Prospekt 45G
125190 Moscow, Russia

Ilyushin's elegant IL-18 (NATO reporting name 'Coot') traces its origins back to a post war Aeroflot request for a medium-range airliner able to carry 75-100 passengers and operate from unpaved runways.

Ilyushin's initial offering was a conventionally laid out 66-seater powered by four ASh-73TK piston engines. This original 'IL-18', designed by A Shvetsov and first flown in July 1947,was tested and rejected by Aeroflot who felt it was too advanced for their current operations.

In the mid-1950s, Ilyushin re-used the IL-18 designation on their new four-engined high-speed mass transportation airliner, originally known as the 'Moskva'. The turboprop-powered IL-18 which first flew in July 1957 and was revealed to the public at Vnukovo that month was vastly different from the early IL-18; however it did retain the same wing area and fuselage diameter. The new IL-18 was reportedly the first large Soviet-built passenger airliner to dispense with the military-style glazed nose in favour of one with an enclosed weather radar. The prototype, and the early production aircraft, were all powered by Kuznetsov NK-4 turboprop engines, while all IL-18s built after aircraft No 21 were fitted with the remarkable Ivchenko AI-20 engine.

All IL-18s were built at GAZ No 30 at Khodinka, near Moscow, where the first series was soon replaced by the IL-18B

that had an increased maximum take-off weight and a reconfigured cabin seating 84. The 90/100-seater IL-18V first appeared in 1961 and this became Aeroflot's standard version. The IL-18D, originally designated IL-18I, first flew in 1964 with the more powerful AI-20Ms and a longer passenger cabin created by moving the rear pressure bulkhead. This could seat 122 passengers in the summer, when the winter coat wardrobes were removed. The IL-18E was similar to the IL-18D but had the same fuel capacity as the IL-18V.

More than 100 IL-18s were exported, with many examples being sold to operators of the IL-14, particularly in Africa and Eastern Europe. Although the civil IL-18 production line closed around 1970, various military versions based on the IL-18 continued to be built until the mid-1970s. The IL-20 is an Elint/reconnaissance aircraft, the IL-22 an airborne command post and the IL-38 (NATO reporting name 'May') is used for maritime patrol. A civil version of the IL-20 is the IL-24N used for fishery patrols.

The Russian Air Force still operates 20 IL-18/IL-22s while the Navy has 38 IL-38s. Civilian use is now confined to operations, mostly freight, in the FSU, Cuba, Africa and the Middle East.

Details

Span: 37.40m (122ft 9in)
Length: 35.90m (117ft 9in)
Engines: Four 3,170kW (4,250shp)
   Ivchenko AI-20M turboprops
Cruise speed: 675km/h (365kt) max
Accommodation: 122 maximum

First service: Aeroflot, April 1959
Number built: 569
Number in service: 40

Current Operators

Africa: ALADA, Compagnie Africaine d'Aviation.
Asia: Air Koryo, Expo AV.
Former Soviet Union: Aerovista AL, Astair, Grizodubova Air, Irbis, Lviv AL, Pecotox Air, Phoenix AV, Russia State Transport Company, Sevastopol-Avia, Vichi Air, Yuzhnaya Kazakhstan AL.
South America: Aerocaribbean.

Note the extended tail support on this IL-62M RA-86566. This is SAT Airlines' (Sakhalinskie Aviatrassy) only IL-62. (Colin Ballantine)

ILYUSHIN IL-62

Ilyushin Design Bureau
Leningradsky Prospekt 45G
125190 Moscow, Russia

Designed primarily as a replacement for the long-range Tupolev Tu-114 turboprop airliner, Ilyushin's IL-62 (NATO reporting name 'Classic') was first revealed to the West at the 1965 Paris Air Show. Looking remarkably like the Vickers VC-10, the IL-62 was advertised as able to fly non-stop from Moscow to New York.

Five prototypes were built at Moscow-Khodinka prior to production switching to Kazan (GAZ No 22). The flying prototypes were all transferred by road to Zhukovsky for their first flights and because the planned Kuznetsov NK-8 turbofans were not ready, the first IL-62 flight was made on 2nd January 1963 using four 75kN (16, 750lb) Lyulka AL-7 turbojets. In trials, the IL-62 initially suffered low-speed handling problems, but these were eventually solved by fitting huge leading edge extensions to the outer wings. First regular service with Aeroflot was a freight run between Moscow and Khabarovsk followed by full passenger service from Moscow to Khabarovsk and Novosibirsk commencing in March 1967.

About 95 of the standard IL-62 version were built before the availability of more efficient Soloviev engines allowed Ilyushin to fly the upgraded IL-62M in 1971. This version first appeared at the Paris Air Show that year and had a greater fuel capacity, improved clamshell thrust reversers, a revised cabin, new cockpit avionics and various modifications to the wings and baggage holds. Nearly 200 IL-62Ms were built and the first service was in 1974.

The higher weight IL-62MK was launched in 1978 with stronger wing structure to increase the fatigue life, revised cabin interior with a wider aisle and overhead lockers and a new main undercarriage with wider bogies. Production finished at Kazan around 1993, although a few unsold examples remained at the factory until they eventually found buyers in the late 1990s.

Nearly 90 IL-62s were exported to countries such as China, Cuba, Czechoslovakia, East Germany, North Korea, Poland and Romania. The type (mostly IL-62Ms) still remains in service in Cuba and North Korea while more than 50 operate passenger services within the FSU. The largest fleet there is operated by Domodedovo Airlines with 11. Several IL-62s are also used as Russian VIP transports with additional communications equipment housed in an extended dorsal fin.

Details

Span: 43.20m (141ft 9in)
Length: 53.12m (174ft 4in)
Engines: IL-62, four 103kN (23,150lb) Kuznetsov NK-8-4 turbofans; IL-62M, four 107.9kN (24,250lb) Soloviev D-30KU turbofans
Cruise speed: 900km/h (485kt) max
Accommodation: IL-62 186; IL-62M 198; IL-62MK 195

First service: Aeroflot, March 1967
Number built: 285
Number in service: 90

Current Operators

Africa: Gambia New Millenium Air, Jetline.
Asia: Air Koryo, Mekong Air Intl.
Former Soviet Union: Airstars, Air Ukraine, Aviaenergo, Dalavia, Domodedovo AL, East Line AL, Grizodubova Air, KAPO Aviakompania, Kokshetau AL, Kras Air, Magadon AL, MCHS Rossii, Quadrotour-Aero, Russia State Transport Company, SAT AL, Tbilaviamsheni, Ukraina Air Enterprise, Ulyanovsk Higher Civil AV School, Uzbekistan AW, VIM AL.
South America: Cubana.

This nicely coloured Il-76TD is one of two that operate freight flights for Tehran-based Qeshm Airlines. (Author)

ILYUSHIN IL-76

Ilyushin Design Bureau, Leningradsky Prospekt 45G, 125190 Moscow, Russia
Tashkent Aircraft Production Corp (TAPO) 61 Elbek St, Tashkent, 700016, Uzbekistan

With more than 30 years of service, the IL-76 is one of the most successful and reliable aircraft to be built by the USSR since the Second World War. Designed partly to replace the Antonov An-12, the IL-76 (NATO reporting name 'Candid') was developed as a long-range turbojet freighter, mostly for the Soviet military. Work on the first of three prototype/pre-production aircraft began in December 1969. First flown by E Kuznetsov at Moscow's Khodinka airfield in March 1971, it made its Western debut at the 1971 Paris Air Show.

All production IL-76s were built by the Chkalov Aircraft Production Association in Tashkent/Chkalovskaya. In July 1975, an IL-76 with a crew led by Ya I Vernikov and A M Tiuriumin broke 25 world records and in the same year the first civilian IL-76 was delivered to Aeroflot.

Cargo is loaded via the rear loading ramp, assisted by on-board gantry cranes that move on tracks in the cabin ceiling. On the IL-76 they are able to lift up to 10,000kg (22,040lb). The last item loaded with these cranes is often the unique tow-bar, designed to fit around the nose mounted radar. The entire cabin is pressurised (unlike the An-12) and has a permanent station for the loadmasters.

The IL-76 has excellent short field performance and is able to operate fully loaded from unpaved runways as short as 6,000ft (1,820m) partly due to the multiple-wheeled undercarriage that distributes the weight on 20 low-pressure tyres fitted to 16 main wheels (on four legs) and four nosewheels.

Initial production consisted of armed and unarmed IL-76T and IL-76M freighters, followed in the early 1980s by the longer range IL-76TD and 'MD. Another eleven versions of the IL-76 are believed to have been built, including an IL-76DMP fire-bomber, the IL-78 tanker, a flying hospital and the military A-50 AWACS (NATO reporting name 'Mainstay') on which Beriev is the main contractor.

The upgraded and stretched (6.60m, 21ft 8in) IL-76MF (civil version is the MT) first flew in August 1995. It has a four-crew 'glass' cockpit and is powered by Perm PS-90AN turbofans. In 2004, after the prototype had completed 1,500 test flights, the Tashkent Aircraft Production Enterprise (TAPO) was contracted to build the second and third prototype IL-76MFs. They will be used for Russian State trials in 2005. The Russian Air Force has signed for 10 IL-76MFs although they actually require 100-120.

A major programme is under way to re-engine IL-76TDs and MDs with the PS-90A-76 engines for the Air Force. The first IL-76MD-90 should fly in early 2005 and serial conversions should start in 2006.

Details

Span: 50.50m (165ft 8in)
Length: 46.59m (152ft 10in)
Engines: Four 117.7kN (26,455lb) Aviadvigatel (Soloviev) D-30KP or D-30KP-2 turbofans. (IL-76MF has four 156.9kN [35,275lb] PS-90AN)
Cruise speed: 800km/h (430kt)
Payload: IL-76T 40,000kg (88,185lb) max; 'MF 52,000kg (114,640lb) max

First service: Soviet AF 1974, Aeroflot 1976
Number built: 950
Number in service: 294 in civil operation, mostly in the Former Soviet Union

Current operators

Africa: Aerolift, Angola AC, Avient AV, Azza Transport, Buraq AT, East West Cargo, Equatorial Cargo, Faso AW, Gira Global, Goliaf Air, Jetline, Libyan AC, Tobruk Air, Trans Attico, Yemenia.

Asia: Air Koryo, China United.

Europe: Atlant Hungary, Hunair, Hungarian Ukrainian AL, Kosmas Air.

Middle East: Qeshm AL, Syrianair.

FSU: Abakan-Avia, Aerocom, Aeroflot, Airlines 400, Airline Transport, Airstars, Alrosa, Atlant Soyuz, Atran, Atruvera, Aviacon Zitotrans, Aviaenergo, Aviaprad, Aviast, Azal Cargo Air Company, Azov-Avia AL, Botir-Avia, Dobrolet AL, Domodedovo AL, East Line AL, Euro-Asia Air, GATS, Gazpromavia, GST Aero, Ilavia AL, Inversia, Jet Line Intl, KNAAPO, Kras Air, Krylo Magadan AL, Kyrgyzstan AL, Lviv AL, MCHS Rossii, Sayakhat, Silk Way AL, TAPO Avia, Tesis, Trans Avia Export, Turkmenistan AL, UAA, Ulyanovsk Higher Civil AV School, Ukrainian Cargo AW, Uzbekistan AW, Vladivostock Air, Volare AL, Volga-Dnepr AL, Yer-Avia, Yuzhmasavia.

Rarely seen in the West, the Il-86 was the Soviet's first wide-bodied airliner. UK-86012 is based at Tashkent. (Hans Oehninger)

ILYUSHIN IL-86

Ilyushin Design Bureau
Leningradsky Prospekt 45G,
125190 Moscow, Russia

When Aeroflot asked the three major Soviet manufacturers, Antonov, Ilyushin and Tupolev to submit plans for a wide-bodied airliner, the Boeing 747 was already flying. Ilyushin's winning design evolved eventually from an 'oversize' IL-62, into a conventionally-shaped aircraft, similar in layout to the Boeing 747, except for the position of the cockpit and the addition of a fourth, centreline undercarriage leg. The IL-86 also had a low-level passenger door with built-in stairs to allow boarding at airfields without walkways. The fact that the Soviet engine manufacturers could not at that time produce a high-bypass ratio turbofan, appears not to have deterred Ilyushin from completing their IL-86.

First flown at Khodynka in December 1976, the IL-86 (NATO reporting name 'Camber') was instantly derided by the West as having significantly less range than the 5,000km (3,106 miles) first promised. However, because Aeroflot had very few long-range/high-capacity routes, the wide-bodied IL-86 still proved very useful to them, especially on the high-density/medium-range routes, such as Moscow to the Black Sea holiday resorts. It made its first commercial service from Moscow to Tashkent in December 1980.

Production models were all completed at factory No 64 at Voronezh-Pridacha where 103 were built. The only new IL-86s sold outside the USSR were the three examples delivered to Urumqui-based China Xinjiang Airlines in 1993. In 1997, 17 airlines operated nearly 100 IL-86s but currently only 62 are in service with 13 operators.

By the time production ceased at Voronezh in 1994, just over 100 examples of this, Russia's first wide-bodied airliner, had been built. These included four special order versions for the Soviet Government that were highly modified for use as airborne command posts. Flown in full Aeroflot colours, they are easily identified by the large dorsal antenna that contains satellite communication equipment and the underwing pods that provide extra electrical power to all the onboard equipment. All the cabin windows are also blanked off as part of the shielding against nuclear blasts.

Currently, the IL-86 can only be found in service with airlines from the Former Soviet Union and it is banned in the EU because of its inability to meet current noise restrictions. Plans to re-engine IL-86s with the much quieter and more efficient CFM56-5C2 appear to have been abandoned.

Details

Span: 48.06m (157ft 8in)
Length: 59.54m (195ft 4in)
Engines: Four 127.5kN (13,000kg) Kuznetsov NK-86 turbofans
Cruise speed: 950km/h (512kt)
Accommodation: 350 maximum

First service: Aeroflot, Dec 1980
Number built: 105
Number in service: 62

Current Operators

Former Soviet Union: Aeroflot, AJT Air Intl, Armenian AL, Atlant Soyuz, Continental AW, East Line AL, Kras Air, Pulkovo, Sibir AL, Ulyanovsk Higher Civil AV School, Ural AL, Uzbekistan AW, Vaso AL.

The Russia State Transport Company operates a huge fleet of types on VIP services including two Il-96-300s for President Putin. (Richard Vandervord)

ILYUSHIN IL-96

Ilyushin Design Bureau
Leningradsky Prospekt 45G
125190 Moscow, Russia

Designed to rectify the shortcomings in range of its sister IL-86, the Ilyushin IL-96-300 has a shorter fuselage and a new supercritical, 'wingletted', wing with less sweep. It also features fly-by-wire controls, new avionics and a six-screen colour EFIS cockpit. Unlike the IL-86, the IL-96-300 and IL-96M do not have the lower deck passenger entry door.

The IL-96-300, IL-96M and IL-96T were designed to meet the Stage 3/Chapter 3 noise restrictions and unlike previous 'Soviet' airliners, they reveal a change in practice by NATO, because they were not allocated a reporting name.

When the IL-96 was first proposed, the possibility of using Western-built engines was suggested, but this arrangement had to wait until the IL-96M was built. With seats for 300 passengers, the first IL-96 was given the designation IL-96-300 and it first flew at Khodinka in September 1988. Russian certification was granted in December 1992 and it entered service with Aeroflot the next year. During the spring of 1996 the Russian State Transport Company 'Rossiya' took delivery of an IL-96-300 to act as a presidential transport. This was later demoted to the equivalent of 'Air Force 2' after a new IL-96-300PU (PU = Putin!) was delivered in 2003.

In 1991, Ilyushin teamed with Pratt & Whitney to obtain PW2337 engines for the IL-96M (originally called the IL-96-350). The higher-powered engines enabled the designers to increase the size of the original -300 until it was slightly longer than the IL-86. The prototype IL-96 was converted into an IL-96M at GAZ.40, Voronezh in 1992 and was first flown from Moscow City Airport in April 1993. Two months later it was displayed at the Paris Air Show. The IL-96M had a two-crew EFIS cockpit, complete with GPS, FMS, GPWS and EICAS. The freighter version of the IL-96M was the IL-96T and this entered service prior to any production passenger versions. It had a 3.60m (11ft 10in) by 2.60m (8ft 6in) main deck cargo door in the forward port fuselage and could carry standard size containers and pallets up to a maximum payload of 92,000kg (202,820lb). Both the IL-96M and -96T designs were cancelled in 2001.

VASO delivered the first new IL-96-300s to an airline in 2004 after a break of five years when Kras Air received two in June and September. Also in 2004, the Cuban President ordered two IL-96-300Ms for Presidential and Cubana use; they will be delivered in mid 2005.

The current development is a PS-90-powered version of the stretched IL-96M called the IL-96-400. The freight version, the IL-96-400T, has been ordered by Atlant Soyuz.

Details

Span: IL-96-300/400 & -96M 60.10m (197ft 3in)
Length: IL-96-300 55.35m (181ft 7in); IL-96M & -96-400 63.94m (209ft 9in)
Engines: IL-96-300 & 400, four 156.9kN (35,275lb) Aviadvigatel PS-90A turbofans; IL-96M/T four 164.6kN (37,000lb) P&W PW2337 turbofans.
Cruise speed: IL-96-300 900km/h (485kt); IL-96M 870km/h (470kt)
Accommodation: IL-96-300, 300; IL-96M, 386

First service: Aeroflot, mid 1993
Number built (ordered): 16 (20)
Number in service: IL-96-300, 14

Current operators (IL-96-300)

Former Soviet Union: Aeroflot, Atlant Soyuz, Domodedovo AL, Kras Air, Russia State Transport Company.

Although the IL-114 was intended to replace the ageing An-24s and 26s, it has failed to sell in significant numbers. (Author's collection)

ILYUSHIN IL-114

Ilyushin Design Bureau, Leningradsky Prospekt 45G, 125190 Moscow, Russia
Tashkent Aircraft Production Corp (TAPO) 61 Elbek St, Tashkent
700016, Uzbekistan

Designed in the mid-1980s to replace the Antonov An-24/26/30 and 32s that were becoming older and less economical to operate, this regional advanced turboprop airliner is very similar in shape to the British-built BAe ATP/Jetstream 61. Typically for a Russian aircraft, it has been designed with a sturdy tricycle undercarriage enabling operation from unpaved surfaces. It also has an APU and a forward airstair for operations at remote airfields. The aircraft has no underfloor storage hold, so baggage is either stored near the front or rear doors, or in the overhead lockers.

The IL-114 features Stupino CB-34 low-noise six-bladed carbon fibre constant speed propellers, and, in a bid to encourage potential buyers from abroad, the IL-114-100 (initially reported as the IL-114PC) was proposed with Western-built turboprops. Both the Allison GMA2100 and the Pratt & Whitney Canada PW127 were considered but it was a PW127-powered version that first flew in January 1999. Uzbekistan Airways received their first of ten IL-114-100s in December 2002 but the second was delayed until 2004 due to currency problems.

The prototype IL-114 was first flown at Zhukovsky in March 1990, and made its Western debut at the 1991 Paris Air Show. Test flying and certification was delayed due to the loss of one of the pre-production aircraft in July 1993. CIS

certification was completed in 1993 and although 350 'orders' for Aeroflot were announced, they were subsequently cancelled. Production commenced at the Chkalovskaya plant in September 1996.

Other versions proposed include the heavier and more powerful IL-114M with TV7M-117engines and the IL-114MA with P&WC engines. The all-cargo IL-114T, developed initially for Uzbekistan Airways, has a removable roller floor and a large 3.25m x 1.71m (10ft 6in x 5ft 6in) rear freight door. The prototype IL-114T made its first flight in September 1996, was certified in 1997, and commenced service in Uzbekistan colours in 1998. Russian carrier Vyborg is currently using IL-114s leased from Uzbek lessor Uzavialising.

Military versions proposed include a freighter with a rear loading ramp, an electronics ECM model, a maritime patroller and a photographic version with a glazed nose and raised cockpit similar to the An-30. In May 2003 the Russian Air Force announced that it had selected the IL-112VT as its new lightweight transport. This is a developed IL-114 with a high wing, T-tail and TV7-117S engines.

Despite Aeroflot's initial interest, the IL-114 has, like the similar ATP/J61, failed to achieve significant orders. Around 1997, the possibility of establishing an IL-114 production line in Iran was seriously discussed as this country had found it difficult to acquire

modern turboprop airliners due to the various trade sanctions imposed, but it has now rectified this but setting up a factory to build Antonov An-140s. Some hope of finishing some of the uncompleted aircraft came in 2004 when the UAE and China announced orders for 15 IL-114-100s. TAPO also has an MoU for three aircraft from Azerbaijan Airlines.

Details

Span: 30.00m (98ft 5in)
Length: 26.88m (88ft 2in)
Engines: Two 1,839kW (2,466shp) Klimov TV7-117-3 or two 2,051kW (2,750shp) P&WC PW127H turboprops
Cruise speed: 500km/h (270kt)
Accommodation: 64 maximum

First service: 1993
Number built (ordered): 10 (unknown)
Number in service: 3

Current Operators

Former Soviet Union: Uzbekistan AW, Vyborg North West AT.

One of South East Asian Airlines' nine Let 410UVP-E Turbolets is seen here at Busuanga in February 2004. (Peter J Bish)

LET L-410 TURBOLET

Letecké Závody
A S, Kunovice 1177
686 04 Czech Republic

LET started building aircraft in 1950 and throughout the second half of the 20th century they were a well-respected company with high quality products that sold worldwide. Apart from the L-410 Turbolet they also built the famous Blanik series of gliders.

The initial design work on the L-410 started in 1966 and work on the prototype led to the first flight in April 1969 and its appearance at the Paris Air Show a few months later. This aircraft, and about 30 early production models, were all powered by imported Pratt & Whitney PT6A turboprops because the intended M601 engines were not yet available.

Early sales to the Czech domestic airline Slovair were soon followed by a batch of L-410A for Aeroflot trials in Siberia and Uzbekistan. The Russian's delays with their Beriev Be-30 twin-turboprop and the successful trials of the Turbolet prompted Aeroflot to order the L-410. A total of 559 Turbolets of various marks were eventually delivered to Aeroflot.

Design features include a strong single-wheel undercarriage designed for rough field operations, optional metal ski landing gear and double upward-opening doors that can be removed for parachuting.

Continuous improvement and adaptation for customers produced a large number of models. These included the early L-410AF with a glazed nose for aerial survey work, the camera-equipped L-410FG, the Walter/Motorlet powered L-410M and 'MA, and the 17-seat 'MU, equipped especially for Aeroflot. Other versions offered included VIP, ambulance, executive and freighter.

The L-410UVP series (UVP = STOL) first flew in 1977 and sold in huge numbers. This had a taller tail with dihedral on the tailplane, longer wings with spoilers and redesigned flaps. The L-410UVP-E first appeared in 1984, it had M-601E engines, wingtip tanks and four extra seats thanks to the rearrangement of the toilet and luggage areas. Other versions were the Let-410UVP-E10 with Bendix/King avionics and the Medevac -E16. Other suffixes were allocated to denote the countries that each type was certified in.

The M601F-powered L-420 first flew in November 1993 and was designed to meet Western certification standards, it was granted FAA type certification in 1998. Letecké Závody became responsible for the Let-410/420 programme from 2001 but filed for bankruptcy in October 2003 after completing only five aircraft in 2003.

Details

Span: 19.98m (65ft 6in)
Length: 14.42m (47ft 4in)
Engines: Two 560kW (750shp) Walter M601E turboprops
Cruise speed: 380km/h (205kt) max
Accommodation: 19 maximum
(Details above are for L-410UVP-E)

First service: Slov Air, 1971
Number built: 1,108
Number in service: 292

Current Operators

Africa: Air Express Algeria, Air Leone, Avion Express, Blue Bird AV, Blue Sky AS, Buraq Air, Business AV, Cabo Verde Express, Citylink, Comores AS, Comores AV, Compagnie Aérienne Maouene, Coptrade AT, Eagle Air, Eastern Air, Easy Link AS, Eldinder AV, Jetair, Madagascar Flying Service, Mombasa Air Safari, Planar, Precisionair, Rossair, STA Trans African AL, Transairways, Trans Air Congo, United AL (Kenya), United AL (Nigeria), West Coast AW, Zanair.

Asia: Asian Spirit, South East Asian AL, Tengeriin Ulaach Shine.

Europe: ABC Air Hungary, Aero Vodochody, Air Max, Air Polonia, Air Scorpio, Alpe Air, Antares, Benair, Bud Air Plzen, Budapest Aircraft Services, Dubnica Air, Farnair Hungary, Heli Air, Hemus Air, Indicator AV, Job Air, Laus Air, LR AL, Scorpion Air, Seagle Air, Silver Air, Sky Service, Solinair, Trade Air, Vera AT, White Eagle AV.

Former Soviet Union: Aeroflot Nord, Aerovista AL, Air Test, Apatas, Avia Ekspress AL, Avies Air Company, Berkut Z K, Concors, ILIN, Kazair West, Kazan Air, Kharkov State Aircraft, Kostroma Air, Petropavlovsk-Kamchatsky Air, Rivne Universal Avia, Rubystar, State Flight Academy of Ukraine, Vostock AL, Zhezair.

South America: Aero Costa Sol, Aerocaribe, Aerodomca, Aeroejecutivos, Aeroeste, Aerolineas Sosa, Aeropacifico, Air Santo Domingo, Atlantic AL, Atlantic AL de Honduras, Aviheco, Caribair, Caribinter, Ciaca AL, Comeravia, Cruser Taxi Aereo, EL Sol de America, Heliandes, SADI, SAP, SASCA, SEARCA, Sundance Air, TAG, Taxi Aereo Cusiana, TEAM, Tikal Jets AL, Tranaca, Transaven, Tropical AW, West Caribbean AW.

After retaining this superb colour scheme for more than 40 years, in 2004 Ethiopian decided to drop it for a fashionable all-white fuselage. (Chris Witt)

LOCKHEED L-100 HERCULES

Lockheed Aircraft Company
Marietta,
Georgia, USA

The L-100 commercial variant of the world famous Lockheed C-130 Hercules military transport first appeared ten years after the prototype YC-130A had flown at Burbank, California.

Marketed as the L-100, the Lockheed Model 382, which was based on the C-130E, first entered civilian service by supporting the oil exploration business on the Alaskan North Slope. Early sales to airlines were hard to achieve, but Continental Air Services bought two for operation in Laos, and Zambian Air Cargoes acquired five. Other companies that operated early examples, like Delta Airlines, Pacific Western and Interior, found that even though the Hercules was not a great load carrier, the low-slung fuselage with a rear loading ramp and its ruggedness and versatility made the L-100 ideal for freight operations especially where ground equipment was minimal.

Twenty-one of the civilian, short fuselage L-100 Hercules were delivered before the L-100-200 (Model 382E), with a 2.54m (8ft 4in) fuselage stretch, was placed into production. This version, with a 20% increase in volume floor space, first flew in April 1968 and entered service with Interior Airways in October that year. Thirty-four were delivered, including some that were converted from short-bodied L-100s.

Another stretch (2.03m/6ft 8in) of the fuselage in 1969 created the definitive

L-100-30 (Model 382G). This design was encouraged by Saturn Airways because of their requirement to transport three Rolls-Royce RB211 TriStar engines from England to the TriStar production line in California, all inside one Hercules. The -30 first flew in August 1970 and other early orders came from Safair (South Africa) and Southern Air Transport (USA). Safair still operate a fleet of 7 L-100-30s in 2005, one of which they have had for 32 years. Angolan-based Transafrik International currently has the largest civil Hercules fleet with 12 examples.

Specially adapted versions include the five L100-30HS built for Saudi Arabia in 1984/1985. These are equipped as airborne hospitals and are often flown in support of the Saudi Royal family. Other conversions include the former military Hercules that were used as water-bombers by Hemet Valley Flying Service in California. These appear to be grounded as of mid 2004 due to problems with the FAA. Six Hercules 'combi' versions were specially converted by Southern Air Transport to carry 18 passengers in a palletised module and five freight pallets.

The civilian version of the latest Allison AE2100-powered C-130J was originally known as the 'Advanced L-100'. The new L-100J is offered with a two-crew EFIS cockpit, six-bladed props, an optional side cargo door and much reduced operating and maintenance costs.

Details

Span: 40.41m (132ft 7in)
Length: 34.37m (112ft 9in)
Engines: Four 4,508kW (3,362ehp)
    Allison 501-D22A turboprops
Cruise speed: 583km/h (315kt) max
Payload: 23,183kg (51,110lb) max;
    97 passengers when converted

First service: Alaska Airlines, Mar 1965
Number built: 112 civil versions
Number in service: 40

Current Operators

Africa: Air Algérie, Ethiopian AL, Libyan AC, Safair, Transafrik Intl, Yemenia.
Europe: Air Contractors.
North America: First Air, Lynden AC, Prescott Support, Tepper AV.
South America: LADE.

Seen at Bournemouth International airport in 2004, G-FIJV is an L-188C Electra freighter belonging to Coventry-based Atlantic Airlines. (Tony Best)

LOCKHEED L-188 ELECTRA

Lockheed Aircraft Corporation
Burbank,
California, USA

Designed in 1954 to meet an American Airlines requirement for a short to medium stage airliner, the L-188 Electra was to become the first and only significant turboprop airliner to be designed and built in the USA.

In June 1955, Eastern Airlines and American Airlines ordered a total of 75 L-188A Electras and Lockheed commenced production at Burbank with hopes of further significant sales. Indeed, by the time that the first Electra flew in December 1957, 144 had been ordered, including 12 for KLM in the Netherlands.

Unfortunately for Lockheed, three major US Airlines, American, Braniff and Northwest Orient all suffered major Electra crashes within 15 months of them entering service. Two of the crashes involved the in-flight break-up of the aircraft. Even though subsequent major modifications to the engine nacelles, wings and propellers cured the faulty resonance problems, the orders dried up leaving Lockheed to complete only 170 Electras. The last one off the line was delivered to Garuda Indonesia in January 1961. Of the 170, 55 Electras were built to L-188C standard for Northwest Orient Airlines and Western Airlines. These had extra fuel tanks, higher weights and a 1,389km (750nm) increase in range.

In 1968 the Lockheed Aircraft Service Co started converting 40 Electras into L-188AF and 'CF freighters. The conversion involved the fitting of a reinforced floor and a large 3.56m x 2m (11ft 10in x 6ft 6in) forward cargo door. Some aircraft were also modified with an additional 2.44m x 2m (8ft x 6ft 6in) cargo door aft of the port wing. The first order was for six conversions for Northwest Orient and later orders followed from Western, Overseas National and Universal.

By the mid 1970s, the Electra had disappeared from 'front line' passenger service, but was proving itself as a reliable and effective freighter in places like Colombia, Ecuador and throughout the USA.

The hugely successful P-3 Orion is a long-range maritime patrol version of the Electra. With over 700 built, including some assembled in Japan, it currently flies with about a dozen air forces. Some early Orions have now been civilianised and converted to fire-bomber configuration in the USA. Surviving Electras, some of them now upgraded with a two-crew cockpit, TCAS, GPS and modern avionics are all now flown as freighters. In the USA, Zantop still have 13 while in Europe, Coventry-based Atlantic Airlines operate 11.

Details

Span: 30.18m (99ft 0in)
Length: 31.81m (104ft 6in)
Engines: Four 2,795kW (3,750shp) Allison 501D-13A Turboprops or 3,022kW (4,050shp) '501D-15
Cruise speed: 652kmp/h (405mph) max
Accommodation: 99
Payload: L-188C/F 15,331kg (33,800lb)

First service: Eastern Airlines, January 1959
Number built: 170
Number in service: 29

Current Operators

Africa: ATO.
Europe: Amerer Air, Atlantic AL.
North America: Air Spray, Neptune Aviation Services, TMC AL, Zantop Intl AL.
South America: Mexjet.

105

Despite being registered in Sierra Leone, this TriStar was based in Jordan and operated by CBJ Cargo of Antigua and Barbuda. (Author)

LOCKHEED L-1011 TRISTAR

Lockheed Martin
86 South Cobb Drive, Marietta
Georgia 30063-0264 USA

In response to a 1966 American Airlines request for a twin-engined, wide-bodied airliner for short/medium ranges, both Lockheed and Douglas produced aircraft of conventional design but with an added third engine in the tail. The major difference between the Lockheed and Douglas design was the position of the third engine. In the L-1011, the engine was inside the rear fuselage fed by a huge air duct from the base of the tail, whereas the DC-10's third engine was inside a pod mounted on the fin above the rear fuselage. Continuing Lockheed's penchant for naming their products after heavenly bodies, the three-engined L-1011 became the TriStar.

Lockheed constructed a huge building complex at Palmdale in the California desert specifically to piece together L-1011 TriStar parts that had been produced in various factories in the USA and abroad. Lockheed chose Rolls-Royce's RB211 engine for the TriStar, but their lack of power compared to the DC-10's chosen General Electric CF6 initially restricted the TriStar's range and payload. By the time that modifications and adjustments to the engines had achieved the planned performance, the TriStar had lost many sales to the DC-10. When TriStar production ceased in 1984 with the 250th aircraft, Douglas had produced nearly 400 DC-10s and still had a large order to complete for the USAF.

Various versions of the TriStar were produced, some of them being conversions of earlier models. Original build series were the -1, -100, -200 and -500. The -500 was developed as a long-range derivative of the -1, with the fuselage being shortened by the removal of two sections, one (1.57m/5ft 2in) aft of the wing and the other (2.54m/8ft 4in) forward. The TriStar 500 was first used by British Airways in 1979 and had a maximum range of 9,655km (6,000 miles). After production finished, Lockheed offered modification packages to convert TriStars to -50, -150 and -250 series.

The Royal Air Force have the world's largest current fleet of nine former civilian Tristar tanker/troop carriers, (note that the RAF drops the capital 'S' from Lockheed's registered trademark name). Saudi Arabia has two executive TriStar 500s fitted out as VIP transports that fly in full Saudi Arabian Airlines colours for the Saudi Royal Family. One TriStar was converted by Marshalls of Cambridge to carry an experimental satellite-launching rocket in its belly while Lockheed Aeromod in Tucson converted another into a flying hospital with two surgical stations, 12 pre-op beds, 12 post-op beds and 50 seats. This aircraft is sadly out of use and stored at Tucson in Arizona. More than 60 other TriStars are currently in storage.

Details

Span: 47.34m (155ft 0in);
  -500 50.09m (164ft 0in)
Length: 54.16m (178ft 0in);
  -500 50.05m (164ft 0in)
Engines: Three 187-222.4kN (42,000-50,000lb) Rolls-Royce RB211 turbofans
Cruise speed: 948km/h (512kt)
Accommodation: 400 maximum. (330 in Series 500)

First service: Eastern, April 1972
Number built: 250
Number in service: 37 plus 9 military

Current Operators

Africa: Air Rum, Air Universal, Hewa Bora AW, International AS, Joasro AV, Northeast AL, Star Air.
Asia: Kampuchea AL, Orient Thai AL, Sky Eyes AV.
Europe: Air Luxor, Euro Atlantic AW, Gee Bee AL, Yes.
Middle East: Sky Gate Intl.
South America: CBJ Cargo, North East Bolivian AL.

The ever-expanding EVA Air from Taiwan operates both the MD-11F and the Boeing 747-400F for worldwide freight services. (Author)

McDONNELL DOUGLAS MD-11

Boeing Commercial Airplanes
PO Box 3707, Seattle, Washington
98124-2207. USA

In the late 1970s, Douglas was considering various design updates for the DC-10. These included the DC-10 'Super 60' series that was proposed in three versions including a 390-seater DC-10-63 with a 12.19m (40ft) fuselage stretch, longer wings and CF6-80 or JT9D-7R4 engines. However, these projects were all shelved when the public image of the DC-10 was shattered by a series of unconnected accidents that shook the flying public's confidence and made the airlines cancel their orders.

In 1981, McDonnell Douglas borrowed a DC-10 from Continental Airlines to fit and study the effects of winglets on aircraft performance. The encouraging results of this, plus the emergence of new, more powerful engines, saw proposals and projects evolve into the two-crew MD-11 in 1984. Formally launched in December 1986, the first MD-11 orders came from current DC-10 operators, Federal Express, British Caledonian, Korean Air, Thai International, SAS, Varig and Swissair.

As with many new airliners, various sub-assemblies were built at aerospace factories around the world and shipped to Long Beach for final assembly. Main suppliers were McDonnell Douglas (Canada) who built the wings in Toronto and General Dynamics' Convair Division who built most of the fuselage.

First flown in January 1990, the MD-11 was available in three versions, a basic 405-seater airliner (normally equipped with 250-330 seats), the all-freight MD-11F (first operated by FedEx) with a large forward cargo door and stronger undercarriage, and the 'Combi', with a rear cargo door and a variety of optional cabin configurations. In 1991, an MD-11CF 'Convertible Freighter' was announced and ordered by Martinair Holland. First delivered in April 1996, the 13,400km (7,240nm)-range MD-11ER variant had been ordered by Garuda and World Airways.

The lack of promised range (a 5% to 10% reduction) initially dogged the MD-11, prompting MDC to introduce various Performance Improvement Packages. These 'phased' modifications reduced weight and drag to such an extent that the MD-11 was eventually able to exceed its original design range. These mods included such diverse items as seals on the wing slats and new windscreen wipers!

Further variations to the MD-11 using a new wing were studied but not built. One had a 6.70m (22ft) fuselage stretch and the other was a -LR Long-Range version. In early 1997, McDonnell Douglas was taken over by arch rival Boeing and the MD-11 line was closed in 2000. The last two MD-11s were delivered to Lufthansa Cargo in 2001. Boeing now offers an after-market cargo conversion.

Current largest fleet is with FedEx who have 42 while more than 40 (mostly passenger versions) are currently stored.

Details

Span: 51.70m (169ft 6in)
Length: 61.20m (200ft 10in)
Engines: Three 266.9kN (60,000lb) P&W4460 or 274kN (61,500lb) GE CF6-80C2D1F turbofans
Cruise speed: 945km/h (510kt) max
Accommodation: 405 maximum
Maximum payload: MD-11F 91,077kg (200,970lb)

First service: December 1990, Finnair
Number built: 200
Number in service: 180

Current Operators

Asia: China Eastern AL, Eva Air, Korean AL, Thai AW.
Europe: Alitalia, Catran, Finnair, KLM, Lufthansa Cargo, Martinair.
North America: FedEx, Gemini AC, UPS AL, World AW.
South America: VARIG.

Spirit Airlines of Fort Lauderdale fly more than 30 MD-80s including MD-83 N833NK. In May 2004 they ordered Airbus A319s and A321s. (Kevin Irwin)

McDONNELL DOUGLAS MD-80

Boeing Commercial Airplanes
PO Box 3707, Seattle, Washington
98124-2207. USA

The MD-80 designation did not relate to one specific type of aircraft, but to a family of variants that were produced after the DC-9-50. The MD-81, MD-82, MD-83 and MD-88 are all externally the same. The short-fuselage MD-87 is described on page 110.

Original plans for the MD-80 carried various designations, DC-9-60, Series 50RSS (Re-fanned Super-Stretch) or Series 55, but by the mid-1970s, this had been changed to DC-9 Series 80, or DC-9 Super 80. The '80' in the designation related to the forthcoming new decade.

The MD-80 series was officially launched in October 1977 with orders from Swissair, Austrian Airlines and Southern Airways. The first aircraft, an MD-81, first flew in October 1979, and FAA Certification was granted in August 1980.

By June 1983 the 'DC' designation had been dropped in favour of the more appropriate corporate identity 'MD', (the Douglas Aircraft Company then being a wholly-owned part of McDonnell Douglas) thereby creating the MD-80. Apart from the new 'big fan' engines, the main differences between the DC-9-50 and the MD-80 were the stretched fuselage, the longer wings with greater chord at the wing root, the larger tail fin and the updated cockpit with optional EFIS.

In April 1979, the MD-82 (JT8D-200 engines for hot-and-high operations and

greater range) was announced. With extra fuel tanks, strengthened undercarriage and airframe, the extended range MD-83 was launched in January 1983 and first delivered to Alaska Airlines in February 1985. The MD-88 was announced in January 1986 with a large order from Delta Air Lines. It first flew in August 1987 and had an updated cockpit and a revised cabin interior with wider aisles and new overhead lockers. The low-drag 'screwdriver' tail-cone of the MD-87 was fitted to all MD-80s from mid 1987, it was also retro-fitted to earlier MD-80s by some operators.

In 1985, MDC signed an agreement with the Shanghai Aviation Industrial Corporation (SAIC), and the China Aviation Supply Corporation (CASC) to allow production of MD-80s in China. 35 aircraft (MD-82 and MD-83) were assembled in Shanghai from kits supplied by MDC.

After the Boeing/McDonnell Douglas 'merger' in 1997, the MD-80 series became surplus to Boeing's requirements and the line was wound down with the last one being delivered in 2000. Current conversions planned include a Stage 4 exhaust mixer/silencer for the JT8Ds and a Boeing/TAECO freighter modification.

Details

Span: 32.87m (107ft 10in)
Length: 45.06m (147ft 10in)
Engines: Two Pratt & Whitney PW JT8D turbofans rated 82.3-93.4kN (18,500-21,000lb)
Cruise speed: 925km/h (500kt) max
Accommodation: 172 maximum

First service: Swissair, Sept 1980
Number built: MD-81 132; MD-82 569; MD-83 265; MD-88 150.
Number in service: 1,155

Current Operators

Africa: 1 Time, Comair, Kulula.com, Nouvelair, Orion Air, Rwandair Express, Safair, Sosoliso AL.
Asia: Airfast, Bouraq, China Eastern AL, China Northern AL, China Southern AL, Far Eastern AT, JAL Domestic, Lion AL, Myanmar AW Intl, Star Air.
Europe: Air Adriatic, Alitalia, Arnoro AL, Austrian, Blue Line, Bulgarian AC, Eurofly, Finnair, Helvetic AW, Iberia, Jet X, Meridiana, Nordic Airlink, SAS, Spanair, Viking AL.
Middle East: AMC AL, Freebird AL, Luxor Air, MNG AL, Onur Air.
North America: Alaska AL, Allegiant Air, American AL, Continental AL, Delta AL, Jetsgo, Midwest AL, Spirit AL, Transmeridian AL.
South America: Aerolineas Argentinas, Aeromexico, Aeropostal, Aerorepublica, Allegro AL, Austral, Avianca, Dutch Caribbean AL, SAM, Surinam AW, West Caribbean AW.

Allegiant's MD-80s fly schedules out of Las Vegas in Nevada. MD-82 N864GA was previously operated by SAS in Norway. (Kevin Irwin)

Yet another revision to the JAL colour scheme sees even more white on this MD-87 JA8372 seen at Osaka Itami in June 2004. (Hiro Murai)

Iberia's smallest mainline jet is the 101-seat MD-87. EC-EYY was delivered new from Long Beach to Madrid in August 1980. (Author)

McDONNELL DOUGLAS MD-87

Boeing Commercial Airplanes
PO Box 3707, Seattle, Washington
98124-2207. USA

With the MD-80 series selling well, McDonnell Douglas reasoned that because the DC-9 Series 30 had been the most popular version of the first DC-9 series, then an MD-80 with a similar fuselage length would be a good idea. Operators of the first generation DC-9s could then replace their noisier and thirstier jets with up-to-date equipment with refanned engines and an EFIS cockpit.

The designation MD-87 was allocated to show the year of planned first service (1987), and the project was officially announced in January 1985 on the back of orders from Finnair and Austrian Airlines that were received the previous month.

The aircraft was generally similar to the rest of the MD-80 series, but with a fuselage shortened by 5.3m (17ft 5in). The MD-87's JT8D-217Cs were quieter and used 2% less fuel than the -217As fitted to the MD-82. In addition to the shorter fuselage, the MD-87 differs from the other MD-80s in the size of its tail fin. This has an extension fitted above the tailplane to restore the aerodynamic stability that was disrupted by shortening the fuselage.

The MD-87 was the first in the MD-80 series to fit an EFIS cockpit, complete with an optional head-up display and an AHRS (Altitude/Heading Reference System), it was also the first to fit the extended low-drag 'screwdriver' tail-cone. This device was later fitted to all new MD-80s and was retro-fitted to earlier versions. It reportedly gave a 0.5% reduction in fuel burn. The MD-87 was also available as an Extended Range version with two extra fuel tanks situated in the underbelly cargo hold.

First MD-87 flight was in December 1986, followed by FAA certification in October 1987. Both Finnair and Austrian received their first examples the following month. The last MD-87s were delivered to SAS in spring 1992. At the time of the Boeing/MDC merger, all outstanding orders had been built, so Boeing deleted the type from their portfolio. Only ten customers originally bought the MD-87, making this version hard to find, particularly in the USA. In total, 75 were delivered and the current largest fleets are with Iberia and SAS.

Details

Span: 32.86m (107ft 10in)
Length: 39.75m (130ft 5in)
Engines: Two 108.9kN (20,000lb) or 93.4kN (21,000lb) Pratt & Whitney JT8D-217C or -219
Cruise speed: 811km/h (438kt)
Accommodation: 139 maximum

First service: Finnair, November 1987.
Number built: 75
Number in service: 75, most in Spain and Scandinavia

Current Operators

Asia: JAL Domestic.
Europe: Austrian, Iberia, SAS, Spanair.
North America: Allegiant Air.
South America: Aeromexico.

Sad to say that this beautiful JAS colour scheme will disappear as each aircraft is repainted in the new white JAL colours. (Author's collection)

McDONNELL DOUGLAS MD-90

Boeing Commercial Airplanes
PO Box 3707, Seattle, Washington
98124-2207. USA

The 'third generation' of the DC-9/MD-80 family was officially launched in November 1989 after Atlanta-based Delta Air Lines ordered 50, plus many more on option.

The MD-90 was a straightforward update of the MD-80, easily identifiable because of the relatively huge V2500 engines and the slightly stretched (1.37m/4ft 6in) forward fuselage. Other features included the enlarged tail fin and 'screwdriver' tail-cone of the MD-87, carbon brakes, new cabin interior with hand rails on the overhead luggage bins, a four-screen EFIS flight-deck, and a more powerful APU, mounted in the tail-cone.

The MD-90 was built at Long Beach on the same production line as the MD-80s, with which it shared many components. Sub-assemblies produced in Australia, China, France and Spain were built into fuselage modules at the Salt Lake City plant before transfer to California. The first MD-90 flight was on schedule on 22nd February 1993 and was followed by No 2, six months later. FAA certification was granted in November 1994 by which time the three flying MD-90s had over 1,900 hours in the air. Delta received their first aircraft in February 1995 and commenced scheduled services in April on the Dallas to Newark route.

The baseline version was the MD-90-30. Two examples of the MD-90-30ER (Extended Range) were built for AMC

Aviation in Egypt in 1997. Proposed versions that were not built included the extended range -50 and -55 that, if they had been built, would have had more powerful V2528 engines with stronger wing spars, fin and tailplane.

In 1992, MDC announced a $1,000m contract with the Shanghai Aviation Industrial Corporation (SAIC) at Dachang to build the 3 MD-82, 17 MD-82T and 20 MD-90-30T under license. The MD-90-30T, known as the TrunkLiner, was designed with dual tandem landing gear with four main wheels for Chinese domestic use, but due to lack of orders, only two were completed when production stopped in 2000 and the last one was delivered to China Northern Airlines.

After the Boeing/MDC merger in 1997, the MD-90 (and MD-80 series) order book was closed; however, production of outstanding orders continued at Long Beach until the final MD-90 was delivered in 2000. The largest fleet currently in service is operated by Saudi Arabian Airlines who have 26.

Details

Span: 32.87m (107ft 10in)
Length: 46.51m (152ft 7in)
Engines: Two 111.2kN (25,000lb) IAE V2525-D5 turbofans
Cruise speed: 809km/h (437kt)
Accommodation: 172 max, 153 typical

First service: Delta Air Lines, April 1995
Number built: 114 by MDC, 2 by SAIC
Number in service: 106

Current Operators

Asia: China Eastern AL, China Southern AL, Eva Air, JAL Domestic, Uni Air.
Europe; Hello, SAS.
Middle East; Saudi Arabian AL.
North America: Delta AL.

With Japan rapidly retiring its YS-11 fleets, Thailand and the Philippines are buying them up. YS-11A-500R HS-KVO is based in Bangkok. (Avimage)

NAMC YS-11

Nihon Aeroplane Manufacturing Co Ltd
Toranomon Building, No.1, Kotohira-cho
Shiba, Minato-ku, Tokyo, Japan

The YS-11 was the result of a joint effort by six Japanese companies that commenced design work in 1959 to produce a medium sized passenger airliner especially for the Japanese domestic market. Mitsubishi Heavy Industries, Kawasaki Aircraft Co, Fuji Heavy Industries, Shin Meiwa, Nippi and Showa Aircraft were all individually responsible for the production of different parts of the YS-11. The main parties involved were Mitsubishi, who built the fuselage, and Kawasaki, who were responsible for the wings.

Construction of two prototypes commenced in March 1961, leading to the first flight in August 1962. Powered by Rolls-Royce's most powerful version of their Dart turboprop, the YS-11 is externally similar in layout to another Dart-powered aircraft, the BAe (HS) 748. The engines are mounted forward and above the wing in large nacelles that also house the main undercarriage legs. The circular cross-section fuselage is pressurised and has front and rear airstairs on the standard passenger versions.

Airline and military operators in Japan accepted the initial deliveries from March 1965, and by late 1966, a small number had been exported to the Philippines and to Hawaii. By the mid-1970s the type could be found on every continent except Australia. Operators at this time included Olympic Airways, Piedmont

Airlines, Cruzeiro do Sul and Transgabon.

Several versions were built, starting with 49 of the original YS-11-100. In 1967, production switched to the higher weight YS-11A Series in the hope of sales on the export market. First delivery from this series was a YS-11A-200 to Piedmont in June 1968. Next came the 'Combi' YS-11A-300 and the all-freight YS-11A-400, both with large cargo doors. The final series offered were the heavier YS-11A-500, -600 and the unbuilt -700.

The last YS-11A delivery was in February 1974 to the Japanese Self-Defence Force. They still operate the type for transport duties as well as for ECM and navaid calibration missions. Although the type is still in operation 40 years after its first service, the YS-11 can not be considered a success, as its production costs and disappointing sales caused NAMC to make a loss of $600 million.

With eight aircraft in mid 2004, Japan Air Commuter currently owns the largest civilian fleet of YS-11s, but since the arrival of their brand new Bombardier Dash 8s, JAC, now the only Japanese airline to still operate YS-11s, has been selling them off especially to the Philippines and Thailand.

Details

Span: 32.00m (105ft 0in)
Length: 26.30m (86ft 3in)
Engines: Two 2,280kW (3,060shp) Rolls-Royce Dart Mk.542-10K turboprops
Cruise speed: 478km/h (253kt) max
Accommodation: 60
Maximum payload: 6,670kg (14,704lb)

First service: TOA Airways, April 1965
Number built: 182
Number in service: 29

Current Operators

Asia: Aboitiz Air, Air Link Intl AW, Asian Spirit, Japan Air Commuter, Phuket AL.
South America: Alcon Servicios Aereos, Gacela AC.

Ten years old in August 2004, Moldavian Airlines' tiny fleet consists of two Saab 340s and a Saab 2000. They fly mostly to Budapest. (Author's collection)

SAAB 340

SAAB Aircraft AB
Linköping
SE-581 88, Sweden

Announced in January 1980, this joint US/European regional airliner was originally built by SAAB-Scania and Fairchild Industries. Designated the SAAB Fairchild SF340, the conventional design featured General Electric CT7 engines with Dowty Rotol slow-turning four-bladed composite propellers.

With a 65% SAAB/35% Fairchild split in the design, the resulting aircraft was completed in Sweden with the wings, tail and engine nacelles provided by Fairchild. For several years, the furnishing and final painting was completed by Metair, from West Malling in the UK.

Crossair, the Swiss regional airline, became the launch customer and the first of the three prototypes was first flown in January 1983. In June 1984 the SAAB Fairchild SF340 received its joint European and American certification. In November 1985, SAAB took full control of the design, due to Fairchild's withdrawal from the aviation business; however, Fairchild still supplied parts until 1987. The 'F' was subsequently dropped from the designator, allowing the type to be marketed as the SAAB 340.

Before production switched to the upgraded 340B, 159 of the initial 'A' series were built. The 'B had a longer span tailplane, higher weights, and more powerful engines. The 340B first flew in April 1989 and once again Crossair

became the launch customer, accepting their first aircraft in March 1994. A 'Combi' version with 19 seats and space for 1,500kg (3,310 lb) of freight was also available. The last variant, the 340B Plus, has lower maintenance costs, better performance, and cabin improvements and refinements borrowed from the SAAB 2000 including its 'active noise control' for a quieter passenger cabin. The first 340B Plus was delivered to American Eagle/Wings West in April 1994. A highly modified AEW&C version (known as the Tp100B) was built for the Swedish Air Force while the Japanese Maritime Safety Agency bought two special search & rescue examples. A few 340s have been fitted out as corporate/executive transports.

By 1999, the lack of sales, particularly of the SAAB 2000, forced SAAB to stop production and the last two 340s were delivered to Japan Air System in August and September 1999. The type can still be found worldwide especially in the USA where the commuter airline American Eagle has the largest fleet. More than 100 SAAB 340s are currently withdrawn and in storage.

The 340B can now be converted to all-freight 3,856kg (8,500lb) layout. SAAB Aircraft AB and Field Aircraft Company of Canada carry out the modifications. The first one was certificated in September 2002 followed by its delivery to Castle Aviation in April 2004.

Details

Span: 21.44m (70ft 4in)
Length: 19.73m (64ft 9in)
Engines: Two 1,395kw (1,870shp) GE CT7-9B turboprops
Cruise speed: 523km/h (285kt)
Accommodation: 37
(Data above for SAAB 340B)

First service: Crossair, June 1984
Number built: 459
Number in service: 320, mostly in USA

Current Operators

Africa: Flamingo AL.

Asia: Cosmic Air, Hokkaido AS, Japan Air Commuter, Shandong AL, Yeti AL.

Australasia: Air Nelson, Air Rarotonga, Macair AL, Regional Express.

Europe: Aurigny AS, Carpatair, Crossair Europe, City Air, Finncomm AL, Golden Air, Lagun Air, Loganair, Nordic Airlink, OLT, Skyways Express, Swedline Express.

Former Soviet Union: Moldavian AL.

North America: American Eagle, Calm Air, Castle AV, Chautauqua AL (US AW Express), Chicago Express (ATA Connection), Colgan Air (US AW Express), Corporate Express, Fina Air, Mesaba AL (Northwest Airlink), Murray AV, Penair, Provincial AL, shuttle America (US AW Express), Transwest Air, Vee Neal AV.

South America: Aerolitoral.

When Swissair collapsed, it was replaced by Swiss International Airlines using a reduced fleet. Saab 2000 HB-IZR departs from Basle in July 2004. (Author)

SAAB 2000

SAAB Aircraft AB
Linköping
SE-581 88, Sweden

In 1983, the successful Swiss regional airline, Crossair, (now Swiss International Air Lines) was the launch customer for the SAAB Fairchild SF340. By 1986, Crossair's pleas for SAAB to build a stretched version of this popular design were taken seriously and, after two years of deliberation, SAAB formally launched their high performance 50-seater Model 2000 in December 1988 with an order from Crossair for 25, plus options for an additional 25.

Although originally specified for delivery in September 1993, problems with certification delayed production, such that Crossair did not receive their first SAAB 2000 until September 1994. Initial production costs and design workload were significantly reduced by using many parts from the SAAB 340, including the cockpit, forward fuselage, tail empennage, nose gear and various systems. Several European aerospace companies assisted in the manufacture of the SAAB 2000 with Westland in the UK making the rear fuselage, CASA of Spain making the wing, and Valmet of Finland, the tail.

The 2000 features a revolutionary Ultra Electronics 'active noise reduction system' for cabin quietness, an APU, six-blade Dowty propellers, three-abreast seating and FADEC engine controls. The cabin interiors were fitted out by UK company Standard AIM Aviation. With its remarkable jet-like speed, the SAAB 2000 is still very popular with passengers and Swiss International Air Lines, who have the current largest fleet, regularly achieve 685km/h (370kt) on short haul flights, easily matching the block-to-block times for jet aircraft on the same route.

Apart from the initial large orders from Crossair, airline purchases of the SAAB 2000 were disappointingly slow and only 63 were built. These included three 36-seater executive model SAAB 2000s sold to General Motors to replace their ageing Convair 580s for 'scheduled' services out of Detroit.

In the late 1990s SAAB tested a 'combi' passenger/ freight version of the 2000. Two configurations were tried, one with 39 seats plus 16.4m³ (508ft³) of freight capacity, and the other with 16 passengers and 29.6m³ (1,046ft³). Just like the SAAB 340, an AEW&C version was also developed and the Japan Civil Aviation Bureau had two 2000FI versions built for Navaid checking. Along with the SAAB 340, the model 2000 production line was shut down in 1999 with the last example being delivered to Crossair in April that year.

Details

Span: 24.76m (81ft 3in)
Length: 27.03m (88ft 7in)
Engines: Two 3,093kW (4,152shp) Rolls-Royce Allison AE2100A turboprops
Cruise speed: 665km/h (360kt)
Accommodation: 58 maximum

First service: Crossair, Sept 1994
Number built: 63
Number in service: 51

Current Operators

Europe: Blue 1, Carpatair, Crossair Europe, Eastern AW, Europe Continental AW, Golden Air, OLT, PGA Express, Regional (Air France), Soder AL, Swedline Express, Swiss Intl AL.
Former Soviet Union: Lithuanian AL, Moldavian AL.

The largest operator of Skyvans in the world is Milwaukee-based North Star Air Cargo. N53NS was photographed at Myrtle Beach. (Author)

SHORTS SKYVAN/SKYLINER

Short Bros PLC
Airport Road, Belfast, BT3 9DZ,
Northern Ireland

Tracing its lineage back to a joint Miles and Hurel-Dubois design study that was tested on a highly-modified Miles Aerovan, the Skyvan's twin-engined, high aspect ratio wing and sturdy fixed undercarriage design in turn became the forerunner of the successful Shorts 330 and 360 regional airliners.

The Shorts SC.7 Skyvan project commenced in 1959 using a high aspect ratio wing mated to a boxy fuselage able to accept loads via a rear, under tail freight door. The first flight was delayed somewhat because of Shorts' preoccupation with their Belfast freighter so it was not until January 1963 that the Series 1 Prototype first took to the air. This was originally powered by two Continental 290kW (390hp) GTSIO-520 piston engines; however it was later re-engined with 390kW (520shp) Turboméca Astazou II turboprops and flown as the Series 1A in October 1963. Nineteen production Series 2s with more powerful 545kW (730shp) Astazou XII were built, starting in October 1965.

Poor hot-and-high performance of the Astazou-powered Skyvan led to the adoption of the Garrett AiResearch TPE331-201 engines in 1967. This created the definitive Skyvan Series 3, which won steady orders, mostly from the USA, Canada and Australia. The Series 3 first flew in December 1967. Some Series 2 aircraft were later modified to accept the TPE331 engines.

The increased weight Series 3A was developed with a full airline standard interior by upgrading the passenger cabin and fitting an airstair. This first appeared at the 1970 Farnborough Airshow with the name 'Skyliner'. Very few were built; British European Airways (BEA) used a couple in the early 1970s in Scotland to replace de Havilland Herons, while Gulf Aviation in Bahrain took delivery of the first production Skyliner in August 1972. After 1981, production continued very slowly until the last Skyvan was delivered to the UAE Air Force in April 1986.

A few military Skyvan Series 3Ms and 3M-200s are still in service, Oman use theirs for general transport, SAR and Coastal Patrol, Ghana has four, Yemen has two and Denmark has recently grounded theirs in favour of the C-130J. The largest civil fleet is operated by Milwaukee-based North Star Air Cargo but other Skyvans have found a new life as paradroppers thanks to their large rear door that can be opened in flight.

Details

Span: 19.79m (64ft 11in)
Length: 12.21m (40ft 1in)
Engines: Two 535kw (715shp) Garrett TPE-331 turboprops
Cruise speed: 324km/h (175kt) max
Accommodation: 19 maximum
(Details above are for Series 3)

First service: Aeralpi, June 1966
Number built: 150
Number in service: 34

Current Operators

Africa: SAL, Swala AL.
Asia: Deraya Air Taxi, Layang Layang Aerospace, Pan-Malaysian AT, Wirakris.
Europe: CAE AV, Danish AT.
North America: All West Freight, Arctic Circle AS, GB Airlink, North Star AC, Pioneer AW, Summit AC.
South America: Helicargo, Skylift Taxi Aereo.

Another Shorts operator from Milwaukee is Air Cargo Carriers. They have the largest remaining fleet including this ex-US military Sherpa. (Author)

SHORTS 330

Short Bros PLC
Airport Road, Belfast, BT3 9DZ
Northern Ireland

Originally given the designation Shorts SD3-30, the aircraft was launched in May 1973, assisted by a UK Government grant to help with the cost of development.

The Shorts 330 is basically a stretched (3.78m/12ft 5in) and improved Skyvan with the same fuselage cross-section, twin tail fins and wing design, but with a retractable undercarriage and more powerful PT6 engines with five-blade props. The wing span is increased by 2.97m/9ft 9in allowing for a 60% increase in fuel capacity compared to the Skyvan.

Because of the similarity in design to the Skyvan, the prototype SD3-30 was completed quickly, leading to first flight in August 1974. In the same month, Command Airways of Poughkeepsie, New York became the launch customer when they ordered three aircraft. In December 1975, the maiden flight of the first production Shorts 330 led to an order from Time Air (Canada). This was followed by further orders from DLT, Golden West, Henson Aviation, ALM Antillean and Hawaiian Air. UK CAA certification was granted in February 1976 followed by US FAR Pt25 and Pt36 approval in June.

With the ICAO designation 'SHD3' for air traffic control and flight plan purposes, the aircraft was soon given the unfortunate nickname 'Shed' by both pilots and controllers. This was quite appropriate considering the aircraft's boxy shape!

The initial Series 100 was powered by PT6A-45A and 'B engines, while the definitive Series 200, which was first revealed at the 1981 Paris Air Show, had -45R engines. The Series 200 also had a greater fuel capacity and adopted many of the earlier models' optional extras as standard. Other versions included the 330-UTT (Utility Tactical Transport), which had a strengthened cabin floor and an inward opening passenger door for parachuting, while the C-23A Sherpa was a freighter/paratroop version with a rear loading ramp for operation with the US military. One US military Sherpa was later converted for counter intelligence and electronic warfare work.

After 95 Shorts 330s had been sold to airlines worldwide, the assembly line in Belfast closed in September 1992. The last civil version was delivered to Quebec in June 1991; the last few off the line were delivered to the US military as Sherpas.

Many 'Sheds' that were originally used for passenger services are currently employed as paradroppers or cargo carriers. The box-shaped cabin with the large forward freight door has, when stripped of all passenger comforts, proved ideal for small freight operators worldwide. The largest fleet of 330s is currently operated by Milwaukee-based Air Cargo Carriers who have 11 Series 200 freighters. The only operator of the 330 left in Europe is Liverpool-based airline Emerald Airways.

Details

Span: 22.76m (74ft 8in)
Length: 17.69m (58ft 1in)
Engines: Two Pratt & Whitney Canada
PT6A-45 turboprops;
Series 100, 875kW (1,173shp)
Series 200 893kW (1,198shp)
Cruise speed: 356km/h (192kt) max
Accommodation: 30

First service: Time Air (Canada), August 1976
Number built: 136
Number in service: 28

Current Operators

Asia: Deraya Air Taxi.
Europe: Emerald AW.
North America: Air Cargo Carriers, Arctic Circle AS, Corporate Air, Freedom Air, McNeely Charter Service, Mountain AC, Skyway.

Seen here at Guernsey in the Channel Islands is SH360 G-XPSS of BAC Express while on lease to Aurigny in March 2004. (Frank McMeiken)

SHORTS 360

Short Bros PLC
Airport Road, Belfast, BT3 9DZ,
Northern Ireland

Announced in July 1980, the Shorts 360 is a stretched and improved version of the Shorts 330. By selecting a new, more powerful version of the PT6, Shorts were able to stretch the 330's fuselage by 0.9m (3ft) and fit two extra seat rows, allowing six additional passengers while retaining the same fuselage cross-section, three-abreast seating and basic wing design. The most obvious change to the Shorts 330 layout was the adoption of a conventional and elegant single tail fin.

Because of the similarities between the two types, prototype construction in Belfast was swift, and the Shorts 360 first flew in June 1981, six months ahead of schedule. Certification was achieved in September 1982 followed by the first of many deliveries to North American commuter airlines including Suburban, Simmons, Mississippi Valley and Newair. The first upgrade to the type appeared in 1985 when the Shorts 360 'Advanced' with more powerful -65AR engines was announced. This was followed in 1987 by the ultimate version, the Shorts 360-300. This entered service in March with again more power from the -67AR engines, new six-bladed propellers, improved passenger comforts and a significant reduction in noise levels inside and outside the aircraft.

In addition to passenger services, the type is currently used by many small freight airlines. The -300F Freighter version can carry five LD3 containers, or 3,300kg (7,280lb) in its 32m³ (1,130ft³) hold. The 1.4m (4ft 8in) by 1.7m (5ft 6in) forward loading door is the same as that used on the smaller Shorts 330.

Although the production line was shut down in late 1989, the last 360-300 was only completed and delivered to Rheinland Air Service in Germany in August 1991. Currently, the largest fleet of civil Shorts 360s is operated by Florida-based Skyway who have 11 series 200 freighters.

In a rather strange conversion project between 1995 and 1998, 28 former civil Shorts 360s were modified for the US Army National Guard in Clarksburg, West Virginia to C-23B+ Sherpas. The conversion involved the replacement of the 360's single tail with the twin tail and 'beaver door' of the Shorts C-23 Sherpa/Shorts 330.

Details

Span: 22.81m (74ft 9in)
Length: 21.58m (70ft 10in)
Engines: Two 990-1,062kW (1,327-1,424shp) Pratt & Whitney Canada PT6A-65R, AR or -67R turboprops
Cruise speed: 390km/h (215kt) max
Accommodation: 39 max, normally 36

First service: Suburban Airlines, November 1982
Number built: 164
Number in service: 92, mostly in the USA

Current Operators

Africa: Air Seychelles, Associated AV.
Asia: Deraya Air Taxi.
Australasia: Sunshine Express AL.
Europe: Aerocondor, BAC Express AL, Emerald AW, Nightexpress.
North America: Air Cargo Carriers, Corporate Air, Freedom Air, IBC AW, Pacific Coastal AL, Pacific Island AV, Roblex AV, Skyway, Trans Air.
South America: Aeroperlas, Air Santo Domingo, Islena AL, La Costena, SAP.

Kazair West have two Tu-134s in their small fleet. UN-65900 is a Tu-134A-3 that has previously seen service with Aeroflot. (Author's collection)

TUPOLEV Tu-134

PSC Tupolev
17 Tupolev Embankment
105005 Moscow, Russia

Initially designed as a derivative of the Tu-124, the USSR's home produced short/medium-range airliner was designed with rear mounted engines to emulate the cabin quietness of the French-built Sud Caravelle. The all-new 35° swept wing carried Tupolev's trademark fairings to house the retracted main undercarriage, and the nose was fitted with a glazed navigator's position with the weather radar under the cockpit floor.

Because it was based on the Tu-124, the new design was originally given the designation Tu-124A; however, the new airliner first flew as the Tu-134-1 in July 1963. Like the British built T-tailed BAC 1-11, the Tu-134 development aircraft suffered deep stall problems that were later rectified by modifications to the tailplane. In September 1967, after extensive trials, the production model Tu-134 (NATO reporting name 'Crusty') entered service with Aeroflot. Of the 78 early series Tu-134 built, many were exported to countries such as Bulgaria, East Germany, Hungary, Poland and Yugoslavia.

In 1969, the 76-seater Tu-134A appeared with a 2.1m (6ft 10in) stretch, and improvements including more efficient Soloviev D-30-2 turbofans, with thrust reversers. This became the standard production model and achieved dozens of foreign sales including several for military use.

Some Tu-134As were upgraded to Tu-134A3 standard at the rework facility in Minsk. The further updated model, the Tu-134B, dispensed with the famous glass nose and after its first appearance in 1980, it was exported to North Korea, Syria and Vietnam.

Production ceased in 1984, and of more than 800 built, possibly 300 are still active, most of them in the FSU. With the current high cost of aviation fuel, these early jets are now very expensive to operate; however, many companies in the FSU still retain their Tu-134s because of the high import tax applied to non-soviet types and the lack of a suitable replacement. Many military examples, some of them much-modified for experimental and military work, still operate in Russia, while countries such as Syria, Vietnam and North Korea still fly schedules with their Tu-134s.

Due to its inability to meet current noise regulations, all models of the Tu-134 are banned from the EU unless they are on Government or humanitarian work. Because of this and because of the delays in building the Tu-334, various operators in the CIS are investigating proposals by the Minsk Aircraft Repair Plant to re-engine their 134s with Stage 3 compliant D-436Ti-134 engines. If it goes ahead, the cabin and cockpit would also get a facelift extending the airframe life by 15 to 20 years.

Details

Span: 29.00m (95ft 2ins)
Length: 37.30m (122ft 4ins)
Engines: Two 66.7kN (14,990lb) Soloviev D30-2 srs 2. turbofans
Cruise speed: 850km/h (459kt)
Accommodation: 90
(Details above are for Tu-134B-1)

First service: Aeroflot, August 1967
Number built: 852 (inc 199 military)
Number in service: 286

Current Operators

Africa: Marsland AV, UTAGE.
Asia: Air Koryo, Benin Golf Air.
Middle East: Syrianair.
Former Soviet Union: Aeroflot, Aeroflot Don, Aero Rent, Airlines 400, Air Kharkov, Air Moldova, Air Ukraine, Alania, Alrosa-Avia, Alrosa, Altyn Air, Antex-Polus, Armenian AL, Astrakhan AL, Atyrau AW, Aviaenergo, AVL, AZAL Azerbaijan AL, BAL, Belavia, Bukovyna AL, Chernomor-Avia, Chuvashia AL, Daghestan AL, East Line AL, Enkor, Euro-Asia Air, Gazpromavia, Georgia National AL, Gromov Air, ISD Avia, Itek Air, Izhavia, Kaliningradavia, Karat, Kazair West, Kirov Air, KMV, KNAAPO, Kolavia, Komiinteravia, Kosmos AL, Kyrgyzstan AL, Meridian Air, NAPO-Aviatrans, Orenburg AL, Perm AL, Primair, Progress TSSKB, Pulkovo, Rusair, Rusline, Russia State Transport Company, Samara AL, Shans Air, Sibaviatrans, Sirius-Aero, South AL, Tajikistan AL, Tatarstan Air, Tbilaviamsheni, Ukraina Air Enterprise, Um Air, UTair AV, Vichi Air, Volga-Aviaexpress, Yamal AL, Zapolyarye Aviakompania.

Unless the re-engining programme is successful, this is a sight we won't see again; a Tu-134 at London Gatwick Airport. (Author)

Ural Airlines' Tu-154B-2 RA-85459 is seen landing at Malta International Airport with a load of holidaymakers from Ekaterinburg. (Author)

All of Caspian Airlines' Tu-154Ms are due to be replaced by brand new Tu-204-100s. This is EP-CPN taxying out at Sharjah in 2004. (Author)

TUPOLEV Tu-154

Tupolev Joint Stock Co
17 Akademika Tupoleva
Moscow 111250, Russia

Early in the 1960s, Tupolev was given the task a designing a replacement for Aeroflot's fleet of IL-18s, An-10s and Tu-104s. When the layout for the resulting Tu-154 was revealed to the West at the 1966 Paris Air Show, it appeared to owe much to the Boeing 727 (first flown 1963) and the HS Trident (first flown 1962). Designed with a wide-track, six-wheel main undercarriage to allow operation from dirt or gravel runways, the Tu-154 (NATO reporting name 'Careless') became Aeroflot's standard medium-range airliner in the 1970s and 1980s.

The first of six test aircraft flew from Zhukovsky on its maiden flight in October 1968 and was first seen in the west at the Paris Air Show in 1969. By late 1970, Aeroflot had the type in use for training and for occasional freight flights and they flew their first Tu-154 service from Moscow to Mineralnye Vody on 9th February 1972.

The initial Tu-154 was followed by the Tu-154A in 1973 with higher weights and an automatic approach and landing system. The heavier Tu-154B had more cabin space and was refined into the 'B-1 and 'B-2 models, while some Tu-154B have been converted to cargo door equipped Tu-154S (in Cyrillic script – Tu-154C) freighters. Just over 600 of the Kuznetsov NK-8-powered Tu-154 series were built at Samara prior to production switching to the Tu-154M.

The longer-range/heavier Tu-154M with the quieter and more efficient D-30KU engines first appeared from the Samara factory in 1982. Aeroflot received their first Tu-154M in 1984 and since then, over 300 have been built. NPO Saturn, who build the Tu-154M's engines, are working on a series of mods that would allow it to continue flying into the EU until the middle of the next decade.

In 2001, the Russian Aerospace Agency, Dvigatel (the engine designer) and Tupolev were funding further work on a dual-fuel gas-powered version known as the Tu-156. Powered by both regular aviation fuel and liquid natural gas, the NK-89-engined experimental Tu-156 was preceded by the LNG-powered Tu-155.

The Tu-154 series was exported widely to pro-Soviet countries including Cuba, Mongolia, North Korea, Syria, Afghanistan and China. Production of the Tu-154M ceased in 2002 leaving a few unfinished examples awaiting buyers.

Details

Span: 37.55m (123ft 2in)
Length: 47.90m (157ft 2in)
Engines: Three 104kN (23,380lb)
   Aviadvigatel D-30KU-154-II turbofans
Cruise speed: 950km/h (513kt) max
Accommodation: 180 maximum
(Details above are for Tu-154M)

First service: Aeroflot, February 1972
Number built: 920
Number in service: 448, mostly in FSU

Current Operators

Africa: Air Libya.
Asia: Air Koryo, Shaheen Air Intl.
Europe: BH Air, Bulgarian AC, Hemus Air, VIA.
Middle East: Aria Air, Caspian AL, Iran Air Tours, Kish Air, Mahan Air.
Former Soviet Union: Aerobratsk, Aerocom, Aeroflot, Aeroflot Don, Aerokuzbass, Aerotrans, Airlines 400, Air Ukraine, Alrosa, Altyn Air, Armenian AL, Asia Continental AL, Atlant Soyuz, Atyrau AW, Aviaenergo, AVL, AZAL Azerbaijan AL, BAL, Belavia, Chernomor-Avia, Chitaavia, Continental AW, Daghestan AL, Dalavia, East Line AL, Enkor, Gazpromavia, Gromov Air, Imair, Itek Air, Kaliningradavia, Karat, KMV, Kolavia, Kras Air, Kyrgyzstan AL, Lugansk AL, Magadan AL, Omskavia, Orenburg AL, Perm AL, Pulkovo, Russia State Transport Company, Samara AL, Sayakhat, Sibaviatrans, Sibir AL, Tajikistan AL, Tatarstan Air, Tesis, Turan Air, Ukrainian Cargo AW, Ulyanovsk Higher Civil AV School, Ural AL, UTair AW, Uzbekistan AW, Vladivostock Air, Yakutia AL, Yamal AL, Yuzhnaya Kazakhstan AL.

Krasnoyarsk Airlines operate three PS-90A-powered Tu-204-100s including RA-64019. The red title is the aircraft name 'Ivan Yarygin' (Avimage)

TUPOLEV Tu-204/214/224/234

Tupolev Joint Stock Co, 17 Akademika Tupoleva, Moscow 111250, Russia
Kazan Aviation Production Association, Dementieva St 1, 420036
Kazan, Russia

Plans for a new generation airliner to replace the Tu-154s, and to some extent IL-62s, were originally announced in 1983. By 1986, the design emerged as the Tu-204, a Boeing 757 look-alike that promised excellent sales with Aeroflot and other airlines.

First flown in January 1989 with PS-90A engines, much emphasis was given to state-of-the-art features and the potential for sales in the West. To this extent, the Tu-204 design included fly-by-wire controls (the first for a Soviet-built airliner), a full-colour six-tube EFIS two-crew cockpit and an efficient high aspect ratio wing with winglets.

With poor early sales, the Aviastar company at Ulyanovsk, who initially built the Tu-204, teamed up with London-based BRAVIA (British-Russian Aviation Corporation) to fund and market a version powered by the Rolls-Royce RB211-535. Originally called the Bravia 204 or Tu-204-220, it first flew in August 1992 becoming the first Russian airliner to fly with Western-built engines.

In 1994, Aeroflot announced they would order 500 Tu-204s and although they trialled the aircraft (a Series 204C freighter) in 1995, they didn't like it, preferring to lease Boeing 737-400s.

The early Tu-204 series proved hard to sell and by early 1995 only 16 had been completed. Several examples were parked-up waiting for buyers and in the hope of attracting sales, the

manufacturers offered an ever increasing number of variants which now number more than 20.

Versions include the improved Tu-204 Series 100, and the windowless, freight door equipped Tu-204C freighter. The Kazan-built Tu-214 (previously reported as the Tu-204-200) that was shown at the 1996 Farnborough airshow was a long-range/higher-weight version with extra fuel tanks in the wing and fuselage. Although the BRAVIA initiative failed, several Rolls-Royce-powered variants are still marketed. These include the Tu-204-120C freighter, the -122 with Rockwell Collins avionics, the heavier -220 and the freighter 220C. A proposed high-winged freight version is the Tu-204-330.

Another variant is the 160-seater, 6m (20ft) shorter fuselage, PS-90-powered Tu-204-300 (sometimes referred to as the Tu-234). Built by modifying the prototype Tu-204, this version was rolled out at Zhukovsky in August 1995. Both Transaero Airlines and Vladivostok Avia have placed orders for the 9,500km-range, 100/110-seater Tu-204-300D (Tu-234D). Deliveries are due to start in 2005.

Financing this design has always been a problem so it was good news when in 2003 the Russian government arranged finance to allow production of 46 aircraft over the next six years. In 2004 the Iranian Transport Ministry ordered 20 PS-90-powered Tu-204-100s for delivery to Caspian and Kish Airlines later in the year.

Details

Span: 42.00m (137ft 9in)
Length: 46.16m (150ft 11in) Tu-234/204-300 40.20m (131ft 9in)
Engines: Two 156.9kN (35,275lb) Aviadvigatel PS-90A or 193kN (43,100lb) Rolls-Royce RB211-535E4 turbofans
Cruise speed: 830km/h (448kt)
Accommodation: Tu-204/214 214 max Tu-234/204-300 166 max.

First service: Vnukovo Airlines, February 1996
Number built (ordered): 37 (9)
Number in service: 23

Current Operators

Middle East: Cairo AV.
Former Soviet Union: Aviapaslauga, Aviastar-Tu, Dalavia, KAPO, KMV, Kras Air, Pulkovo AL (3 on order), Russia State Transport Company, Sibir AL, Vladivostok Avia (2 on order).

The Tu-334 has suffered from political interference and money problems; however, it now has firm orders from Aerofreight and Atlant Soyuz. (Chris Doggett)

TUPOLEV Tu-334

Kyiv State Aviation Plant
100/1 Peremohy Prospect, Kyiv
03062, Ukraine

Many airliner projects in the FSU take years before they are ready for service, but the Tu-334 programme must be one of the longest ever. Designed as a replacement for Yak-42s and Tu-134s in the USSR, initial design work started in 1986; however, the economic disaster caused by the collapse of USSR caused a chronic funding shortage that allowed the programme to slip several times.

Although it is a Tupolev design, the project was originally marketed by the RSK MiG concern after they had contributed $25m towards costs. Tupolev built the first prototype, but it did not fly until the 8th February 1999. The production standard second prototype (completed by Aviant) first flew in November 2003 and, thirteen years after it was supposed to have entered airline service, the Russian authorities granted it its provisional AP-25 Russian type certification in December 2003. This prompted a revival in the programme in 2004.

Before granting a full type certificate, the Russian authorities normally need a third prototype to enter the flight test programme, but even though the third aircraft (RR-powered and built by Aviant) had not flown, full certification was granted in June 2004.

In partnership with several banks, Tupolev has set up the 'Project 3000' firm. Subject to them finding customers this company will lease Tu-334-100s to airlines providing they can guarantee 3,000 hours annual utilisation. Contracts have been signed with Aviant and KAPO to build 20 and 100 aircraft respectively.

The basic model is the Tu-334-100. This features a cockpit identical to the Tu-204; in fact the Tu-334 shares a considerable number of component parts and systems with the 204 including the fuselage design. It is also extremely quiet and is designed to comply with the ICAO Chapter IV noise restrictions. For the future, two westernised versions are proposed powered by Rolls-Royce BR715-56 engines – the Tu-334-120D and a stretched 126-seater Tu334-220. Also planned are the -100D and the stretched 126-seat Tu-334-200 both powered by the higher power D-436T2 engines. The stretched version is also reported as the Tu-354.

Since it first appeared in the West at the Dubai 2000 Air Show, political chicanery and a change in the leadership at RSK MiG have delayed the type's progress. Recent political wrangling because of MiG's major stake in the project has led the Russian Government and Rosaviacosmos to consider re-allocating the workshare to reduce the work earmarked for MiG. They are building a factory near Moscow but at the moment Tu-334 production will be carried out at Aviant in Kyiv and KAPO in Kazan. Aviant build the wings and centre fuselage, Aviastar the front fuselage, Tavia the tail and empennage and RSK MiG the engine nacelles.

Atlant-Soyuz and AeroFreight Airlines both ordered 5 aircraft in August 2004 and 15 Russian airlines have reportedly signed 'Letters of Intent' (LoIs) to buy 130 Tu-334s. The first Tu-334-100 should be delivered to either Atlant-Soyuz or Aerofreight Airlines in 2005. Since inception, Tupolev have invested $1bn in the project

Details

Span: 29.77m (97ft 8in)
Length: 31.26m (102ft 7in)
Engines: -100 Two 73.6kN (16,535 lb)
  ZMKB Progress/Motor Sich D-436T1
  turbofans; -200 Two 80.5kN (18,100lb)
  D-436T2; -120D & -220 Rolls-Royce
  BR715-56.
Cruise speed: 820km/h
Accommodation: -100/120D 102;
  -200/220 126.

First service: planned 2005
Number built (ordered): 3
  (10, plus LoI for 130)
Number in service: None

Current operators

None

Shanxi Airlines is one of the few remaining in China that operate the Y-7. B-3701 is one of their three Y7-100s based in Taiyuan. (Romano Germann)

XIAN Y-7/MA-60

Xian Aircraft Company
Yanliangqu, PO Box 140-84, Xian, Shaanxi
710089, China

Approximately 42 Soviet-built Antonov An-24 turboprops were operated by the Chinese state airline CAAC on domestic services, the first one being accepted in 1969. At the same time, the Xian Aircraft Company, based in Shaanxi Province, obtained the rights to build the An-24 under license. Known as the Y-7 (Yunshuji 7/Transport Aircraft No 7), the prototype was first flown in December 1970. The main differences from the Antonov-built version include the fitting of Chinese-built Dongan engines and the slightly wider fuselage and larger wing. The Y-7 was given its Chinese certificate of airworthiness in 1980, and production of a batch of 20 commenced around 1984.

In 1985, a Y-7 was flown to Hong Kong and converted by HAECO to Y-7-100 standard. This involved the fitting a new three-crew cockpit with new nav/com equipment and the total re-design of the cabin interior. The Y-7-100A model later appeared with winglets and became the standard model for many Chinese airlines. Powered by 2,051kW (2,750shp) Pratt & Whitney Canada PW127 turboprops, the stretched 60-seat Y-7-200A was intended for overseas sales. It also had Hamilton Standard propellers and Collins avionics. To reduce some costs for the Chinese domestic market, Xian also offered the Dongan-engined -200B. This had the same stretched fuselage and the Collins avionics, but no winglets.

Other versions included the 'hot-and-high' Y-7E, and the Y-7F freighter first delivered in June 1992. Mention must be made here of the military Y-7H and civilian Y-7H-500 that made its debut at Asian Aerospace 96. These are derived from the Antonov An-26 and are Dongan WJ5E powered freighters with the rear loading ramp and optional winglets.

In China, the Y-7 became the standard turboprop transport with many domestic airlines and the PLA Air Force and Navy, while foreign sales were confined to a few examples sold in Laos. After a Wuhan Airlines Y-7 accident in June 2000, the Chinese CAA banned all scheduled commercial passenger flights in Y-7 aircraft from June 2001.

Making its debut at the Zhuhai Air Show in 2000 was the MA60 'Modern Ark' version of the Y-7. Powered by Pratt & Whitney PW-127 engines, it has Hamilton Standard props, a Honeywell APU and Rockwell Collins avionics. An MA60H-500 freight version and an MA60-100 upgrade are also proposed. The launch customer for the MA60 was Sichuan Airlines who ordered five plus five on option. In 2004 the MA60 was temporarily grounded after reliability problems and runway overruns.

Details

Span: 29.63m (97ft 3in)
Length: 23.70m (77ft 9in)
Engines: Two 2,080kW (2,790shp) Dongan WJ-5A-1 turboprops MA60, two 2,050kW (2,750shp) P&W PW-127J turboprops
Cruise speed: 476km/h (257kt) max
(Details above are for Y7-100)
Accommodation: Y-7: 52. MA60: 56.

First service: CAAC, April 1986.
Number built (ordered): unknown
Number in service: 23 Y-7, 6 MA60, mostly in China

Current Operators

Asia: Changan AL (Y-7), CCAFC (Y-7), China Eastern AL (MA60), China United (MA60), Royal Phnom Penh AW (Y-7), Sichuan AL (MA60), Shanxi AL (Y-7).

Odessa Air has four of these 30-seater Yak-40s including this 1973 example UR-87327 seen at Kyiv-Zhuliany in July 2004. (Richard Vandervord)

YAKOVLEV Yak-40

Yakovlev Design Bureau
68 Leningradsky Prospekt, 125315
Moscow, Russia

The Regional Jet concept is not a recent one; Yakovlev's Yak-40 (NATO reporting name 'Codling') preceded all the Canadairs, Avros and Embraers by nearly 30 years. It was created in response to an Aeroflot request for a replacement for their IL-12s, IL-14s and Li-2s.

Yakovlev, who had never before built a civil airliner, commenced design work around 1964, unusually deciding to use three AI-25 turbofan jets and an unswept wing. The Yak-40 was extremely strong and the rugged single-wheel undercarriage was sturdy enough to operate from unprepared or grass runways. The three-engine layout was adopted to allow operations from short or 'hot-and-high' runways; it also allowed for better control in the event of an engine failure after take-off.

First flown in October 1966, the Saratov-built Yak-40 was mostly completed as a 3-abreast 27-seater for Aeroflot domestic services. Other variants were a freighter with a 1.6m x 1.5m cargo door, and the unbuilt, stretched 40-seater (Yak-40M). An alternative interior arrangement that is still offered as a retrofit by Yak is an executive 'Salon' model. On all versions passenger entry is via the ventral air-stair under the tail, while the two pilots can use a small door on the port side. All baggage has to be carried into the cabin and there is only one overhead rack in the airline examples. Although it was only produced in one size, various sub types were built including the Yak-40AT, D (longer range/International flight equipment), DTS (Troop carrier/Paramedic) EC, FG, K (Cargo/passenger convertible), KD, P, REO (Airborne electronics testing), TL, V (Export model with AI-25T engines). There is also a Navaid calibrator and the Avka, Liros, Fobos, Shtorm and Meteo for meteorological work. In 1987, a Czech Yak-40 was flown as an aerial testbed with an M-602 turboprop engine fitted in the nose.

Unusually for a Soviet-built airliner, it was promptly certificated and it entered Aeroflot service between Moscow and Kostrom in September 1968. 130 were exported to 17 countries including Germany and Italy.

Currently, even though the type is expensive to operate, large numbers of former Aeroflot Yak-40s can be found in the CIS and FSU. A programme, announced in 1991, to convert Yak-40s to twin engine configuration (Yak-40TL) using two 31.1kN (7,000lb) Textron Lycoming LF507-1Ns, never came to fruition.

Details

Span: 25.00m (82ft 0in)
Length: 20.36m (66ft 10in)
Engines: Three 14.7kN (3,300lbst)
Ivchenko AI-25 turbofans
Cruise speed: 297kt/550kmh max
Accommodation: 32 maximum.
Freighter 3,200kg (7,054 lb).

First service: Aeroflot, Sept 1968
Number built: 1,011
Number in service: 368

Current Operators

Africa: Air Jet, Air Libya, GEASA, Premium Air Shuttle, UTAGE, Weasua AT.

Europe: Hemus Air, Linair.

Middle East: Syrianair.

Former Soviet Union: Aerobratsk, Aero-Charter AL, Aerorent, Aerostar, Aero Vista AL, Air Moldova, Aist-M Airclub, Alliance Avia, Armenian AL, Asia Continental AL, Avial, Aviastar-Tu, AZAL Azerbaijan AL, Belavia, Belgorod Air Enterprise, Berkut Air, Berkut Z K, Blagoveshchensk AL, Botir Avia, Bravia, Bugulma Air Enterprise, Bylina, Center-South AL, Challenge Aero, Columbus Avia, Constanta AL, Dniproavia, Don Avia, Elbrus-Avia, Euro-Asia Air, Evenkiya, Gazpromavia, Gromov Air, GST Aero, Ilyich Avia, ISD Avia, Karat, Khantyavia, Kirovohradavia, KMPO, Kokshetau AL, Komiinteravia, Kras Air, Kyrgyzstan AL, Lukoil-Avia, MCHS Rossii, Motor Sich, Nikolaevsk-Na-Amwe Air, Novosibirsk Air, Odessa AL, Orel Air, Orenburg AL, Perm AL, Petropavlovsk-Kamchatsky Air, Polet AL, Rosneft-Baltika, Rusair, Rusline, Russia State Transport Company, Samara AL, Saratov AV Plant, Saturn Avia, Semeiavia, Severstal Air, Sibaviatrans, Sirius Air Company, Skol Aviakompania, Sverdlovsk 2nd Air Enterprise, Tajikistan AL, Tatarstan Air, Tatneftaero, Tbilaviamsheni, Tomskavia, Transavia-Garantia, Tulpar AL, Tura Air Enterprise, Turkmenistan AL, Tuva AL, Ukraina Air Enterprise, Ules-Avia, Ulyanovsk Higher Civil AV School, Unitemp-M Industrial, UTair AV, Uzbekistan AW, Vladikavkaz Air Enterprise, Vladivostock Air, Volga-Dnepr AL, Vologda Air Enterprise, Vostotsnaya Neftyanaya Kompania, Yakutia AL, Yamal AL, Yuzhmashavia, Zhezair, Zhetysu.

South America: Aerocaribbean.

This is Lat Charter's ex-Chinese Yak-42D YL-LBU arriving at EuroAirport Basel-Mulhouse-Freiberg from Riga in July 2004. (Author)

YAKOVLEV Yak-42

Yakovlev Design Bureau
68 Leningradsky Prospekt, 125315
Moscow, Russia

The Yak-42 (NATO reporting name 'Clobber') was originally conceived as a simple and reliable short/medium-range airliner to replace the Tu-134, the An-24 and IL-18. Designed very much as a scaled-up Yak-40, Aeroflot's requirements dictated the use of the same three-engined layout for engine redundancy and for short/rough-field performance.

The first of three pre-production Yak-42s, fitted with the early twin-wheeled main undercarriages, flew in March 1975. Prototype trials with two wing sweep designs delayed the revenue service entry until November 1980 when it flew Aeroflot's Moscow-Krasnodar route. The type was grounded for two years from 1982 after an Aeroflot accident in Belorussia caused by the failure of tail stabiliser screw-jack. Later Yak-42s re-entered service with over 2,000 modifications and have since proved safe and reliable.

The production models featured two airstairs, one beneath the tail, the other on the forward port-side fuselage. The two-crew cockpit had an automatic navigation and flight control system and the undercarriage was beefed-up with four-wheel main bogies. The three-shaft Lotarev D-36 engines were the first true turbofans (rather than a bypass jet) to be developed in the Soviet Union and were fitted without thrust reversers.

The 'Export' Yak-42A was developed with a new on-board oxygen system permitting higher cruising levels and avionics that comply with ICAO Category 2 standards. The Yak-42F was designed for aerial photography and had two large underwing containers with electro-optical indicators. The upgraded Yak-42D-100 (then called the Yak-142) was demonstrated at the 1993 Paris Air Show with AlliedSignal (now Honeywell)-built 4-screen EFIS and upgraded engines allowing it to comply with the west's Stage 3/Chapter 3 noise restrictions. (The basic Yak-42 only has Stage 2 compliance).

In 1987 Yak announced the stretched 168-seater Yak-42M; however, this was dropped in 1993 in favour of the experimental Yak-242 which was proposed with two rear-mounted PS-90A turbofans. In 1997, the stretched Yak-42-200 was announced. It was 6.03m (19ft 10in) longer than the Yak-42 allowing for a maximum capacity of 150 in a single-class layout.

The current model is the long-range Yak-42D that was first certified in 1988. It has greater fuel capacity and a revised cabin arrangement that can accommodate up to 126. The updated cockpit has GPS, TCAS, GPWS and RVSM authorisation. VIP, cargo and combi versions are also offered. Yak is currently working to fit new D-436 engines with thrust reversers. The Yak-42 was still in production at Saratov in 1999 and is reportedly still available from the manufacturers.

Details

Span: 34.88m (114ft 5in)
Length: 36.38m (119ft 4in)
Engines: Three 63.74kN (14,330lb) ZMKB Progress (Lotarev) D-36 turbofans
Cruise speed: 750km/h (405kt)
Accommodation: 126 maximum

First service: Aeroflot, Nov 1980
Number built: 175
Number in service: 120, mostly in FSU

Current Operators

Africa: Aerolift, Aero Service, Sudan AW.

Asia: Aero Asia, China United, Shaheen Air Intl.

Former Soviet Union: Adjaria, Aero Rent, Air Moldova, Alania, Astair, Aurela, Centre Avia, Dniproavia, Domodedovo AL, Donbassaero, Elbrus-Avia, Enkor, Gazpromavia, Irbis, Izhavia, Karat, Kras Air, Khozu-Avia, Kuban AL, LAT Charter, Lukoil-Avia, Lviv AL, MCHS Rossii, Motor Sich, Samara AL, Saravia, Shar Ink, Tatarstan AV, Tavrey Aircompany, Tulpar AL, Ulyanovsk Higher Civil AV School, Volga Aviaexpress.

South America: Cubana.

AVIC 1 Commercial Aircraft ARJ21

First details were revealed in 2001 but the ARJ21-700 78/85-seat Regional jet wasn't launched until September 2003 with an order for five from Shanghai Airlines. Powered by two GE Aircraft Engines CF34-10A, the proposed versions include the 105-seater stretched ARJ21-900, the ARJ21-700B Bizjet and freighter ARJ21-700F. With 41 orders by November 2004, (ten from Shandong Airlines, five from Shanghai Airlines, twenty from Shenzhen Financial Leasing and six from Xiamen Airlines) the first ARJ21-700 should enter commercial operations in 2008 after flight tests at Shanghai and Xian. Components are under production at Chengdu, Shanghai, Shenyang and Xian and final assembly will be at Shanghai. (Photo courtesy *Airliner World*)

Sukhoi Su-80

With fewer orders for their military types, the Sukhoi Design Bureau decided to expand into the commercial market. It is the design team leader in the RRJ and it is also testing this 30-seater twin turboprop airliner. First flown in September 2002, it is powered by two 1,305kW (1,750hp) GE CT7-9Bs similar to those used on the CASA/IPTN CN235. The twin-boom design has a rear-loading ramp and production examples will have a 1.4m longer fuselage, a 5-screen LCD cockpit display and increased fuel capacity. The aircraft are built at Komsomolsk-on-Amur in eastern Siberia. (Photograph Author)

Antonov An-148

The prototype of this twin-engined 75-100 seater was moved from AVIANT hangar at Kyiv in October 2004 prior to its first test flight. Five variants (-100A, -100B, -100E, -200A and -200B) with two fuselage lengths are planned seating up to 100 in a 5-abreast layout. The engines are ZMKB Progress D-436-148s with 14,100lb thrust and the cockpit has a two-crew EFIS with 5 screens and uses mostly Russian and Ukrainian avionics. The second of the three prototypes made the type's first flight on 17th December 2004. Russian certification is planned for the first quarter of 2006 after 600 test flights. Interest in the type has been shown by KrasAir, Pulkovo Airlines, Aeroflot-Don and Aerosvit. (Photograph Dmitry Karpezo)

Bombardier CSeries

In July 2004, Bombardier revealed the first computer pictures of their new commercial aircraft design, to be known as the 'CSeries'. Looking remarkably similar to the Embraer 170 series, this is a conventional layout twin-jet seating 110 to 135 passengers. It has underslung engines mounted on a wingletted wing, a sleek fuselage and a low-mounted tailplane. Four variants with two fuselage lengths are planned. Initially announced with International Aero Engines (IAE) turbofans, in late 2004 Bombardier announced that CFM engines could also be considered. The official launch is expected in mid 2005 with service entry in 2010. (Photograph Bombardier)

Russian Regional Jet

The neat-looking RRJ series of regional jets was announced in 2003 and was designed from the start to meet all the West's certification standards. Led by Sukhoi, the RRJ manufacturing consortium includes Boeing and Beriev. Three versions RRJ-60, RRJ-75 and RRJ-95 seating 60, 75 and 95 respectively are proposed and the first flight is planned for 2005. All models share the same wing, landing gear and Snecma/Rybinsk Motors-NPO Saturn SaM146 engines. Aeroflot Russian Airlines has signed a Letter of Intent (LoI) for 30 aircraft and Sibir have ordered 50 RRJ-95Bs. First flight is planned for October 2006. (Photograph Author)

International Aircraft Registration Prefixes

Prefix	Country	Prefix	Country	Prefix	Country	Prefix	Country
AP	Pakistan	HS	Thailand	TS	Tunisia	3D	Swaziland
A2	Botswana	HZ	Saudi Arabia	TT	Chad	3X	Guinea
A3	Tonga Islands	H4	Solomon Islands	TU	Ivory Coast	4K	Azerbaijan
A4O	Oman	I	Italy	TY	Benin	4L	Georgia
A5	Bhutan	JA	Japan	TZ	Mali	4R	Sri Lanka
A6	United Arab Emirates	JU	Mongolia	T2	Tuvalu	4X	Israel
A7	Qatar	JY	Jordan	T3	Kiribati	5A	Libya
A8	Liberia	J2	Djibouti	T7	San Marino	5B	Cyprus
A9C	Bahrain	J3	Grenada	T8A	Palau	5H	Tanzania
B	People's Republic of China	J5	Guinea Bissau	T9	Bosnia-Herzegovina	5N	Nigeria
B-H	Hong Kong	J6	St. Lucia			5R	Madagascar
B-M	Macau	J7	Dominica	UK	Uzbekistan	5T	Mauritania
B	Republic of China (Taiwan)	J8	St. Vincent and Grenadines	UN	Kazakstan	5U	Niger
C	Canada	LN	Norway	UR	Ukraine	5V	Togo
CC	Chile	LV	Argentina	VH	Australia	5W	Samoa
CN	Morocco	LX	Luxembourg	VN	Vietnam	5X	Uganda
CP	Bolivia	LY	Lithuania	VP-A	Anguilla	5Y	Kenya
CS	Portugal	LZ	Bulgaria	VP-B	Bermuda	6O	Somalia
CU	Cuba	N	USA	VP-C	Cayman Islands	6V	Senegal
CX	Uruguay	OB	Peru	VP-F	Falkland Islands	6Y	Jamaica
C2	Nauru	OD	Lebanon	VP-G	Gibraltar	70	Yemen
C3	Andorra	OE	Austria	VP-L	British Virgin Islands	7P	Lesotho
C5	Gambia	OH	Finland	VP-M	Montserrat	7Q	Malawi
C6	Bahamas	OK	Czech Republic	VQ-T	Turks & Caicos Islands	7T	Algeria
C9	Mozambique	OM	Slovakia	VT	India	8P	Barbados
D	Germany	OO	Belgium	V2	Antigua and Barbuda	8Q	Maldives
DQ	Fiji Islands	OY	Denmark	V3	Belize	8R	Guyana
D2	Angola	P	North Korea	V4	St. Kitts & Nevis	9A	Croatia
D4	Cape Verde Islands	PH	Netherlands	V5	Namibia	9G	Ghana
D6	Comores Islands	PJ	Netherlands Antilles	V6	Micronesia	9H	Malta
EC	Spain	PK	Indonesia	V7	Marshall Islands	9J	Zambia
EI	Ireland	PP/R/T	Brazil	V8	Sultanate of Brunei	9K	Kuwait
EK	Armenia	PZ	Surinam	XA/B/C	Mexico	9L	Sierra Leone
EP	Iran	P2	Papua New Guinea	XT	Burkina Faso	9M	Malaysia
ER	Moldavia	P4	Aruba	XU	Cambodia	9N	Nepal
ES	Estonia	RA	Russia	XY	Myanmar	9Q	Congo/Kinshasa
ET	Ethiopia	RDPL	Laos	YA	Afghanistan	9U	Burundi
EW	Belarus	RP	Philippines	YI	Iraq	9V	Singapore
EX	Kyrgyzstan	SE	Sweden	YJ	Vanuatu	9XR	Rwanda
EY	Tajikistan	SP	Poland	YK	Syria	9Y	Trinidad and Tobago
EZ	Turkmenistan	ST	Sudan	YL	Latvia		
E3	Eritrea	SU	Egypt	YN	Nicaragua		
F	France	SU-Y	Palestine	YR	Romania		
G	Great Britain	SX	Greece	YS	El Salvador		
HA	Hungary	S2	Bangladesh	YU	Serbia and Montenegro		
HB	Switzerland (including Lichtenstein)	S5	Slovenia	YV	Venezuela		
HC	Ecuador	S7	Seychelles	Z	Zimbabwe		
HH	Haiti	S9	Sao Tome & Principe	ZA	Albania		
HI	Dominican Republic	TC	Turkey	ZK	New Zealand		
HK	Columbia	TF	Iceland	ZP	Paraguay		
HL	South Korea	TG	Guatemala	ZS	South Africa		
HP	Panama	TI	Costa Rica	ZR	Macedonia		
HR	Honduras	TJ	Cameroon	3A	Monaco		
		TL	Central Africa	3B	Mauritius		
		TN	Congo	3C	Equatorial Guinea		
		TR	Gabon				

RUSSIAN AIRLINES
AND THEIR AIRCRAFT

Dmitriy Komissarov & Yefim Gordon

ARRIVALS & DEPARTURES
North American Airlines 1990-2000

John K Morton

We hope you enjoyed this book . . .

Midland Publishing titles are edited and designed by an experienced and enthusiastic team of specialists.

Further titles are in preparation but we always welcome ideas from authors or readers for books they would like to see published.

In addition, our associate, Midland Counties Publications, offers an exceptionally wide range of aviation, military, naval and transport books and videos for sale by mail-order around the world.

For a copy of the appropriate catalogue, or to order further copies of this book, and any of many other Midland Publishing titles, please write, telephone, fax or e-mail to:

Midland Counties Publications
4 Watling Drive, Hinckley,
Leics, LE10 3EY, England

Tel: (+44) 01455 254 450
Fax: (+44) 01455 233 737
E-mail: midlandbooks@compuserve.com
www.midlandcountiessuperstore.com

US distribution by Specialty Press –
see page 2.

Following the ending of Aeroflot's monopoly in 1992 and the break-up of the Soviet Union, the Russian civil air transport scene has been considerably transformed.

This full-colour album covers the major airlines operating in Russia today, illustrating the types operated by each carrier, their equipment and the various colour schemes worn by them. A brief history and fleet information are provided for each airline, as are detailed photo captions.

Softback, 280 x 215 mm, 160 pages
449 full colour photographs
1 85780 176 8 **£19.99**

This is a photographic record, with extended captions, of new and departed North American airlines during the last decade of the 20th century. It is divided into three sections: 'Arrivals' contains 32 airlines which began operations during the period and were still operational at the end of it; 'Arrivals and Departures' features 24 carriers which came and went, and 'Departures' covers 29 airlines which went out of business in the 1990s. Included here are famous names such as PanAm, Eastern and Tower Air.

Softback, 280 x 215 mm, 112 pages
168 full colour photographs
1 85780 200 4 **£14.99**

AIRLINES WORLDWIDE
Over 360 Airlines Described and Illustrated in Colour (4th edition)

B I Hengi

AIRLINES REMEMBERED
Over 200 Airlines of the Past, Described and Illustrated in Colour

B I Hengi

AIRLINES WORLDWIDE
76 Older Types, Worldwide, Described and Illustrated in Colour

Tom Singfield

Airlines Worldwide, first published in 1994, has established itself as a trusted and sought-after reference work. It aims to give an overview and illustrate the world's leading or more interesting airlines, including smaller national operators, with their history, routes, aircraft fleet and operations.

This latest edition is more than ever revised and updated, notably in the light of the turbulent events and rapid changes in the airline industry over the past couple of years.

Softback, 240 x 170 mm, 384 pages
c360 colour photographs
1 85780 155 5 **£18.99**

In the same format as the enormously popular *Airlines Worldwide* and *Airlines Worldwide*, this companion reviews the histories and operations of over 200 airlines from the last thirty years which are no longer with us, each illustrated with a full colour photograph showing at least one of their aircraft in the colour scheme of that era. Operators such as BEA, CP Air, Eastern, Invicta, Jet 24, Laker and Fred Olsen are examples of the extensive and varied coverage.

Softback, 240 x 170 mm, 224 pages
c200 colour photographs
1 85780 091 5 **£14.95**

This companion volume reviews the histories, operations and specifications of 76 airliner types which have been familiar during the last fifty years, and includes over 200 outstanding colour photos showing the airliners both in service and preserved. Included are less well-known yet significant types, for instance the Dassault Mercure, Breguet Deux Ponts, Saab Scandia, and VFW-614. Of course, all the appropriate Boeing, Douglas, Antonov, Lockheed, Ilyushin, and Tupolev types appear.

Softback, 240 x 170 mm, 160 pages
over 200 colour photographs
1 85780 098 2 **£13.95**